First Class Research

A guide to your research project or dissertation

in accounting and finance

Chris Brooks

AIMS OF THIS BOOK

This book is specifically written to help undergraduate and master's students to write their research projects in accounting or finance. I have been conducting my own research, supervising and marking student dissertations for more than 25 years, and in this guide, I will pass on what I have learned about how to maximise your mark and produce a document of which you can be proud.

KEY FEATURES

- Covers all aspects of writing a project, from finding initial ideas to drafting and polishing the final report
- Focuses specifically on the needs of students in accounting and finance
- Loaded with top tips on how to make quick progress and avoid common pitfalls
- Takeaway messages summarising each chapter
- Access to YouTube videos that map directly onto the key topics covered. Search on the site for Chris Brooks and look for the Finance Books logo or use this URL then select the First Class Research Playlist
- Identification of URLs with free resources for data, literature and software.

First Class Research: A guide to your research project or dissertation in accounting and finance by Chris Brooks
Copyright © 2021 Chris Brooks. All rights reserved

PUBLISHED BY FINANCE BOOKS

Cover design by Sheena Brooks

DISCLAIMER

Only general guidance is given in this book, and following these suggestions cannot necessarily guarantee high marks, for the objectives and required level of the project will vary from one institution to another.

The author does not accept responsibility for the persistence, accuracy or relevance of URLs pertaining to the third-party websites referred to in this book, nor is any assurance offered that this material is or will remain appropriate.

First published, September 2021

ISBN 978-1-915189-02-8

ABOUT THE AUTHOR

Chris Brooks is Professor of Finance at the ICMA Centre, Henley Business School. He was formerly Professor of Finance at the Cass Business School, London. He holds a PhD and a BA in Economics and Econometrics, both from the University of Reading. He has been involved with research for more than 25 years spanning a wide range of subject areas, including finance, economics, real estate, econometrics, investor behaviour, tax, and history.

Chris developed a wide range of modules delivered at the ICMA Centre, and has taught undergraduates, postgraduates and executives. He has supervised numerous research projects as well as more than 25 PhD students through to successful completion. He is also a Senior Fellow of the Higher Education Academy but is probably best known as the author of the first introductory-level econometrics textbook targeted at finance students, *Introductory Econometrics for Finance* (2019, Cambridge University Press), which is now in its fourth edition and has sold around 70,000 copies worldwide.

Contents

II   The investigative part

III	Writing and polishing

List of Tables

List of Figures

PREFACE

The research project is probably the only opportunity during your entire degree programme where you get to choose what to study, how to study it and at what pace. Although you will be working within a well-established framework and given support, guidance and encouragement by your supervisor, nobody is going to be continually telling you what to do. The project is also your chance to produce something unique – so get creative and show the world what you can achieve.

Research can be fun because conducting it allows the investigator (the person doing the research) to solve a puzzle and potentially uncover new knowledge that nobody else has. It is rarely repetitive since, by definition, academic research involves doing something different than what has been done before, so it can be a gratifying experience. In addition, the project allows students to select a topic of direct interest or relevance to them and is often useful in developing time-management, report-writing, and many other skills. The final document can often provide a platform for discussion at job interviews or act as a springboard to further study at the taught postgraduate or doctoral (PhD) level.

The phenomenal growth that has taken place in the types and volumes of data available makes this a fascinating time to be embarking on a research endeavour. New sources of data have arisen due to social media and on-line searching and investing, newsrooms and forums, all of which are conducted electronically, leaving a digital footprint of the activity that could be analysed. Many companies, such as Google, make their data available to researchers in aggregated or anonymised forms, often free of charge. Using such data opens up exciting possibilities for kinds of investigation that were not previously possible, such as examining the disclosures that firms might make through social media before other channels or which types of communications media yield the most significant market impacts.

Technological progress has also made the task of conducting research easier in many ways and more fun. If you get stuck along the way, there will probably be a video on YouTube or a question-and-answer forum that covers precisely what you need. Statistical software can automatically format your regression results to drop into your project document, while survey packages can code the results and output them straight into a spreadsheet, both of which will save countless hours of dull and error-prone data-entry.

Despite all of the positives, many students dread the idea of having to write a research project or dissertation: 'What will I write about?' 'How will I organise the work?' 'Where will I get the data?' 'There is so much already out there, how can I do something better, or even different?' 'How will I overcome issues as they arise?' 'My time management is bad, and I know I'll leave it until the last minute.'

Well, fear not – this book is written specifically to help you navigate the process from the beginning to the end – with the aim to arrive at the point where you submit a great project that you are proud of and with which your supervisor is impressed. Have some faith in your abilities and the structures your department will have put in place to guide you through. Very many students have already completed the same journey – the vast majority without facing any significant difficulties. Completing a dissertation will always be a rollercoaster ride to some extent. There will be good days and bad days with problems faced then overcome, but seeing the finished product will provide an enormous sense of satisfaction.

Why is another book on how to do a research project needed?

Having reviewed the current work in this area, I felt that all of the existing textbooks were lacking by being too broad-based or not using the latest pedagogy or sources. This book aims to make maximum use of contemporary methods and resources. The suggestions for further reading and data are deliberately focused on electronic sources, freely available where possible. Traditional paper-based material is kept to a minimum because you won't follow those up anyway as you don't have the time.

More importantly, there is so much variation in research approaches across subjects that a book written for English literature or biology students won't cut it for someone in an accounting and finance department. Our field sometimes considers itself a science and sometimes a social science. We are, therefore, fortunate that the subject area draws its methods from both and embodies a range of approaches so that quantitative and qualitative research are employed. Nonetheless, the methods used and the conventional writing style in accounting and finance are somewhat different from those in other disciplines. Most existing 'how to do research' books are written by sociologists or professors of education, which leads these texts to miss key aspects of what a marker in our subject would expect a project to contain.

In addition, many extant books on writing a research project are simply too abstract. I skimmed through several of them as I was preparing this manuscript, and

I wondered whether students would be able to apply what was written in those books to their situation and chosen topic. By contrast, this text aims to cover the nuts and bolts of the research process, and where intangible concepts are used, clear examples and applications to the accounting or finance context are provided. In some cases, I have used illustrative examples from my own (usually co-authored) research. While this is perhaps somewhat self-indulgent, it does ensure that I know the material well, and I don't have to be concerned about infringing someone else's copyright.

For whom is this book written?

The book is aimed primarily at undergraduate or master's students researching a project or dissertation in accounting or finance. It might also prove useful for those studying in cognate areas such as economics, business studies or management.

I have tried to adopt an informal and engaging style as far as possible, and readers might also observe that I have used gender-neutral pronouns in the plural ('them' and 'they') when discussing an unspecified person even when I am referring to one individual.

Outline of the remainder of this book

The book develops as follows. Chapter 1 covers the essential background information needed to make an effective start to working on a dissertation, including what research is, how it might differ between the undergraduate and master's levels and the differences between the kinds of research conducted by academics and practitioners. This chapter also encourages you to consider, at this early stage, what a good research project might look like, and what markers are looking for. Forming a solid and productive working relationship with your supervisor is paramount to a smooth and successful experience, and handling your supervisor is also discussed at length in this chapter, alongside suggestions on how to organise your time.

Chapter 2 provides a brief introduction to the philosophy of research as it is conducted in social sciences, with a specific focus on accounting and finance. A distinction is drawn between the positivist tradition of the empirical study of large datasets and the interpretivist approach using interviews and case studies to extract detailed information within specific contexts. Various approaches to classifying research and learning are discussed, providing useful frameworks that make it easier to understand where different types of research fit within the body of knowledge.

Chapter 3 examines a wide range of issues around the choice of project topic to investigate. This is the first, and in many ways most important, challenge. Making a bad decision can render the entire process thereafter much less rewarding – both emotionally and in terms of the mark received at the end – than it would have been if more careful consideration had been given at the outset. Tips on where to look for inspiration and the kinds of research areas that might be acceptable are presented alongside coverage of some of the aspects that can go wrong and how to avoid that outcome.

The ethical issues that arise in the production of research are covered in chapter

4. The chapter examines the Data Protection Act and discusses the ethics approval process that students are likely to have to go through if their research uses live subjects rather than anonymised secondary data. There then follows a detailed examination of plagiarism, including what it is, how markers detect it, and how to avoid it. Other issues are examined around ethical behaviour in research, including falsification of data or results, the importance of accuracy and honesty, and how to prevent conflicts of interest.

Chapter 5 continues the work begun in chapter 3 by covering all aspects of how to write a research project proposal, which is formally assessed alongside the final document on some programmes. The chapter discusses in detail the document structure and sections likely to be required, including how to construct a Gantt chart or timeline.

Chapter 6 is the first of two that cover an essential component of all dissertations, namely the literature review. This chapter examines how and where to find the source material to incorporate in the review, including accessing journal articles, books, websites, working papers and PhD theses. It also offers suggestions on how to ensure the quality of your reading material, how to focus your search if there is too much literature, and how to read quickly.

Chapter 7 then proceeds to discuss how to pull all of the material together to write the literature review. It discusses issues around both style and content, including suggestions for structure, how to write critically while at the same time presenting a balanced argument, and how to cite existing work appropriately. The chapter ends with a discussion of some of the flaws that weak literature reviews could contain and how to fix them.

Chapters 8 and 9 discuss the investigative aspects of a research project, with the first of these focused on methods and the second on data. Chapter 8 explains how the choice of research methods is made and examines how to incorporate theory into a dissertation in accounting or finance, including discussing from where relevant theories come. Chapter 9 continues the focus on the investigation to present the various types of data that can be employed in research projects, distinguishing between primary and secondary data types. The chapter presents pointers on how to conduct surveys and interviews, and outlines the relative advantages and disadvantages of each approach. Case studies, focus groups, mixed methods and issues around data validity are also discussed.

Chapter 10 is the first of two chapters on writing the project document. It begins by discussing the differences between the style of writing employed by academics and those used in other walks of life. Tips are provided on how to make your writing entertaining as well as informative, and the chapter also outlines how to structure the project and what material should be placed in each section or chapter of the dissertation.

Chapter 11 continues the project document theme with a consideration of the further issues regarding refinement and polishing of the draft prior to submission.

Suggestions are provided on how to deal with feedback or comments from supervisors and others, and how to get the most from it. The chapter proposes ideas for improving the project structure and narrative, along with tips on how to respond if your draft is significantly under or over the official word limit. The chapter ends with a checklist of aspects to tick off before final submission.

The book finishes with chapter 12, which comes in two parts. The first provides some suggestions of what to do if things go wrong, including ideas on where to get help and from whom, together with a list of commonly occurring problems and how you might be able to fix them. Finally, the second part of the chapter provides some ideas for getting more out of your project document after submission, including the possibilities of further study or publishing the work in some form – either as a journal article or in a magazine or popular website.

Project foundations

1. INTRODUCTION

Learning outcomes: this chapter covers

✓ Some reasons for doing a research project
✓ The skills needed to complete a dissertation successfully
✓ The difference between academic (scholarly) and practitioner research
✓ How to build your network
✓ How to manage your time
✓ How to handle your supervisor
✓ What a good project might look like

1.1 Background information

1.1.1 Why do a research project?

In some cases, the project will be a compulsory element of a degree course, so you are doing it because you have no other choice. But in other instances, a student might elect to take it rather than one or more taught modules. A university department might require students to complete a research project to demonstrate that they have mastered the skills necessary to be competent, independent researchers. Students will need to show that they can define and execute a piece of research, possibly embodying a minimal degree of originality, within the given time, resource and report-length constraints.

If you elect to do a research project, the process of completing it will help you obtain or strengthen several key skills that you may not be able to acquire from other parts of your programme. These are often attributes that employers value more than subject-specific knowledge, and completing a project will enable you to evidence that you have acquired these competencies as well as providing valuable discussion points for job or further study interviews. The following is a non-exhaustive list of the key skills that you could acquire:

- Independent thinking – not only do you decide what research problem to work on and how to tackle it, but you will also be primarily responsible for resolving any issues that you face.
- Time management – the project is yours to organise from the start until the end. Although there is a support structure in place, you will be responsible for the workflow and keeping progress on track.
- Critical synthesis of a body of existing work – you choose what to read, how to summarise it, and, most importantly, how to identify the flaws in what is already written.
- Identification of opportunities and 'gaps in the literature' – partly leading on from the previous point, once you have filled your head with knowledge about a particular topic, you will be in a position to see where the limitations are – what is missing, where existing research is lacking, and where you could potentially contribute.
- Data collection and organisation – you might need to use some detective work to identify the types of data you need, matched to your project's aims and methodology. Wherever the data come from, they will almost certainly need cleaning and organising in a spreadsheet to get them in an appropriate form for analysis.
- Statistical modelling – quantitative data investigation including econometrics and other approaches are specific skills that will hopefully be covered in other aspects of your programme, but this might be the first instance where you need to select the appropriate techniques and use them in a context that you have chosen rather than being provided with all of the steps.
- Report structuring and writing – organising all the parts of the project's output and adopting a sound writing style that engages the reader and explains the findings clearly is another valuable skill.

These skills are all required to successfully complete a research project, which is why writing one is such a valuable experience. When you complete it and secure a good mark, it will be a demonstration with evidence that you can do all the items on this list.

Research projects need to be highly specific because the available resources – your finances, time, current knowledge of the field, skills in data collection and analysis, and the amount that you are permitted to write will all face some constraints. Working within these boundaries is another important aspect of the process.

Your dissertation might be the only component of your course where you get the opportunity to study a topic in any real depth. Unfortunately, the nature of modern degree programmes in accounting or finance is such that most are 'conversion courses' requiring no prior knowledge of the subject and covering a wide range of subject matter. This breadth means that depth is sacrificed, and each module only skims the surface of popular topics with textbook-style treatments and no time to delve into the research literature.

The dissertation is also probably the only module where you have any genuine freedom to choose what, when and how to study (within some fairly loose constraints). It is an intellectual challenge involving a comprehensive array of skills. The proof that you have acquired those talents will arise from the dissertation document you produce and the mark and comments you receive as validation of its quality.

Most project students are free to select their own topic (see chapter 3), and the same is true of accounting and finance scholars, whose research agendas are usually established based on the direction of their intellectual curiosities. Even though academics have the freedom to research whatever they choose, their outputs can have many benefits for the 'real world' outside the academy. For instance, to offer just a few illustrations, university researchers work on many topics of practical importance such as:

- Environmental accounting
- Dealing with tax avoidance
- Revising and updating accounting standards
- Supporting the efficient running of multinationals with timelier information
- Imputing values for work conducted by the public sector
- Ensuring that banks have sufficient capital to avoid financial distress
- Building portfolios with desired risk characteristics
- Designing new approaches to pension saving
- Determining whether an asset market contains a speculative bubble

Thus, another reason to conduct a student research project is as a first step on a journey to producing knowledge that has genuine practical value to solve some of the issues faced by accountants and financial market participants.

Neither accounting nor finance are modern inventions. Accounting, and in particular bookkeeping, has a very long tradition dating back thousands of years to Mesopotamia or perhaps even earlier (Mattessich, 1989), and the Roman Empire used sophisticated accounting systems (Oldroyd, 1995). Similarly, while the foundations of 'modern finance' were primarily laid in the 1960s and 70s with the advent of portfolio theory, the CAPM and the Black-Scholes option pricing model, financial markets have existed for thousands of years. For instance, medieval monks in England sold their wool to Italian merchants up to 20 years in advance of production using instruments akin to modern-day forward agreements (Bell *et al.*, 2007).

These historical examples demonstrate that even though many people think of accounting and finance as being very recently developed fields, they are millennia old at their most fundamental levels. Research is not only supporting the continuing advancement of the subjects, but also allowing us to understand better how accounts and markets functioned throughout history. Drawing parallels between historical and modern events can help contemporary policy-makers to solve problems by seeing how they were tackled in the past and to what effect.

What is the difference between a research project and a dissertation?

A dissertation is usually thought of as a more substantive (accounting for more credits and with a longer word limit) version of a research project, but there is no strict differentiation between the two terms, which will be used interchangeably in this book. The dissertation or project document is sometimes termed a thesis, especially for PhD-level dissertations.

Research projects vary enormously in terms of their subject matter, and the layout of the final document will reflect that. Some are purely scientific studies that fit the template of approach in any applied science discipline; others are evidence-based opinion pieces; others still will be related to policy or practice and will be focused on providing useful recommendations for non-academic end-users. One of these types is not necessarily favoured over the others, although, as I will discuss below, the standard approach that results in an empirical investigation of secondary data written up in the style of a journal article is the most common approach.

1.1.2   What is it like to do a dissertation?

In some ways, if you have never been involved with research before, it will be an entirely new experience. But the closest you will probably have come is when you have written an extended essay or mini-project. There, you will likely have had to identify your own sources, summarising a little published research, and possibly conducting some empirical modelling. There are two main differences between that and a full dissertation, however. First, the scale of the undertaking: this research project will be much bigger, taking far longer to complete and requiring considerably more writing. Second, the freedom you now have to organise everything yourself: the topic, the aims, the methodological approach, the timescale, and the writing style.

1.1.3   Is a research project in accounting or finance different?

To what extent is a research project in accounting or finance different from one in another field? The basic definition of research, and the core ingredients that every project should embody, are universal and will transcend subject boundaries. An appropriate structure, straightforward writing style, appropriate document length, a review of the relevant literature, rigorous data analysis and appropriate conclusions will all be expected of a research project, whatever the field.

There are, however, several features of accounting and finance as subject areas that distinguish them from other fields. First, as discussed in chapter 2, they straddle the sciences and social sciences, and hence they draw methods from both sides. The most common structure adopts the form seen in scientific papers, although case studies or interviews are also used, and would lead to a style more akin to a sociology or history piece.

What differentiates accounting and finance from the sciences, however, is the importance of the narrative in our subjects. As I describe in detail in chapter 10, having a solid story to tell based on theory is essential for a high-quality project. On the other hand, the results would be written up more dispassionately and probably at less length in the sciences.

1.1.4   Skills needed to complete a good project

Some students will start from the premise that they will never be able to write 12,000 words (a typical length for a dissertation) on the same topic and will be nervous that they do not have the skills to complete it to the required standard. But my experience suggests that, even if you have never written a document of that length before, it is far more likely that you will struggle to keep the length of your project down to the limit than not being able to write enough. This book is approximately 130,000 words long, and I wrote it in around six months (although I was doing other work over the same period), which shows what can be done.

You don't need to be super-intelligent to do good research, nor do you need to be a brilliant writer. Of course, both of those attributes would be helpful, but much more important characteristics are:

- Possessing a genuine interest in learning something new and having an inquisitive mindset
- Having a willingness to put in many hours and to prioritise the project over activities that might be more fun or more financially rewarding
- Being an all-rounder with a mixture of skills, including organising, writing, analysing, programming, etc.
- Remaining doggedly determined to finish and being able to overcome the many issues that will occur along the way rather than becoming disheartened and giving up
- Being confident in working alone without frequent guidance, albeit within a supervisory framework

If you do not enjoy working on the project and find it a chore, you are much more likely to do a poor job or even give up altogether. No student will find pleasure in every aspect of the process – for instance, some people love writing but hate dealing with data and doing quantitative analysis, others vice versa. Consequently, try to focus your energy on the parts that you enjoy the most and make them as big a part as possible of the whole activity. You have the scope to select the kind of project that makes the most of your interests and abilities, as discussed in chapter 3.

1.1.5   How might undergraduate and master's dissertations differ?

Traditionally, it was understood that an undergraduate programme would provide a general education across a field, with a master's qualification building upon the subject matter that was already covered to offer more in-depth, specialist knowledge. In that sense, we might expect that a research project at the master's level ought to be more detailed and at a higher intellectual level, embodying smarter and more novel ideas, more sophisticated models, more depth in analysis, etc. But over recent years, business schools have seen the growth of 'conversion' master's, where no or little prior knowledge of the subject is required for entry onto the programme. While there will be variation across universities, in this context, the level of master's dissertations has arguably slipped so that the expectations for undergraduate and master's courses are now probably fairly similar.

When the term 'master's' is used in this book, it refers to a taught postgraduate (MSc or MA) programme, usually of 9- or 12-months' full-time duration. A 'traditional' UK one-year master's programme involved nine months of taught courses and exams followed by a three-month summer dissertation. In these cases, the research component will be at most a third of the whole programme's credit weighting and possibly as little as 15-20%.

However, many universities also offer MRes or MPhil degrees, which are more specialist research-based programmes. The MRes is likely to involve some modules that specifically support the project (for example, in research methodology or the philosophy of research), and these will probably be assessed separately from the dissertation itself. But an MPhil is a pure research degree where only the final thesis is assessed, which would generally be of two years' full-time duration.

1.1.6   Steps in doing a research project

A standard 'student journey' to completing a research project involves several stages:
1. Organising and planning
2. Reading and thinking
3. Data collection
4. Data analysis
5. Writing up
6. Polishing and review

Each stage is an essential part of the process covered in this book and needs to be devoted sufficient time.

Stage 1 involves setting everything in place so that the remaining steps progress as smoothly as possible. Establish your timetable, consider access requirements or other constraints, and seek ethical approval if it will be needed. Also, reflect on any training needs at this point to speed up the later stages – e.g., sourcing electronic literature, data collection, coding or econometrics.

Stage 2 is the literature review phase that is discussed in detail in chapter 6 and chapter 7 of this book. It also involves refining and honing your research questions and finalising your methodology so that you obtain the appropriate data in step 3.

Stages 3 and 4 constitute the project's investigative work and together will probably comprise the most time-consuming aspects. If you are using secondary data from existing databases, it should be reasonably straightforward to download everything you need. Still, it might take a while to become familiar with the interface and get the information into the correct format for input into a spreadsheet or statistical package. On the other hand, if you elect to use a survey or interviews, the third step could take considerably longer. Stage 4 will be conducted using spreadsheets and statistical software, but as well as generating the results, it will take significant time to interpret them and reflect on what they mean.

Stage 5 is the part that that many students dread the most – where you start to collect the pieces together and write the first draft. If you have been writing up the aspects above as you got to them, this stage will progress more quickly, but it is still common to leave all the writing until the end.

Stage 6 is a crucial aspect despite many students believing that they have pretty much finished at step 5, and so it is the subject of an entire chapter of this book. If there is a requirement to submit a (now rather old-fashioned) bound hard copy (or two copies), then you will need to allow time for printing and binding as well.

1.1.7   Does a research project need to be original?

For an undergraduate or taught master's degree dissertation, it is unlikely that the project would be expected to have a significant original contribution. At best, it will probably be an 'enhanced replication study' that re-analyses an existing problem with a new dataset or a very slightly different empirical approach. But if your project is outstanding, it might have a more noteworthy contribution, in which case you should naturally give this aspect as much prominence in the write-up as possible. But equally, if you are struggling to identify or articulate where your originality is, then do not be overly concerned, as that is often the case for students engaged in their first piece of research. This situation is unlike a full research degree, such as a DPhil or PhD, where making a clear and evident contribution to knowledge will be an absolute requirement for getting the qualification.

1.1.8   Practitioner research compared with scholarly research

If you compare an article published in an academic journal with a report written by a management consultant or a researcher working for a bank or auditing firm, you will notice several systematic differences between them. As well as differences in the writing style, which will be discussed at length in chapter 10 and chapter 11, there will be variations in the purpose and nature of the research itself.

Academic research tends to be primarily interested in solving puzzles – in other words, determining why a particular phenomenon occurs or explaining the factors that affect the extent of that phenomenon. Such research does not necessarily need to have any specific use outside of the academy and is sometimes called blue skies, curiosity-driven, or basic research. Note in passing that the term 'basic' does not imply that the investigation is simple or intellectually low-level; instead, it means that it is not yet applied or focused on a particular practical problem. In such research, there will be an emphasis on the rigour, validity and reliability of the findings. Contrast this with practitioner research, where the focus will be on producing something directly useful to the organisation. In the practitioner world, the study's drafting is directed to demonstrate the value of the approach with the robustness of the findings merely a secondary consideration or not of interest at all.

For instance, in the asset pricing branch of finance, academics have given a considerable amount of attention to documenting and explaining pricing anomalies, where systematic patterns are found in stock returns. Their research efforts have been directed primarily at trying to explain the anomalies, why they might have occurred, whether they are still present in various other settings, and whether risk-based or behavioural explanations are most plausible.

On the other hand, a practitioner writing on this same subject would be more concerned with how big the returns might be to a trading strategy that sought to exploit the anomaly and how risky such a system would be, together with details about the transactions costs of implementing it. In essence, their focus would be on whether they could make money from the research, and if so, how much. However, these technical aspects would probably not be of much interest to academic researchers since they would argue that this information would not help our understanding of how financial markets work or why they operate in that fashion.

Research programmes that have a strong practice-basis, such as those that are part of an MBA or DBA, and research projects that firms sponsor, will need to combine elements of both the practitioner and scholarly foci. Their studies would need to simultaneously satisfy the two audiences by producing work that is both useful and rigorous, which is quite a challenge – see also subsection 1.3.7.

1.1.9 Establishing your network

Doing research can be a lonely experience, and for researchers at all levels, there will be instances when they feel stuck and unsure how to proceed. At such times, they will call upon someone in their network for help and support. Similarly, for your research process to be as pleasant and smooth-running as possible, you will also need a network. You are more likely to remain on track if you have already considered who is in your network and to whom you can turn for different types of problems rather than letting them build up or curtail your progress. Making a mental list such as the one in Table 1.1 could be useful.

More generally, other students conducting their research in your cohort can be a precious source of support since they are likely to be facing many of the same issues as you at roughly the same time. Discussing your work with them (even though the topic will probably be different) could provide suggestions for the project itself and help diminish any feelings of isolation that are a common aspect of research.

Table 1.1: Potential sources of support if things go wrong

Person	Type of problem they can solve
Friends, siblings, classmates	Feeling isolated, lacking motivation, general problems with progress
Your supervisor	High-level issues, serious problems with data collection or falling behind
Classmates, PhD students	Problems accessing data, faulty computer code
University statistical services	Problems running or interpreting quantitative models
Library services	Finding or accessing prior literature
Departmental administrator	Uncertainty about the format or deadline for the project
Study skills team	Help with organising your time or with writing

1.2   Time management

1.2.1   How much time is needed?

Effective time management is probably the most valuable talent you will need to master to complete the project to the best of your ability. This is an essential skill for the long-term because so many aspects of work and life are improved if you can organise yourself, stay on track, and plan ahead.

Before you get deeply into your research, it is worthwhile to consider how much weight the project has within your overall programme and to allocate your time to it accordingly. In some undergraduate and master's programmes, the dissertation might be only the equivalent of one taught module. So, for example, it might be quoted as '10 ECTS credits', [1] which should be roughly equivalent to 200 hours of total study time, where 60 credits represent a full year of undergraduate student work (and 90 such credits are a notional master's year of work). On the other hand, for some research-heavy programmes (such as an MRes), the dissertation element could be 20 or even 30 ECTS credits and, therefore, the equivalent of 4–6 months of full-time study.

Naturally, the amount of work expected to achieve a given grade and the number of words required are likely to be highly correlated with the number of credits assigned to the project or dissertation module. For a 10 ECTS credits undertaking, the word limit will probably be of the order 8,000 – 12,000 words, whereas for 30 credits, perhaps the limit will be 18,000 – 20,000 words. Note that these are upper limits rather than targets, and it is possible to write an excellent piece of work using fewer words, particularly if the nature of the subject matter involves a lot of equations and tables rather than detailed arguments. This point will be discussed extensively in

---

[1] https://ec.europa.eu/education/resources-and-tools/european-credit-transfer-and-accumulation-system-ects_en

section 11.4.

The volume of completed work must be at least commensurate with the number of credits. In other words, if you are supposed to have spent approximately 200 hours on the project overall (including reading, data collection, analysis and writing), will your submission give the impression that you spent that long on it?

An essential aspect of the time-management involved in doing a research project is to develop self-discipline. One of the most exciting features of conducting research is that you will have considerable latitude to run the project at your own timescale and in the order you want. This freedom also brings a responsibility to pace yourself and to make progress continually. If you leave it until the last minute, how will you complete the expected 200 hours of study in a few days? 'Pulling an all-nighter' might work with an essay or assignment, but a research project is simply too big an undertaking to be able to complete in an intensive couple of days.

Initially, the amount of time you have available to complete the project might seem vast, but the weeks and months will simply fly by. You might, for instance, have three months from beginning to submission deadline, and it is that amount of time for a reason – because that is approximately how long a typical student will need. So you need to get started straight away and regularly work on the project until it is completed.

Equally, it is important not to put in so many hours from the outset that you burn out. Think of the project as a marathon, and to get to the finishing line, you will need to pace yourself. If you set off too quickly, you will tire and run out of steam. On the other hand, if you stop off for a series of long breaks along the way, you won't get to the end either.

The supervision of dissertations is very 'hands-off' so that nobody will be standing behind you on a day-to-day basis telling you what to do, meaning that you must motivate yourself to make gradual progress with the work to stay on track and complete on time. In particular, successfully finishing requires a certain amount of mental resilience – not only to keep working on it when there always seem to be other calls on your time but also to keep plugging away at it when things seem to be going wrong. It would be easy to lose heart and give up in such circumstances, so every completed dissertation implies a certain amount of dogged determination and triumph in the face of adversity on the part of the person who wrote it.

Since there are so few real deadlines during the dissertation completion period, you need to set some artificial ones and try to stick to them. And as you progress towards the final stages, always make sure that you aim to finish well before the official deadline to allow for a careful last check through and have some slack in case things go wrong.

The guidance on what to do and when is likely to be at arm's length, and hence you need to impose your own structure to avoid falling behind and feeling a lot of stress as you rush at the end. Most aspects of a university degree have a framework where you are answerable to someone (usually a tutor or essay marker) within a fairly narrow time window, but the project is much less structured, and hence you will need to learn to become answerable to yourself. In some ways, the situation is akin to being self-employed, where you have to establish your own goals and be disappointed with yourself if you fail to achieve them.

The best approach is to start working on the project right away and set aside time every week to make progress with it. Draw up a rough timeline to completion like the ones discussed in subsection 5.2.7 and try to stick to it. It is also useful to build in a contingency at the end for unforeseen problems with the project itself or with other work that unexpectedly eats into your research schedule. Don't overestimate what can be achieved in the time that you have. It is better to complete a solid project on time than to attempt something earth-shattering but only get part-way through it.

To obtain the most out of the research project while keeping your stress at an acceptable level will require you to work efficiently. This means that you will need to focus on what is required in order to get a good mark, something that this book is explicitly designed to help with. You will want to minimise the amount of time you waste with pointless or fruitless work.

You will also need to be able to prioritise, which means that at certain points, any urgent tasks arising are completed first, and important work on your dissertation may have to wait. Some people find that making lists of all the jobs they have to do, and keeping the list up to date, helps them to set priorities and ensure that nothing gets forgotten or falls behind.

1.2.2   Avoiding procrastination

Everyone goes through periods in their working lives where they tend to procrastinate. Procrastination means finding any and every excuse not to undertake an important task, putting it off as long as possible. Completing a dissertation is no exception, and there will be numerous instances where you will be at risk of procrastinating – for example, by doing some housework or tidying a cupboard rather than getting started on drafting your literature review. It is as if you convince yourself that you cannot focus on this big and important task until every small and insignificant distraction is out of the way. Procrastination can manifest itself in many different ways, including:

- Prioritising unimportant tasks that could have waited (or not been done at all)
- Spending excessive amounts of time planning how you will tackle various aspects of the project rather than just getting on with them
- Starting work on a particular dissertation-related task but never making any progress
- Focusing on trivial aspects such as the font size or page layout rather than the substance of the writing.

Procrastination often arises from a 'mental block' where you can't bear to think about doing a particular task because the intellectual exertion required is so considerable. It is essential to tackle outbreaks of procrastination before they eat away at significant portions of the available time. Procrastination usually occurs at points where the effort needed is the most considerable, or the task is deadly dull such as:

- The very beginning of a new aspect of the project, and you don't know where to start
- Any aspect involving writing, as this is the part of the whole task that students typically find the most challenging (and least enjoyable)
- Tackling a massive pile of papers to read and summarise for the review
- Gathering or cleaning the data, which might be time-consuming and monotonous
- Formatting the tables and improving the presentation
- Reading through and polishing a rough draft

The trick to resolving all of these issues is simply to get started. Worrying too much about planning and setting the perfect conditions for progress mean that you delay beginning the task and lose valuable time. Invariably, once you have started, you will discover that you make much quicker progress than you expected. And improving an existing spreadsheet, programming code, or document draft is a much more straightforward and less painful task than beginning from scratch.

Another trick to make progress and avoid blocks is to plan a system of rewards for yourself and resolve not to take a treat, such as a trip to the pub/cinema/clothes shop, until you have reached your self-established target, such as writing 2,000 words of literature review. Don't delay, start right away.

In addition to mental blocks, a further reason why students sometimes progress slowly is their hesitance because they experience 'imposter syndrome' where they doubt their own ability to complete the project. Such feelings are pervasive, and if this happens to you, remember that you were accepted onto the programme, and therefore you must have possessed the requisite skills and qualifications. You have also made it through the programme this far, and thus you have credibility as a project student.All of your classmates will be going through the same steps, and no doubt many of them will be feeling the same trepidation. As you progress through the tasks involved, your confidence will grow.

1.2.3   Organise your time

Some aspects of the project require more focus and mental effort than others. For instance, interpreting results, writing and debugging code, and writing the abstract all need intense concentration. Try to time the tasks to conduct the most demanding parts when you are at your best cognitively and the least distracted. Other aspects, such as formatting tables, inputting results, completing and checking the reference list, require less mental effort and progress with these tasks can still be made when you are somewhat tired or distracted (e.g., waiting for a train or plane). These sorts of tasks can also be dipped in and out of rapidly without the need to 'get in the zone' and so can be accomplished during short stretches of otherwise dead time. Having a tablet or laptop computer rather than just a desktop will help make this possible since you can then work outside of the home and on the move. Never spend time idling when you could be making progress with some aspect or other of your dissertation.

When you are extremely busy at various points in life, the only way to simultaneously stay on top of everything is to work harder than you were previously accustomed to. One way to fit more into the day is simply to make the day longer by, for instance, getting up an hour earlier or going to bed later, depending on whether you are an early riser or a night person. Although, of course, maintaining sufficient sleep is important, getting into the habit of not lying in bed will help you to schedule more work time; once the dissertation is submitted, you will be able to revert to your previous pattern.

Finally, if you are really struggling with a particular aspect of the work or your motivation more generally, seek help from your supervisor, other students, or a university study skills advisor. They will all be well used to dealing with these sorts of issues and geared up to provide support.

Mix it up

Some people naturally have a high boredom threshold and can continue with the same task for a prolonged period without losing enthusiasm or focus. But others experience task fatigue when they have had enough of what they are doing, and their productivity and concentration start to decline. To avoid this, try to mix the tasks so that you can make progress with several aspects more or less concurrently – for example, by writing up the methodology section at the same time as running statistical models to analyse the data. While they are related, the two tasks require different skills and can therefore be interspersed to limit monotony.

1.2.4   Get motivated and get organised: Some initial tips for success

The research project is almost certainly the most significant undertaking of your degree and the most time-consuming, so get motivated and organised. As well as the time management ideas presented above, you might find that working with music in the background helps you concentrate and avoids boredom. It also drowns out other people's noise, although some people nonetheless prefer silence.

I do believe, though, that seeing moving visual images while trying to read or write is a distraction. The radio, Spotify or Amazon Music, etc. are ok but switch the TV, computer games and YouTube off. Also, turn off the notifications from every app on all your devices to have as few disturbances as possible while you are working.

As well as establishing a timeline, think about where, when and how you will study for your project. The more ideal the conditions you can create, the better the quality of the work produced.

Where

Find somewhere comfortable, in a place you won't be disturbed, where there are not too many distractions, and you feel creative. That might be the library, in a garden (weather permitting), or by the window in a coffee shop. It might even be sitting in the lounge on the sofa or at the desk in your room – whatever works for you.

Wherever you work, make your study area clutter-free, which will help you think more clearly. Remember, a tidy desk is a tidy mind.

When

Setting aside regular, timetabled hours is more likely to lead to good progress than irregular blocks. It is best to treat your research as you would a lecture series or a paid job – prioritise it, drop it into your calendar, and fit other things in your schedule around it. If any non-essential activities clash with your allocated research time, then refuse them; when any time is lost from the research schedule, try to replace it somewhere else during that week. Like preparing for participation in a sports event, while missing one training session almost certainly won't affect your ultimate performance, skipping one workout is the beginning of a slippery slope to getting out of the habit altogether and falling far behind.

How

Research is not a process that moves in a straight line with a constant rate of progress. Sometimes things will go awry, and you will waste hours chasing down an alley that leads nowhere. There will also be instances where you are stuck and unsure of how to proceed. Be prepared for these occurrences and don't become disheartened over minor setbacks. Other days, something you anticipate being tricky and time-consuming will turn out to be much more straightforward than you expected. The good days and the bad will balance out to some extent.

   Try to anticipate in advance when you are likely to face delays in waiting for other people to complete tasks, including waiting for your supervisor to read your proposal or comment on drafts of the document, waiting for responses to your survey to come in, or when you have to book access to a terminal for data access. Rather than having dead time when you are not able to make any progress, you could aim to do other work during those periods, such as brushing up on your coding skills or engaging in further reading or writing.

1.2.5   Get your writing abilities up to scratch

All universities will offer some forms of writing support, either using on-line resources or via face-to-face sessions organised through their student services division. If you feel that your writing skills are not up to the job, it is worth enrolling in one of these – not just to improve your dissertation's quality but also to develop your aptitude for writing more generally.

   You could use the requirement to complete the dissertation as a reason to invest the time to upgrade those skills that could be strengthened and that you are likely to continue to use during your future study or career plans. Any relevant skill or knowledge gaps need to be addressed as early as possible during the dissertation registration period since, by the time these attributes are required, it may be too late to develop them.

1.2.6   Keep copies of everything

It is crucial to become accustomed to keeping more than one electronic copy of all of your files in case the primary version becomes lost or corrupted, and indeed, make backups of the backups and backups of the backups of the backups.

Be careful with version control, however, which means, in particular, not dragging a file in the wrong direction from one storage location to another so that you write over a new version of it with an old one. This is a disaster if it happens since there is probably no way to retrieve the more recent version unless you happened to have another backup of it already. One way around this is to rename the file every time you open it by, for example, including the date in the filename such as 'project110221' would be the project draft as of 11 February 2021. This would ensure that you do not write over a file with an older edition, but you need to be vigilant that you always begin working on the latest prior version – a concern that does not arise if you keep the same filename and write over it. Whichever approach you use, take care to use the latest version and not write over it or lose it.

It is probably not helpful to keep each chapter's drafts in separate files since the project is unlikely to have a sufficiently big file size to make this necessary unless your project includes a large number of images or other complexities.

Your university might have some free cloud storage space that you can use, which is ideal for backups since it cannot get lost or corrupted like a flash drive might. If not, or if you require more space to store data, code and documents, several commercial cloud storage options are available. Many of these operate a 'freemium' model, offering a modest amount of space for free, with the opportunity to purchase more if required. For example, at the time of writing, the following are examples of some of the free services available, although there are many others (use a search engine to find them):

- Apple iCloud provides 5Gb, which integrates seamlessly with Apple products and hence is ideal for Mac users[2]
- Google Drive provides 15Gb (shared with other Google products such as Gmail), and an app can be installed to facilitate transfers[3]
- Degoo provides 100Gb[4]
- Mega provides 50Gb, and an app can be installed to facilitate transfers[5]
- pCloud provides 10Gb, and an app can be installed to facilitate transfers[6]

Of course, there is nothing to stop you from making use of the free allocations from several providers and separating your files among them.

You should retain all of your notes, data spreadsheets, code, statistical output, intermediate drafts, and so on until after the point when you receive your final mark.

---

[2]https://www.icloud.com

[3]https://www.google.com/drive/

[4]https://degoo.com

[5]https://mega.io/start

[6]https://www.pcloud.com/lifetime-storage/?ref=1120

Doing this has at least two benefits. First, it will help to safeguard against any corrupted files or version control problems. It will also offer a fall-back in case you need to check something, or you made some changes that you later realise rendered something incorrect when it was previously correct. Second, it would also provide a line of defence if you were to be in the situation where your department alleges that you have not done the work in your dissertation yourself.

1.2.7 Developing resilience

Inevitably, some aspects of your project will work out less well than you might have hoped, particularly relating to the data collection and analysis. For instance, if you anticipated getting 80 participants in your survey, but you ended up with only 32 usable responses. Or if you were aiming to conduct some fundamental analysis by manually going through all current FTSE100 constituents' accounts, but it took longer than you expected so that you only achieved half that number. Or you might have had a brilliant idea for an empirical model only to find when you estimate it that none of the coefficients is statistically significant and some have the wrong signs.

These kinds of issues are all part and parcel of academic research, and your project assessor will appreciate this. You have no choice but to make the best of your data and results, whatever they are and to make the best of your writing, even if this is not your strongest skill. You are primarily being assessed on how effectively you went through the process of conducting research and writing it up rather than the strength of the findings, so none of these difficulties above with data or results would be disastrous, and nor would your mark fall by much as a consequence. And with time and possibly a proof-reader, you could considerably improve the standard of exposition in the draft to deal with supervisor comments, as discussed in section 11.3.

Another situation where you might feel discouraged is if you believe that you have produced an excellent piece of work, only to receive scathing criticism from your supervisor or someone else who reads it. The greater the effort you have put into the draft up to that point, the more bruising such disparagement will be. More detail is given on this point in section 11.3, but the main message is that you must take it on the chin: pick yourself up, dust yourself down and carry on, trying to learn from the feedback.

More generally, there are some excellent free resources available on-line that discuss how to build your mental resilience so that you cope well with minor setbacks and learn to take them in your stride. These include:
- The American Psychological Association[7]
- Greater Good Magazine at Berkeley[8]
- A more detailed report at the Chartered Institute of Personnel and Development[9]

---

[7]https://www.apa.org/topics/resilience/
[8]https://greatergood.berkeley.edu/article/item/five_science_backed_strategies_to_build_resilience
[9]https://www.cipd.co.uk/Images/developing-resilience_2011_tcm18-10576.pdf

- An article specifically on building 'academic resilience' at editage.com[10]

1.3   The role of the supervisor and what to expect

1.3.1   What determines who will be your supervisor?

The usual process is that once you submit a research proposal for the project or you select an idea from a pre-defined list, at that stage, you would be allocated a supervisor based on the subject area and the interest and availability of the members of faculty. Your supervisor will be your primary contact point throughout the entire process, providing support and guidance and acting as the first marker of the finished piece. They will fulfil a range of related roles, and you can reasonably expect that your supervisor should:

- Be knowledgeable about the broadly defined subject area
- Provide comments on your proposal
- Supply suggestions for sources of data and literature
- Offer advice and suggestions at any point where you need them
- Respond to your e-mails in a timely fashion and be available to attend scheduled meetings
- Point you to additional learning resources to enhance your skills and knowledge
- Write you a reference for a job or further study

Do not be concerned if your allocated supervisor has research interests in a different part of accounting or finance than your proposal's subject matter. Academics are used to working across different areas and will be experienced in supervising a wide range of project topics. Their breadth of knowledge will be an asset, not a liability, and their primary role is to supply high-level guidance rather than detailed subject-specific technical information (which is mainly your job to source elsewhere).

1.3.2   When to meet your supervisor

The supervisor will probably set up an initial meeting to discuss the proposal and any issues they foresee. They will provide some suggestions for additional reading or approaching the topic from a different angle. The feedback could be more severe – for instance, that the idea is unworkable, too risky, too ambitious or not feasible within the time available, in which case you may be invited to have a rethink and submit a revised proposal. The supervisor will also discuss your work-plan and whether it is realistic and likely to allow you to finish on time.

After that, you can expect to meet your supervisor infrequently but according to a prescribed schedule – for example, once half-way through the allocated time to see how you are getting on and then once again towards the end to discuss a preliminary draft. Find out from the department or the student project handbook how much total contact time you will receive from your supervisor throughout your

---

[10]https://www.editage.com/insights/7-secrets-to-help-you-build-academic-resilience

project registration. Between approximately two and four hours in total seems likely, spread across perhaps three or four meetings, although, of course, you can contact them at other stages of the process as the need arises if you require advice or when something goes wrong.

Do engage with your supervisor whether you believe that you are well ahead with your study and so not needing any guidance or hopelessly behind and feeling embarrassed. They will be able to help (possibly a lot) whatever your current state of progress, and meeting with them at the required intervals will help ensure that you satisfy the requirements. These meetings will also allow you to gauge your supervisor's expectations about both the investigative part and the project document. Skipping these consultations implies missing out on valuable support and inside tips from the person likely to be the dissertation's first marker.

1.3.3 How to deal with your supervisor

Always keep e-mails to your supervisor friendly but reasonably formal. It is probably polite to address them as 'Dr X' or 'Professor Y': find the correct title and use it (with Professor being the more senior one, so employ that if the person also has a PhD) the first time you make contact with them or any other members of the academic staff. However, you will likely revert to first-name terms when you have got to know them a little better. Some academics take themselves more seriously than others, so it is best to err on the side of formality to ensure that no offence is caused.

Supervisors will differ in terms of their approach to the process, and you will have no choice but to dance to their tune. You can only find out how your supervisor works after you have experienced it. Some will be willing to be flexible about when you meet with them and will respond promptly to your e-mails, even in the evening and at weekends. Others might take a day (or longer) to respond, and you might have to wait a week to have an appointment to see them. Unfortunately, even if they take several days or more to reply to an e-mail, and they are not available to see you for two weeks despite arranging an appointment, there is little that you can do except to ensure that you make up for this tardiness by being even better organised and more efficient yourself so as not to fall behind schedule or waste time waiting for their replies. Hopefully, they will make up for lack of timeliness with particularly useful input, providing high-quality ideas and comments.

Relatedly, some supervisors will be more friendly and supportive than others. Some might ask you about your post-university career ambitions, your family or hobbies as part of polite conversation, while others will want to get straight down to the task at hand. Again, whether you have a more expansive chat with your supervisor or brief interactions based only on the project will depend on their preferences, and it is simplest to conform to that.

Ideally, a supervisor will always be encouraging, combining criticism and suggestions for improvement with praise for what went well. However, some supervisors will focus exclusively on the aspects of your project needing work, passing over any parts that are already strong. Hence, an overall balance of negative comments on draft work should not be taken to imply that the work is weak and will receive a low mark. If you are concerned that the tone or balance of comments indicates serious flaws, you should go back to your supervisor and ask them directly if that is the case. But always reflect on the negative comments, take them on-board and re-work the project accordingly.

Overall, though, one supervisory experience cannot be compared with another, so do not be concerned if your supervisor appears less impressed with your work than other students' supervisors are with theirs. Some academics supply harsh comments but, by comparison, give generous marks, while others might do the reverse. You would only need to be concerned in the unlikely event that the comments were unfounded or incorrect.

Supervisors are usually juggling a range of different roles, so it is vital to use their time effectively. It is a waste of your supervisor's time, which they will find irritating, if you:

- Turn up to meetings late repeatedly or without a very good cause
- Don't prepare, so you have no questions to ask, leaving the supervisor to drive the meeting
- Ignore the advice you are given
- Take offence at mild and well-intentioned criticism of your work
- Expect your supervisor to undertake tasks that are not part of their role
- Expect to receive a high mark while putting in minimal effort
- Leave everything until the last minute and then expect your supervisor to treat your e-mails and requests as urgent

If, for some legitimate reason, you know you will be late for a meeting or delayed in submitting a piece of work, out of politeness, drop your supervisor a note to let them know so that they can adjust their schedule accordingly. Don't just fail to turn up or send a pointless message the next day about what happened. Supervisors will have heard numerous imaginative excuses for late work or failure to attend meetings over the years, so the best strategy is to be refreshingly honest. If you overslept or forgot an appointment, be very apologetic but don't be tempted to lie as it won't wash and would further damage your reputation and working relationship.

As mentioned above, the frequency with which academics check and respond to e-mail varies enormously, so when e-mailing your supervisor, do not expect an instant response and always wait at least a few days before sending a reminder unless the matter is urgent. I met a student once who set e-mails to resend automatically every hour until they got a response! As you can imagine, that technique was not popular with academic staff, and the student was soon persuaded to adopt a more patient approach.

Similarly, while all supervisors will work within a framework established at the department or school level regarding the amount and timing of supervisory contact, each scholar will have different expectations about how much input they will provide to their students and on what basis. Some supervisors will be very 'hands-off', only responding when their students contact them, while others will expect to be much more involved in the process and will be proactive in telling students when to meet them and what they should have achieved at each stage. Many different models for supervision will be acceptable within the department's general guidelines, so, to some extent, you have little choice but to 'go with the flow' and conform to the approach to the process that your allocated supervisor adopts.

Ensure that you pre-arrange meetings with your supervisor or drop by during their office hours, which are set times that each academic commits to being available to see students without an appointment. Avoid just turning up out of those hours unless it is an emergency since your supervisor will be expecting to spend time on other activities rather than seeing you, and so you may receive a less warm welcome than if you had timed your visit more carefully.

When you are due to meet your supervisor, make sure you are well prepared for the discussions. Think beforehand about what you want to achieve from each meeting and plan in advance a list of questions you want to ask. Try to direct the flow of the session yourself to get the outcome that you want. If there are awkward silences with your supervisor having to take charge and question you on how you are doing, the meeting will be less useful to you than it could have been.

Your supervisor's role is to push you forwards from where you were, and so the further you are already into your project, the more in-depth guidance you will receive. Your supervisor might be able to suggest where to start looking for existing research on your chosen topic or which class of models would be appropriate to analyse the data. But it would be a much better use of the time you have with them if you have already nailed down these fundamental aspects to leave the meetings free for a more detailed discussion. In general, your supervisor should be commenting on your ideas rather than establishing the ideas from scratch. If you find that they are driving the agenda, you need to be more proactive and forward-thinking in future.

Your supervisor will probably get to know you better than any other staff member except your personal tutor, so they would be an obvious choice to ask for a reference for a job or further study applications when you leave. That makes it all the more vital that you create a good impression throughout and try your best.

If (or when) you hit difficulties with the project, your supervisor should always be there to offer suggestions or steer you towards another colleague or resource that might be better placed to help. Never be afraid to seek guidance when you need it. This could be for a specific narrow task, such as operating a piece of software or trying to get your head around what should go in an abstract. Or you might require support with something more substantive, such as not knowing where to start or feeling overwhelmed by the enormity of the task ahead. Although you would usually not expect your supervisor to show you how to use a statistical package or to act as a counsellor, they will be aware of some resources that are available if you cannot identify any yourself.

1.3.4   Other sources of support

A vast array of sources of support and guidance is at your disposal, each of which is discussed at various points in this book, including friends and classmates, other academic staff, forums and discussion boards. Having discussions with experts on the subject matter – not only your supervisor but also other academic members of staff and PhD students – can be valuable in providing additional ideas and suggestions. But since you cannot over-use their time, you should refrain from contacting them until you have done enough background research that you could have an informed and worthwhile conversation.

Current or former project students can be another invaluable asset in helping you to overcome the issues that arise as you work on your research. But suppose that no other students are working on the same topic as you in your department. In that case, it is also worth considering whether you can develop an e-support network by looking for students at other universities studying in similar areas. For example, people often post questions to forums and chatrooms; you could do the same, and it is surprising how commonly academics and other experienced researchers reply to these and offer their expert guidance and suggestions for free.

If you are struggling with a particular aspect of your project work, the more clearly you can explain what the issue is, the more targeted help your supervisor or others will be able to give. And the more initiative you have already taken to sort out the problem before contacting them, the keener they will be to offer support because they will appreciate that you have sought alternative solutions rather than over-relying on them.

It is sometimes said that supervisory time is a precious and finite resource, so you must use it wisely. If you waste too much, it may be used up just when you need it the most. An essential aspect of dealing with your supervisor is to demonstrate some independence in your learning. While they are there to help you, they should not always be the first point of contact when you hit a problem or there is something you cannot understand. Show some resourcefulness and investigate other ways to solve problems before turning to your supervisor – a vast amount of information is available on the internet through YouTube videos, forums and blogs. It is probably the case that other students will be having or will have had similar types of problems, so you can also rely on them as a mutual support network.

As well as providing support and guidance towards the completion of the dissertation, your supervisor is also likely to be the first marker of the final project. While they will be doing so within a well-established framework, it would be unwise to put them into a negative frame of mind about you and your work by continually bugging them over relatively minor issues that you could have dealt with yourself. A supervisor who has needed to spend much time telling you in detail what to do or solving problems that you encounter could legitimately consider that the work they now need to mark is partly their own, and they may grade it accordingly by deducting a portion for the part that they feel you didn't do.

It is worth reflecting on what you cannot reasonably expect from your supervisor, as well as what you can. In most cases, your supervisor will not:
- Provide you with an 'oven-ready' research topic
- Provide you with data or code
- Fix your code or statistical programs when they don't work
- Show you how to write any part of the project
- Correct your spelling and grammatical errors

Concerning all these points, your supervisor might have suggestions for where to look or how to sort out the issues, but the primary responsibility in all cases is yours.

Try your hardest not to fall out with your supervisor! Fortunately, this is an infrequent occurrence. As a supervisor for over 25 years, I don't think I ever had a serious dispute with any of my research students, although I considered some of them rude, and some were more fun to work with than others. As a new researcher, you need all the help you can get to obtain the most you can out of the experience and maximise your grade. Most supervisors are consummate professionals, and so they will still provide support and guidance even if you have a bad working relationship with them. But in such circumstances, they might not be willing to go beyond the minimum level that could be expected of them. It would also make the whole experience much less pleasant than it otherwise could have been for both parties.

1.3.5   Should a record be kept of supervision meetings?

Ideally, both parties should make notes of every meeting – the time, place and duration of the meeting, what was discussed, whether there were any deliverables or targets agreed, what would be the next meeting's date, and so on. Taking minutes of the meeting will not only act as an aide-mémoire and ensure that suggestions are acted upon, but it will also help to avoid any subsequent misunderstandings or disputes which can protect both the student and the supervisor if things go wrong.

However, I must be honest at this stage that while such record-keeping is good practice, I have never done so, either when I was a student or, for a much longer period, as a supervisor. I believe that life is too short, and the academy already has so much paperwork that we can no longer function as teachers or researchers, but no doubt many colleagues would regard such a perspective as old-fashioned. I am sure that the day will soon come where meeting logs will be a requirement for both students and their supervisors. If you are willing to take the time to do that, it would be a worthwhile activity.

1.3.6   Can you get departmental funding for research expenses?

As an undergraduate or master's student, it is improbable that you will be able to secure any funding from your department to cover research expenses unless you are funded through a scholarship, and even then, it is an outside chance. But if the costs you believe that you will incur might be high (e.g., expenses involved with conducting a survey, travel for interviews, purchasing a specialist database), it is worth asking your supervisor if the department will offer financial support. But be prepared for a negative response, which means that you will have to rely on your own resources and probably keep any outgoings to a minimum. For this reason, it is essential to consider likely research costs right from the time you are selecting a topic and pick the research methods accordingly.

1.3.7 Sponsored or independent research?

Some business schools are sufficiently well connected with industry that they can offer students the opportunity to work on a specific project with a 'sponsor'. Alternatively, if you can make such connections yourself by linking your dissertation to your job or an association you have with an external organisation, there are potentially several benefits:

- The sponsor may provide the topic ideas and give additional expert guidance from a practical perspective
- Sponsorship may give the student an insight into the kind of research problems that are of interest to practitioners and would probably ensure that the work is practically focused and of direct relevance to the private sector
- The sponsor may provide access to proprietary or confidential data, which will broaden the range of topics that could be tackled
- Most importantly, many students hope that if they impress the firm they are working on their project with, a permanent job offer will follow
- Some funding might be made available for research expenses

The chance to work on a sponsored project is usually greatly sought after by students, but it is very much a double-edged sword and that there are also several disadvantages. A potential drawback of working in such a partnership is that by linking the project with an outside entity, there might be tensions between what the two parties (your university department and the external organisation) want to see from the work. The organisation might wish you to examine something of practical value to them and which they can put to use directly. They might also prefer the work to be written in an entirely non-technical language that non-academics can easily understand. But your supervisor will want to see a report written in the style of an academic paper, using scholarly language with an emphasis on the contribution to knowledge rather than to practice.

The disappointing reality is that the problems of most interest and relevance to practitioners are often (although admittedly not always) of less interest to an academic audience, and vice versa. Fundamentally, the objectives of the sponsor and the university may be divergent. For example, a stereotypical investment firm might like to see a project that compares several technical trading rules and evaluates their profitability. Yet many academics would argue that this area has been well researched before and that finding a highly profitable rule does not constitute a contribution to knowledge and is therefore weak as a research project.

There is a danger that by trying to please two separate audiences, you will satisfy neither of them. Remember that, first and foremost, the project is an academic exercise as part of your degree programme, and so this should always be the primary consideration if there are tensions between what would maximise your mark and what an external party wants. Furthermore, most schools cannot offer such sponsorships and even those that can usually provide them to only a fraction of the class.

In summary, if you have the opportunity to undertake a sponsored project, consider the offer carefully as there could be numerous benefits. But also ensure that you would still be in the driving seat and that your research would be of academic as well as practical value – after all, it will almost certainly be the academic who grades the work. Or consider that you might have to take the time to produce two different versions of the work, one for each of the academic and practitioner audiences.

1.3.8   Can you undertake a group-based project?

It is often more fun and easier to work on a project with other students. As you will have seen (or soon will see), the majority of academic publications (papers and books) are multi-authored by teams of academics working together rather than sole-authored by individuals studying alone. There are several reasons for this: principally, working with others allows much faster progress and permits authors to cover their weaknesses by focusing on the parts of the research process they enjoy and at which they are best.

The same is true of student projects, of course. If you get to choose who is in your group and you make that choice strategically, the whole process could be more enjoyable and less stressful than working alone. You will also be able to add 'teamworking' to the list of transferrable skills that you have assimilated as part of the process.

However, there are risks too, particularly if the people in your group were assigned to you rather you being allowed to choose them since you would lose a certain amount of control over the timeline and the quality of the work. Dealing with strained group dynamics or individuals who refuse to engage with the process can be challenging and traumatic. You would need to clarify in advance the roles and responsibilities of each group member and ensure that everyone makes a substantive contribution. The process of specialisation in the course of a joint project will mean that different group members will take on varying tasks and hence pick-up different skills, with not all people achieving all of the learning outcomes.

Ultimately, the vast majority of degree programmes specifically rule out group projects, instead specifying that the dissertation must be a solo endeavour. That being the case, you would have no choice but to work primarily by yourself. However, it would still be allowable and indeed desirable to discuss ideas with fellow project students, offering each other support with technical issues (e.g., problems getting data or estimating models), and reading each other's drafts. But you would need to select individual topics, do your own reading, conduct your own analysis, and write the project yourself.

1.3.9   Part-time dissertations

Although the majority of students are registered on full-time degree programmes, some are engaged in part-time study. In such cases, the total number of hours of effort expected will be the same as for a full-time schedule but spread over a longer timeframe – for example, six months rather than three. This long horizon may encourage a feeling that there is time to spare, but part-time study is usually even more challenging as the student needs to balance academic study with employment (possibly full-time) or significant family responsibilities.

There is also the danger that the momentum full-time students are able to generate when focusing on their projects is not achievable for part-timers, so that the latter are never able to really get going with it. Therefore, if you are registered on a part-time programme, it is even more important to establish a schedule towards completion and to endeavour to stick to it since the consequences of falling behind are direr: competing time demands will mean that it is not possible to work intensively at the end to catch up.

If you are registered on a full-time programme but are now doing outside, paid work for a significant number of hours per week, it is worth considering applying to switch to part-time registration, which would stretch the period available to complete your project and buy you considerably more time. But be careful – having a job for more than a few hours per week during term-time registration for a full-time degree programme is probably against the rules.

Another difficulty relates to part-time students' scope to visit the campus and engage with their supervisor and fellow learners. Full-time students are generally based at, or close to, their universities for the entire duration of their studies. On the other hand, part-time students might be located a considerable distance away from their university and only visit infrequently for lectures and classes, which can engender a sense of isolation. Consequently, part-time students need to make additional efforts to embed themselves into the academic community at their university, taking every opportunity to engage with their supervisor, other academic staff and students.

1.4   Getting an eye on the finishing line

1.4.1   Attributes of a good project

Most universities in the UK have a similar approach to marking dissertations, in part because they will all be guided by the Quality Assurance Agency (QAA) for Higher Education. This organisation provides subject descriptors for Accounting and for Finance that define what students should have learned and the skills they should have developed when studying for a degree in each of these areas. The requirements for the work's features and quality will nonetheless vary depending on the level (BA/BSc vs. MA/MSc, etc.) of the programme and how many credits are allocated to the project.

As this book proceeds, I will explain in detail how to write the project report and what it should look like. But for now, in summary, the key attributes of a good research project are:

- It is of the right length
- It tackles the brief that was distributed at the outset
- It states and addresses a set of research aims or questions
- It engages with the existing literature on the topic
- It contains competent investigative work
- It has a clear and logical structure
- It is well written and pleasant to read with a good presentation
- It is submitted and on time.

A good project will also contain an in-depth analysis of the issues at hand, rather than a superficial, purely descriptive presentation, as well as an individual contribution. A good project will be interesting, and it will have relevance for one or more user groups (although the user group may be other academic researchers and not necessarily practitioners); it may or may not be on a currently fashionable and newsworthy topic. The best research challenges prior beliefs and changes how the reader thinks about the problem under investigation. Good projects can be primarily of interest to other academics, and they do not necessarily have to be of direct practical applicability. On the other hand, highly functional work must still be well-grounded in the academic approach to research.

1.4.2   How will the research project be marked?

You might be surprised to see a section on the mark scheme for the project in the introductory chapter to this book when you have scarcely thought about where to start. But knowing from the outset what you are aiming for and how it will be evaluated will help ensure that you remain on track and always driven in a direction that focuses on maximising the final score.

There are two broad types of approach to establishing the appropriate grade that the marker might use. The first is where the assessment is separated into discrete sections such as 'context and motivation; conceptual framework and hypotheses development; methodology; results and analysis; . . . ; presentation and structure.' In this case, each section will have a maximum number of points available, and the overall mark for the project will be the sum of the scores awarded for each individual unit.

If your department uses this approach to marking and you are able to obtain a breakdown of the weightings that they attach to each section, it will provide some indication of the amount of effort you should expect to allocate to each aspect, and also how many words you should plan to write. For instance, as I will discuss in chapter 10, students sometimes write literature reviews that are too long and unbalance the project overall. If only 20% of the overall mark weight is attached to this aspect, it would suggest not spending half of your time and a third of your available words on it.

A second approach involves the marker taking a holistic view of the project and awarding a single score. I prefer this marking style, although it provides less structure and requires more experience and insight from the grader. This approach offers opportunities for the marker to assign different weights to each aspect of the project across students. For instance, a student might have had a genuinely novel, ambitious and exciting idea that was severely let down by sloppy empirical work and poor writing. Such a student would likely receive a low mark if based on a grid-style of grading since they will score poorly on all sections unless there is one for originality. But a one-line marking scheme can recognise the challenging nature of what the student was trying to achieve and award a higher mark accordingly.

If there is a research project marking scheme to which students are permitted access, try to get hold of it at the earliest possible stage. This information will provide you with a guide as to what aspects of the project are the primary foci of the assessment, and as you come close to the final submission, you can use it as a checklist to ensure that your document embodies all of the required features. What are markers looking for? In summary, the grader will want to see that you can:

- Find and select your own reading material appropriate to the topic
- Review, summarise and understand the existing literature
- Define an exciting and relevant set of research aims or questions
- Select an appropriate method to tackle the research questions
- Collect data that are relevant given the choice of objectives
- Demonstrate that you can generate and understand your results
- Draw appropriate conclusions supported by your findings
- Pull the whole document together into a coherent, logical and readable piece.

For interest, Table 1.2 shows how to interpret marks within each classification range and the characteristics that a project at that level might typically embody. However, this is just a typecast; naturally, projects will rarely be of a uniform standard across all dimensions; more likely, they will be strong on some aspects and weak on others.

1.4.3 The role of the external examiner

After submission, your dissertation is likely to be marked first by your supervisor, then by another staff member from your department, probably independently (i.e., without the second marker seeing the supervisor's grade and comments until after they have formed their own judgement).

In the UK system, a senior academic from another university will be appointed to examine and approve all of the provisional degree results before they are awarded by a department at each level (bachelor's or master's). This person is known as the external examiner and is a key part of the process of ensuring that standards are comparable across universities. The external examiner will be invited to consider the range of marks awarded for dissertations on a particular programme, examining a sample of them in detail, focusing on any that have failed and any that have received

Table 1.2: Possible mark ranges for projects and their interpretation

Mark	Undergraduate Classification	Postgraduate Classification	Interpretation
80-100	'Starred first'	High distinction	An exceptional project. Very few errors, if any, in all aspects; sensible choice of topic; shows ambition beyond the level expected with an attempt to make and articulate an original contribution; relevant literature cited appropriately and evaluated critically; the research aims are clearly identified; appropriate, sophisticated methods are selected; a detailed and insightful analysis of the findings leading to appropriate conclusions; suggestions for further study and implications for policy or practice are present, together with a thoughtful consideration of the research conducted; the report is well presented with very few grammatical or spelling errors; overall, the work shows genuine creativity and is of the best quality that could reasonably be expected at this level with very few suggestions for improvement. The work might be publishable (with modifications)
70-79	First	Distinction	An excellent project. Treatment of the topic is comprehensive; possibly containing a few minor mistakes, but none of these is sufficiently serious to damage the work significantly; research aims are identified; relevant literature is cited in an appropriate way with a critique; appropriate methods are selected; the findings are analysed in detail with few, if any, errors in interpretation; justified conclusions are drawn; a high standard of presentation with at most a small number of grammatical or spelling issues; very interesting to read; overall, a very high-quality project that could nonetheless have been even better
60-69	Upper second	Merit	A good project. Clear understanding demonstrated of what research is; the literature review is sound, including an appropriate number of relevant sources, although it is unlikely to have developed a critique; there is a solid attempt at investigative work; the results are present and appropriately analysed, although the depth might be limited; there might be some errors, although none of them is fatal so as to make the project worthless; the presentation is good in terms of both the structure and the writing; while there might be some typographical errors, the work will still be pleasant to read
50-59	Lower second	Pass	An acceptable project. Shows some understanding of the subject matter; there will be some aims, but they will be rudimentary and unchallenging; the project makes an attempt to do some investigative work, but there will be weaknesses or a lack of depth in the analysis; there are results that achieve some of the project aims; there will be a relevant literature review, but it might be mostly descriptive; the structure could have been improved but is reasonably logical and can be followed; there could be many grammatical or spelling errors, but the meaning is still evident; there will be a concluding chapter, but it will probably be merely a brief summary and not provide suggestions for future research
40-49	Third	Marginal fail	A project with some obvious flaws. The main ingredients will probably be there in the project, including a literature review and some investigative work; the methods might be inappropriate or incorrectly applied; there will either be serious omissions (e.g., no research aims or no proper conclusions) or problems with the execution that render the findings dubious; referencing will be patchy, containing omissions and inaccuracies; the citations may be limited in number or dated
40	Fail	Fail	A project with serious issues. Important sections will be absent – e.g., no aims stated, no proper literature review, no findings or results tabulated but not analysed, no conclusions; references in a mess, systematically missing, or very small in number; there might be severe misunderstandings about how to apply the methods that render the results invalid; poor sentence structure or hard to read with some parts unintelligible

first class/distinction marks. They will also pay particular attention to any situations where an adjustment of the dissertation mark by a few points would be material to the overall degree outcome. The external examiner, whose decisions are definitive, will look at any anomalous cases or situations where the two internal markers could not agree on the appropriate grading.

Therefore, if your supervisor and second marker agree on your dissertation mark, and your mark is not pivotal to your degree outcome, the external examiner will probably not read it. However, the latter will act as a safety net if there is disagreement internally or where the addition of a couple of extra marks could make all the difference to your classification. The existence of such a three marker approach incorporating the external examiner system should reassure you that the mark you will receive will be fair and an appropriate reflection of the quality of work you have submitted.

Although having some background awareness of the assessment scheme is valuable to have from the outset, equally, it is best not to become too fixated on how the project will be marked. Instead, just try to make your work as good as it can be and focus in detail on the marking criteria at a later stage when you will be able to use it to guide your further time and effort. If you are able to assess roughly how well the current version of your work stacks up against these, you will be able to improve it in an efficient way using the same method of thinking as the person who will ultimately be evaluating it.

Further reading

- If you struggle to manage your time, the book by Carroll (2012) might be useful, and Redfield (2020) provides practical tips to stop procrastinating
- There are numerous self-help resources for people to deal with stress and build their mental resilience. The books by Johnstone (2019) and Wilson (2020) are good starting points
- There are also numerous books on how to enhance the supervisor-supervisee relationship, although most are written from the perspective of the former. Tanggaard (2016) is a good example that includes a student perspective.

Chapter takeaways – top tips for success

- ⊛ Conducting a research project will provide you with many transferrable skills in demand by employers
- ⊛ Successful completion of a research project depends more on putting in the hours and dogged determination than being super-smart
- ⊛ Organising yourself from the outset and preventing procrastination are essential
- ⊛ Keep backups of everything using free cloud storage
- ⊛ Treat your supervisor's time as precious, and don't waste it

Chapter takeaways – continued

- ⊛ Don't expect your supervisor to provide you with a topic or check your spelling
- ⊛ Seek help when you need it, but make use of a range of sources of support
- ⊛ Take sponsorship for your project if you can get it but be aware of the disadvantages
- ⊛ Get hold of the marking criteria as soon as possible and think about how to match up your work with what is required

2. APPROACHES TO RESEARCH

Learning outcomes: this chapter covers

- ✓ The difference between scholarly and everyday research
- ✓ Different philosophies of research
- ✓ The distinction between positivism and interpretivism
- ✓ How to classify research and learning
- ✓ The differences between inductive and deductive research

2.1 What is research?

The Cambridge dictionary defines it as the 'detailed study of a subject, especially in order to discover (new) information or reach a (new) understanding.' This general definition of the word embodies the fact that in everyday parlance, deliberately searching for information to find something out that you did not already know would fit under the research umbrella. If you scoured the internet to find the best type of mortgage for you, given your circumstances, this constitutes research because you did not previously know that information, but after investigation, you will.

However, the academic (or 'scholarly') definition of research is somewhat narrower, such as 'the process of investigation leading to a new contribution to knowledge.' This statement embodies the idea that academic research involves learning something new to everybody, not just new to you. In other words, you would be generating new ideas that could not be found anywhere else in the world before, and hence the example of finding the best mortgage would not fit within the scholarly definition of research. Scholarly research is a strategically planned, systematic and highly organised search for new knowledge. It provides routes to formally testing and evaluating new ideas to determine whether the data support them. Sometimes, research that is new to everyone is termed primary research, whereas when you learn something that others already know, it is called secondary research.

The main purpose of research is to understand the physical, natural and social worlds in detail. This relates to physical or natural occurrences, such as the climate, the migration of birds, or crop yields, but it also involves social experiences, including human behaviour and decision-making. Once scientists or social scientists have firm knowledge about a phenomenon, this can lead to a range of related objectives for further research, including:

- Explaining why these phenomena occur
- Categorising events or occurrences as being of one type or another
- Evaluating the efficacy of various courses of action to control or mitigate something happening (e.g., preventing flooding or stock market bubbles from occurring)
- Forecasting what is likely to happen in the future

Research is important because, although we rarely see it being conducted, its findings influence our everyday lives in so many ways. As well as obvious examples such as the development and testing of vaccines against diseases, product development and choices of which government policies to implement are also frequently supported by research.

2.2   Types of research

There are various ways to typecast and classify research, and this chapter will now examine several approaches to doing this. Being able to categorise research output is useful when trying to identify how your work fits into the bigger picture, and it also helps other researchers when they come to evaluate a particular piece of work.

2.2.1   Four classes of research

The book by Hussey and Hussey (1997) provides a helpful classification of research into four types (although a similar framework is presented by many other authors):

1. Exploratory
2. Descriptive
3. Analytical
4. Predictive

In some ways, this typology also describes how the body of work on a particular topic develops chronologically.

Exploratory research refers to the process of scholars working in a new area where the current extent of knowledge is meagre, no structure has yet emerged, no formal research agenda has been developed, and it is too early to identify any theoretical framework or hypotheses. Such studies will aim to gather evidence that will subsequently be used (probably by other researchers) to develop further and formalise the ideas. Exploratory research usually adopts a case study or observation approach to data collection and analysis, with formal quantitative models rare. This type of research tends to be unstructured, and therefore, while the originality will be evident since the topic area is new, it tends not to fit into an established framework. It may also be accused of lacking the rigour of the other types of research and hence is riskier and less common in accounting and finance.

Descriptive research adds structure to exploratory research, where data about the phenomenon under study are gathered and documented systematically, and the new research area begins to develop some form and establishes concepts. This research may even extend towards a typology (i.e., a classification) of the phenomenon under study. There will be little analysis or depth at this stage, so this is a similarly risky type of research in accounting and finance. While it is more structured than exploratory research, it may be considered somewhat superficial, answering 'what'- type questions rather than 'how' or 'why' a particular phenomenon occurs.

The distinction between *description* and *analysis* is crucial in accounting, finance and economics. When you describe your data, you are merely pointing out interesting features or explaining how the data are, not why they take the values they do, which would be analysis. Similarly, when you describe a phenomenon (such as stock markets tending to rise in January) or a piece of research, you are merely reporting an observation or rephrasing an argument that someone else has already made. But when you analyse it, you are attempting to explain why an event happened, how a piece of research relates to others, and whether the findings are valid and robust.

The majority of research projects in accounting and finance fall under the analytical umbrella. Such research takes a further step from descriptive research in that it tries to understand and explain why a phenomenon occurs or how it has occurred. This extension might involve developing a theoretical or empirical model that consists of specifying causal links between the variables of interest and possibly establishing a set of testable hypotheses. Analytical research is prevalent in accounting and finance because it can lead to profound insights, and it involves a rich and rigorous examination of a phenomenon. However, there are limitations such as a frequent confusion between correlation (two variables tending to move together) and causality (movements in one variable cause movements in another).

Finally, *predictive research* involves taking existing findings and trying to use them to determine whether they plausibly also apply in other places or situations without actually collecting data and testing the latter. In essence, this class of research involves a reapplication of prior knowledge to create additional insights. Many research projects will have a predictive element, although this frequently occurs after conducting analysis rather than as a stand-alone endeavour.

2.2.2   A Framework for Classifying Learning

Another way to think about research is from the perspective of what you have learned through the process rather than the type of research being undertaken. The famous Bloom's classification (sometimes known as Bloom's taxonomy) does this, establishing a 'ladder' with six rungs, each building on the level beneath it. The ladder classifies a researcher's level of familiarity with and understanding of a particular topic. Sometimes the classification is instead conceptually represented as a pyramid rather than a ladder. Bloom was an educational psychologist, and his original scale had three aspects, although only the cognitive one is widely employed in teaching research methods. The ladder is sometimes expressed in the following terms:

Knowledge – being able to remember a particular piece of information, probably without being able to understand or explain it. This bottom rung on the ladder relates to being aware of fundamental concepts and ideas.

Comprehension – not only knowing information but also understanding what it means so that you could explain that meaning to someone else. You could also summarise the information and arrange it in different ways. This level is the minimum required to conduct a literature review, which would not be possible while only at the lowest rung on the ladder (knowledge).

Application – here, you could take information and apply it in different contexts. Hence, this level moves beyond only a conceptual understanding towards being able to use the knowledge in various settings to solve real problems.

Analysis – this involves being able to explain why certain things happen based on linking pieces of information together and identifying causal relationships.

Synthesis – where pieces of information are chosen for a purpose and combined to generate new knowledge and understanding.

Evaluation – the highest level of attainment in the knowledge space embodying the ability to reflect on information and other research to form a viewpoint or verdict on it and to provide recommendations about the best course of action.

Note that the taxonomy should not be taken to imply that only evaluatory research is worthwhile since that is not the case. A good piece of work will demonstrate that all rungs on the ladder have been mastered to a lesser or greater extent.

2.3   The philosophy of research

Numerous books on how to do research begin with one or more chapters on the philosophy of research and different high-level approaches to research. The texts use esoteric words such as ontology and epistemology, positivism versus interpretivism, and so on. These are the foundations upon which the 'house of knowledge' is built, and the ideas relate to how knowledge is gathered and interpreted and what methods are used to obtain it.

You would be able to complete a very successful project by just pushing ahead with the research, applying the knowledge that exists and possibly slightly extending it by working within that framework but remaining blissfully unaware of these concepts or how they underpin research structures. It is certainly not necessary for students studying for a bachelor's or master's degree to know a great deal about the philosophy of research, and it is unlikely that you will need to explain the rationale for your choice of methods using the specialist terminology described here.

But having a basic understanding of these ideas will help you to be able to classify research (yours and others') and to understand how the research paradigm adopted by the investigator leads to a research design that will favour some particular methods over others. Knowing this material will also help you evaluate research, reflect on which methodology might be most appropriate to tackle a specific problem and how different approaches can yield alternative insights. Therefore, this chapter now discusses two of the key concepts in this area – ontology and epistemology – and how they relate to the kinds of research conducted in accounting and finance.

Ontology is concerned with what knowledge exists ('what is out there to know?') while epistemology is about the theory of knowledge and the knowledge gathering process ('what can we find out and how can we find out about it?') Knowledge can be defined as a set of justified true beliefs or true statements. There is more than one ontological view of the world, and the two key ontological positions are objectivism and subjectivism. Objectivists believe that there is one reality that exists independent of the person experiencing it, whereas subjectivists (sometimes known as constructivists) contend that each reality is invented by the person observing it. Therefore, a person's view of 'how things are' is socially constructed and hence all knowledge is subjective.

Epistemology is the branch of philosophy concerned with how knowledge is generated and the techniques we consider best to produce it. Epistemology is sometimes termed the theory of knowledge. Two contrasting epistemological approaches are the starting points for thinking about knowledge creation, known as positivism and interpretivism, which are linked with the objectivist and subjectivist ontological positions, respectively.

The positivist and interpretivist epistemological philosophies are also sometimes termed research paradigms, and they are diametrically opposed, which means that many researchers would argue they cannot be combined in a single study as they are logically incompatible. The key distinction between them arises from how researchers gather knowledge under each paradigm. In other words, the research approaches, including the methods and data collection, are very different, and the main features of each will now be discussed.

2.3.1 Positivism

Positivism is arguably the oldest philosophical approach and dates back to Aristotle, although it is often argued to have been invented by Auguste Comte (1880) and John S. Mill (1881) in the nineteenth century. It is also associated with the French philosopher René Descartes and the French sociologist Emile Durkheim, amongst others. Sometimes positivism is known as the 'scientific approach' to research since it is the methodology for knowledge creation employed in the natural and physical sciences. Its proponents argue that research in the social sciences should be conducted in the same fashion.

According to positivists:

- Research should focus on observable and verifiable phenomena and avoid engaging in conjecture or supposition
- They claim to take an unbiased view of the world when conducting research
- Cause and effect arise and can be captured in a model, and hence the empirical method of collecting and analysing data follows
- Proposing and testing causal relationships is a key objective of research
- There is a congruence between what we observe and how things really are
- They are concerned with facts and not with judgements or values
- The key approach is to use theories to generate testable hypotheses, which are then applied to data
- The methods should be 'scientific' (using mathematics, statistics and large databases and involving repeated sampling)
- Assumptions might be required to test theories or implement models
- Researchers should be unbiased in their views about their research and should be at a distance from their data or test subjects

Positivism was the dominant paradigm for social research as well as scientific exploration up to the 1960s. Until that point, most researchers in the social sciences believed that it was the appropriate epistemological position for all fields of enquiry, while philosophy had also become primarily focused on concrete questions to which there should be an answer.

But in sociology, the consensus around the pre-eminence of positivism started to collapse in the 1950s and continued thereafter. There were several reasons for this decline, including its reliance on some knowledge as being given or certain and the difficulty in answering particular kinds of questions about human behaviour using a hands-off approach with statistics. There was also concern that too much weight was being placed on the outcome of hypothesis tests, whereas in reality, if a hypothesis is rejected, it could be because it is wrong or merely that one of the assumptions built into the theory behind the hypothesis does not hold.

2.3.2 Interpretivism

The concerns outlined at the end of the previous section led to the growth of an alternative epistemological approach, interpretivism, which has a much shorter history. It is in many ways the opposite of positivism, and indeed, it is occasionally referred to as 'antipositivism.' Although some of its ways of working have been around much longer, the development of interpretivism is often credited to German sociologists such as Karl Marx, Georg Simmel and Max Weber.

Interpretivists believe that:

- There is a clear distinction between the natural and social sciences so that the two need entirely different approaches to gather knowledge
- Judgement and fact cannot easily be separated, and therefore all knowledge is tentative
- Purely objective analysis is impossible since all research is a function of the opinions and attitudes of the researcher who conducts it
- Usually, the emphasis is on documenting and understanding phenomena and not on explaining them using causal analysis
- The approach is based on observation, case studies, interviews, etc.
- Detailed investigation of small datasets is preferred over arm's-length analysis of big data
- The context of research is important so that a different researcher in a slightly different environment may obtain starkly varying results
- Assumptions are not needed as the researcher can observe what is happening

The interpretivist researcher understands that findings cannot be independent of the investigator's views or the manner in which the research is conducted. So this dependence is explicitly acknowledged as interpretivists observe each phenomenon in action within its own environment and typically use qualitative techniques as will be discussed in chapter 8.

Positivists would retort that the interpretivist approach to obtaining knowledge is *ad hoc* and unscientific. However, the latter argue that the additional insight gained from a close examination of phenomena and events in their own environments makes a different and more valuable contribution to knowledge that outweighs the lack of replicability or generalisability. The debate about the efficacy of each paradigm continues. Nowadays, positivism has a much more modest role in modern social science research, yet it is still endemic and represents the usual paradigm forming the approach used in virtually all research in finance and economics, with some accounting research fitting under each umbrella.

2.3.3 Critical realism

Between the two extreme epistemological positions sits critical realism, also known as 'post positivism', and as constructivism, realism or pragmatism, which seeks to bridge positivism and interpretivism by both understanding and explaining phenomena. A pragmatist would support strands of the positivist and interpretivist arguments, seeing the value of both large-scale statistical analysis and a fine-grained micro-examination of individual cases. Thus, pragmatists believe that the same methods can be used in natural and social sciences but that an added interpretation is required in the latter case. They support mixed methods research and are willing to use whatever research design is best suited to the particular task at hand. In some cases, that will be a sophisticated econometric analysis of aggregate secondary data, but in others, it could be one-to-one unstructured interviews with key individuals in an organisation (see chapter 10 and chapter 11 for detailed discussions of these methods).

Critical realism retains the key ideology of positivism but recognises that analysis can never be truly objective or certain, so that we should merely hope to obtain a close approximation to the truth rather than its totality. It is a relatively recently developed perspective compared with positivism and interpretivism, drawing ideas from both. Critical realists believe that there is a truth that holds irrespective of how people view it, but how people see this reality can be distorted. These distortions arise both because people cannot gather all relevant information (e.g., they can only gather imperfect historical recollections rather than seeing for themselves what happened in the past) and since their pre-conceived beliefs heavily influence their perspectives. In that sense, reality is, therefore, still to a degree socially constructed, as interpretivists argue. There are also several other paradigms that are again variants of the two primary types, but these are beyond the scope of student projects in accounting or finance and so are not further considered here.

How will you know which ontological or epistemological position to adopt? Rather than trying to answer this question directly, my suggestion would be to focus on your research aims, which will lead naturally to a particular design and a set of methods, as discussed in chapter 8. Incorporating such a statement of your research design will imply that you will have selected a specific epistemological approach, although you will have done so indirectly, and you probably do not need to refer to it directly in your dissertation. But having some idea of where your design sits within the range of possible approaches to knowledge creation will help you put it into perspective.

2.3.4 'Scientific revolutions'

A relevant question to ask when examining how the literature in a particular field develops over time is, 'if all knowledge is tentative, and could later be demonstrated to have been wrong, how does a subject move from one set of widely held beliefs to another?' The American philosopher, Thomas Kuhn (1962), suggested that a field's progress does not follow a continuous path, but there are periods where it develops rapidly and others where it stagnates. He also argued that once a set of ideas – what he called a paradigm – becomes established, it shapes future study as other researchers follow in the footsteps of the tradition developed by those previously working on the same topic.

Even though the ideas might be widely understood to be right at a particular point in time, if, in fact, they did not represent 'true knowledge', then an increasing array of evidence against the notions will emerge. These cases that do not fit in with the established patterns are termed anomalies. Initially, and for a potentially considerable time, any challenges to the established doctrine may be dismissed out of hand, and the anomalies are considered by those working in the mainstream of the field as irrelevant statistical coincidences. But eventually, a particular set of ideas may come to be viewed as inadequate as the number of anomalies, and the weight of evidence against the current perspective grow so substantial that they can no longer be summarily dismissed.

The paradigm then faces a crisis with new ideas that could potentially resolve the puzzles that have been created put forward. Kuhn argued that these new viewpoints might arise through a 'revolutionary scientist' who is perhaps more junior than those who developed the previous paradigm, and they will therefore not be so wedded to it. There will subsequently be a regime change to a completely new way of thinking about the particular issues, which Kuhn termed a 'paradigm shift', an expression that is still in widespread use today. An interesting implication of the occurrence of such paradigmatic breakdown and reconstruction is that the total amount of knowledge does not rise monotonically over time, since shifts involve a requirement to reconsider what we previously thought we knew and for puzzles that we believed were already solved to be reopened. So it is as if the global stock of knowledge is on an upward trajectory but with temporary declines as it is continually re-evaluated.

To offer an illustration of this process of paradigm shift, in finance through the 1970s through to the 2000s, it was widely considered by scholars that financial markets were broadly efficient with prices incorporating relevant information rapidly in most cases. This ties in with the risk-based view of how assets are priced, which purports that investors will be rewarded with higher expected returns for taking on additional risks. Thus, on average, the returns on riskier asset classes are higher than those on lower risk classes (equities outperform bonds, which outperform Treasury bills, etc.)

This era represented what Kuhn would term a period of 'normal science'. However, the global financial crisis of c.2008 spurred a period of 'extraordinary science' in Kuhn's terminology, where new ideas were entertained that previously would not have been taken seriously. The new approaches that emerged are based on the principles of behavioural finance and adaptive markets rather than neoclassical economics. It is possible that a scientific revolution will emerge, but the new ideas have still yet to fully take hold, and the majority of the previously existing models are still in widespread use. The paper by Gippel (2012) provides a highly readable and accessible treatment of this topic.

A particular point of concern among behavioural researchers, which led them to criticise orthodox finance theory, is the vast array of assumptions required to operationalise most of the models employed. For example, the striking list of suppositions stated before deriving the capital asset pricing model (CAPM). Those who adopt an interpretivist perspective might argue that such models are doomed to failure because the assumptions are demonstrably unrealistic (e.g., perfect capital markets, no short sales constraints, all agents have full information).

However, positivist researchers, dating back to Friedman (1953), have argued that the plausibility of model assumptions is not relevant, and a theory or model with questionable suppositions will still be valuable if it can explain observed outcomes.

Indeed, they would argue that the more unrealistic the assumptions the better, since this helps to make theories the simplest they can be so that models can abstract further from the complexities of the real issues. These concerns with the requirement for assumptions so that positivists can do their research led to the development of phenomenology in the 1960s and 1970s, which argued that our understanding of the world flows from the assumptions we make rather than reflecting how the world actually is.

2.3.5 Inductive versus deductive reasoning

Research following the 'scientific approach' involves beginning with a theory formulated into a set of testable hypotheses that are then evaluated using data. This ordering is known as deductive reasoning, or sometimes as a 'top-down' approach, which is prevalent in finance and much accounting research, associated with the positivist paradigm discussed above. The deductive approach involves a structured and formalised approach to analysis.

The converse, known as inductive reasoning, involves starting with empirical data, examining it carefully and then formulating a theory based on what is observed. Hence, according to the inductive approach, the data come first and the theory after as an output of the process, and vice versa for the deductive method where theory is an input. As a result, inductive theories make few assumptions since nothing is taken for granted about the entity under examination, and the researcher begins with a blank page. Inductive research is usually associated with the interpretivist paradigm. The distinctions between inductive and deductive research are summarised in Table 2.1 and explained in further detail in chapter 8.

In practice, most research involves at least a little of both approaches. Researchers using the scientific method might modify and improve their theories after seeing their empirical results, even though sometimes the work is written up to appear as if the theory was fully formulated before the empirical work began. Likewise, inductive researchers might have some initial ideas (perhaps based on previous research) and will not start their investigation with an entirely clean slate, although they will not have fully formulated a theory at the outset.

It might also be the case that researcher X develops a theory based on observing some data (an inductive approach), but then researcher Y reads the resulting study written by X and then takes that theory as a starting point for a new empirical analysis. Is this now a deductive theory? Therefore, in reality, the distinction is blurred, and most theory development is a mixture of both induction and deduction.

2.3.6 Grounded theory research

The grounded theory approach to social science research is attributed to Glaser and Strauss (1967) and is linked with inductive reasoning. It is, in some ways, the antithesis of the conventional scientific method. According to the latter, a theory is developed or implemented first, and it is then 'shown' to the data, with the theory

Table 2.1: The differences between inductive and deductive research

Characteristic	Approach	
	Deductive	Inductive
Alternative name	Scientific approach	Grounded theory approach
Epistemological position	Positivist	Interpretivist
Assumptions	Could be numerous	Not required
Standard research methods	Surveys, secondary data analysis	Case studies, interviews
Standard sample size	Large	Small
Order of steps	Formulate theory ↓ Test theory empirically ↓ Theory is supported or refuted by the data	Empirical observation ↓ Formulate theory to explain observed behaviour

either refuted or supported by empirical observation. Grounded theory does the reverse, where researchers begin *a priori* with observations. They explore the data (or situation) first and then use it to develop a theory that evolves along with their surveillance and is said to be grounded in the data – hence the name. According to the grounded theory approach, a theory emerges as a tentative step to putting assorted findings into a coherent framework and explaining them. It does not begin with a set of pre-determined testable hypotheses, nor would there necessarily even be a literature review before the investigative work begins.

In the management field broadly defined, the deductive approach to research where the theory comes first is sometimes known as structured research since the prior theory places structure onto the process of organising the investigative work and guides how it should be done. In reality, while most research in accounting and finance claims to use the scientific methodology, it is common to refine the theory in the light of the empirical evidence, which would be a hybrid of the two approaches.

Further reading

- There are numerous textbooks on the philosophy that underpins social sciences research, although many of them are specifically aimed at educational research. More general texts that might be of interest to students of accounting and finance include Howell (2012) and Williams (2016)
- Birks and Mills (2015) and Urquhart (2012) both provide focused and accessible introductions to grounded theory research

Chapter takeaways – top tips for success

⊛ Know the difference between academic research and the everyday use of the term

⊛ Be aware of the differences between positivist and interpretivist approaches to conducting research

⊛ Be able to explain the four types of research (exploratory, descriptive, analytical and predictive) and know where your research will fit within this classification

⊛ Think about Bloom's classification and whether your familiarity with your research topic will cover all the rungs on the ladder

⊛ Decide whether your research will be of the inductive or deductive type

⊛ Ensure that you understand the importance of theory for conducting high-quality research and decide what conceptual or theoretical framework will underpin your study

3. CHOOSING THE TOPIC

Learning outcomes: this chapter covers

✓ Where to begin thinking about topic selection
✓ Whether a project has to be 'useful'
✓ How to turn a broad area into a focused idea
✓ How to select a good topic rather than a bad one

3.1 Introduction to choosing your topic

You have made the decision to do a research project or dissertation (or the choice to do so has been made for you), and now you need to decide what to study. In some ways, it is a misnomer to talk of a 'choice of topic stage' since the majority of dissertation topics will continue to evolve right until the point that the investigative work is completed. Therefore, a first point to note is that you should not be concerned about being somehow boxed in by what you write in your research proposal. You can and probably will end up producing something somewhat different, even though it will usually be in the same general area as the proposal.

Armed with some knowledge about what research is and how it is structured, this is the first of two chapters that aim to steer you in the right direction regarding the subject to undertake your research on (this chapter) and how to write up your initial ideas into a plan document (the next chapter).

Selecting the topic is arguably one of the most, if not the most, crucial part of the whole process. You will be spending a significant amount of time on the dissertation – probably somewhere between the equivalent of one and three entire modules just on this single project, so the topic must maintain your interest for that long, and you need to choose carefully. Being able to generate novel yet feasible research ideas is a valuable skill that even many career academics never fully master. It is not easy, and for those who are new to research with little prior reading completed, it is even tougher.

You need to select a sufficiently challenging topic that it will push you to learn and achieve more than you have before and will allow you to showcase your abilities across a range of aspects. But on the other hand, it needs to be within your scope given the time available and not be so out of reach that it leaves you floundering, permanently worried, and making no progress.

If you find the subject boring, then reading and writing about it will be a chore from beginning to end, and your lack of passion for it will probably show through in your writing. If your response to this statement is that you find all research dull or that none of the topics within the subject is enjoyable, then it is time to see if there is still an opportunity to do something else instead of a dissertation.

There are significant variations in the amount of choice that students are given to select their project topic, but we can characterise there being three degrees of optionality:

1. Your department may tell you precisely what topic you will write your dissertation on, in which case, of course, you will have no choice regarding the subject, although you may still have flexibility about how you tackle it – for example, choosing the data, methods and models to employ.
2. A more likely, scenario is that you are presented with a list of topics from which you have to select one (again in each case, probably having some further flexibility regarding the data and methods).
3. A final scenario is where you have a completely free hand to study whatever you want so long as the subject lies within your degree programme's field boundaries.

As student numbers in accounting and finance departments have grown over the past two decades, supervising projects has become more challenging for the staff. In some instances, departments have responded by making the project optional where it was previously compulsory or by reducing its scope. If you are presented with a selection of titles from which to choose (a so-called semi-closed list corresponding to the second possibility in the list above), you have less freedom, but you should still give the decision careful consideration as the amount of work you will need to put in will still be non-trivial. So think along the lines shown in this chapter regarding your interests, skills and aspirations.

Even more limiting is where a department has diminished the research project's scope to a replication, which is an exercise in taking an existing study, implementing the same models, and writing up the results. This situation would be a hybrid of 1 and 3 in the list above, whereby the student chooses the study to replicate but the research design and methods would follow those of the existing study. In some ways, this is regrettable and severely restrictive as it limits the range of transferrable skills that you could acquire through the process of working on the project, but it does make the choice of topic considerably more straightforward as you would merely be selecting the paper to replicate.

If you have the opportunity to examine previous successfully completed dissertations, then do take this up as it will give a clear idea of what you are aiming at and might spark some inspiration. Of course, you should not be tempted to copy any aspects of the work, and even the topics might not also be an appropriate choice for you. Still, you can get useful ideas on the kinds of subjects that could be chosen, how a completed document might look, what sections are included and in what order, and how the work is formatted and presented.

3.2   Where to start looking for ideas

The remainder of this chapter presumes that you have a free hand to select your own subject area rather than picking from a pre-established list. So, where do you start? It is advisable to stick within the remit of the research areas covered in your department and relevant to your degree programme. If you are studying for an Accounting and Business degree, for instance, your project ought to be on one of those areas – indeed, you might not be permitted to engage in a topic on something else. Working on a subject you have studied on a taught module will use your existing knowledge and reduce the amount of groundwork you have to undertake initially.

It is possible to approach the task of topic selection strategically, thinking about your strengths and weaknesses and focusing the choice to make the most use of the former and the least of the latter. Working on a subject that you have studied in a taught module will reduce the amount of groundwork that you have to undertake initially.

Alternatively, you could treat the whole exercise as a learning experience and use it as a way to maximise opportunities for that. For example, if there are particular new quantitative techniques or programming languages that you feel could be valuable for other parts of your degree programme or to put on your CV to impress potential employers, then select a topic that will require those skills and provide you with a concrete motivation to develop them. Be realistic, though, about the extent to which you can develop your techniques in the time available, given that you also have to do the research and write it up.

Try not to be in a hurry to select a topic immediately, and similarly, don't be overly concerned if some of your classmates say that they already know what they are going to work on. Preparing well at this stage and selecting the idea judiciously will pay dividends at a later stage. You need to choose something that will hold your attention, is challenging but feasible with your skills and time constraints, and is likely to generate as high a mark as possible. Making this selection will probably

Figure 3.1: How to focus your ideas to select a topic

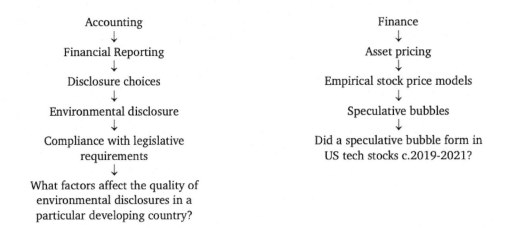

Accounting
↓
Financial Reporting
↓
Disclosure choices
↓
Environmental disclosure
↓
Compliance with legislative
requirements
↓
What factors affect the quality of
environmental disclosures in a
particular developing country?

Finance
↓
Asset pricing
↓
Empirical stock price models
↓
Speculative bubbles
↓
Did a speculative bubble form in
US tech stocks c.2019-2021?

require extensive information retrieval and detailed thought and reflection, which will take time.

Sometimes a student will have a very focused idea from the outset – if it is something they always wanted to study, or if someone else has presented them with an 'oven-ready' idea that they can just get cracking on. But in most cases, it is a process of starting with an expansive area and gradually narrowing down the perspective until an idea that is manageable within the available timeframe emerges. In this case, there are several stages in the process:

- Define a broad area for research
- Narrow this to pinpoint a research problem
- Articulate the research problem in a statement
- Separate the statement into several practicable aspects
- Draft the statements into a set of research aims, questions or hypotheses

Focusing your ideas beginning with a very broad idea and successively narrowing it down until you have a workable title could operate as in Figure 3.1,for particular ideas in accounting and finance, respectively.

When you have pinned down a broad topic area for your project, one way to think about converting your general ideas into a manageable plan is to transform them into a question or set of questions because, ultimately, the whole purpose of research is to provide answers to problems.

If you have a broad area in mind but not yet a specific topic, it is worthwhile to proceed by reading introductory-level treatments of that topic. It is advisable not to dive straight into the latest, cutting-edge thinking since the level of assumed knowledge and detail will be too great. Trying to penetrate such work at this stage might be off-putting and may give the incorrect impression that you will never understand any of it and need to choose a different, less challenging field. Instead, start with an introductory-level treatment such as a textbook, lecture notes, or even Wikipedia. Although the source is much maligned by scholars and should never be the only point of reference, it is often a good starting point since it is quick, free, and easy to access. Wikipedia will provide you with basic, foundation-level knowledge from which you can build by moving to gradually more specialist and advanced treatments once you are determined that this is the topic for you. Even if the Wiki pages suffer from some omissions or contain some inaccuracies, that does not matter at this stage if you are starting from the position of having virtually no prior knowledge.

Have a browse through some recent editions of relevant journals and practitioner magazines. Browsing used to be a much different experience in days gone by where it was common to wander into the library and peruse the physical copies. Nowadays, the journals are all on-line, but browsing can still be useful. If you go to your university library's website, you should be able to search the e-journals available to find those in the subject area you are interested in (e.g., management accounting, quantitative finance, etc.). There are many accounting and finance journal lists available on the internet, including the Academic Journal Guide, which is very comprehensive (see chapter 6 for a discussion of this and more detail on how to search for and download the papers).

Another useful tip is that most research articles end their concluding sections with an 'ideas for further research' paragraph, which does precisely what the name suggests, where the authors provide a list of new research ideas that lead on from what they did (and did not do). Obviously, there are no guarantees that these ideas are sound or even feasible, and if the article is old, the suggestions may have already been taken up subsequently by those authors or other researchers. Looking at this concluding paragraph in high quality, recent studies might provide you with some suggestions, although to be able to go down this route, you would need to know which studies' conclusions to look at. This issue is discussed in the remainder of this chapter and chapter 6.

3.2.1   Where to look if you have no ideas whatsoever

Inspiration for topic choice may come from several sources, so if you have absolutely no idea what to study or where even to start looking for a topic, initially cast your search net very wide and see what you can catch. The following headings provide some ideas.

Successfully completed projects

Your department might have a library of previously completed projects – either in a display cupboard somewhere in the department or on-line in an intranet folder. Even if not, they might be willing to circulate a list of previously submitted project titles. If so, while it would not be wise to select an identical topic, it might spark some related research ideas.

Table 3.1: Subject areas in accounting and finance

Accounting	Finance
Management accounting	Bonds and money market securities
Financial accounting and financial reporting	Investments and asset pricing
Tax	Derivatives and financial engineering
Business finance / financial management	Corporate finance
Business strategy: an accounting perspective	Ethics for finance
Critical accounting	Mathematical finance & econometrics
Quantitative techniques for accountants	Risk management
Public sector and charity accounting	Portfolio management
Social and environmental accounting	Alternative investments
Governance and ethics in accounting	

Consider the subject areas that interested you the most

One way to begin thinking about what to study is to make a list of all of the modules covered in a degree programme in accounting or finance and deciding which of these you find the most interesting. Although this will not provide you with a research topic, it will at least allow you to select a research area, which then makes the choice of the topic more straightforward since you will have a better idea of where to look and who to ask (journals, books, academic staff and PhD students in that subject area). A list of subject areas in accounting and finance could be as given in Table 3.1.

If one area from the list above is particularly appealing, it is worth spending time talking to the corresponding module(s)' instructors to gain their advice on the exciting and plausible topics in their subject areas.

A related avenue to explore for research ideas would be to re-examine a topic that you have already studied in a taught module. For example, one where you have done some reading and written an assignment that interested you and for which you scored a high mark, indicating a solid understanding of the material. However, if you go down this route, take care not to self-plagiarise from what you have already written (see chapter 4).

Practitioner magazines and hybrid journals

Academic journals are often not ideal as sources of inspiration for research projects since they are so great in number, and the articles are frequently esoteric and spanning such a wide-ranging subject matter that it is hard to know where to look.

Journals aimed at practitioners or hybrid journals spanning both academic and industrial environments can be more useful for beginner researchers since they deal with practical problems in accounting or finance and tend to be more accessible than more squarely academic papers. Care is needed since some of these are more magazine than journal, and your research topic will still need to fit within the scholarly framework for research discussed in subsequent chapters of this book. But examining recent studies published in these outlets might spark some exciting ideas, and the list below contains a few suggestions for such journals, although note that some charge subscriptions to view the full article unless the outlet is included in your university's bundle.

Accounting practitioner journals
- Accounting Horizons[1]
- CPA Journal[2]
- Journal of Accountancy[3]
- Strategic Finance[4]

Finance practitioner journals
- Financial Analysts Journal[5]
- Journal of Alternative Investments[6]
- Journal of Asset Management[7]
- Journal of Fixed Income[8]
- Journal of Portfolio Management[9]
- Journal of Risk[10]

Practitioners

If you know any accounting or finance practitioners, it could be valuable to chat with them and try to find out about the problems they face in their roles that might be amenable to academic research. If they are working in an area of interest to you as a potential future career, this could serve two purposes. Even better, if you already have some relevant experience from the industry, you might be able to identify an exciting subject that has practical relevance from your role there.

Forums

Numerous web-based interest groups have established discussion forums, and by looking at the threads on these, you will get a good idea of the kinds of practical issues people are writing about. For example, in finance:

---

[1] https://aaahq.org/Research/Journals/Accounting-Horizons

[2] https://www.cpajournal.com

[3] https://www.journalofaccountancy.com

[4] https://sfmagazine.com

[5] https://cfainstitute.org/en/research/financial-analysts-journal

[6] https://jai.pm-research.com

[7] https://www.palgrave.com/gp/journal/41260

[8] https://jfi.pm-research.com

[9] https://jpm.pm-research.com

[10] https://www.risk.net/journal-of-risk

- Citywire has an investing forum where members discuss ideas and challenges on that topic[11]
- The Wilmott Quantitative Finance forum[12]

There are also forums in accounting such as:

- Accountant Forums[13]
- Proformative[14]
- Accounting Web[15]

By linking it with the relevant academic literature, it might be possible that you can turn one of these questions or responses into a dissertation topic.

An internet search

As I will discuss in chapter 6, internet searches can be enormously valuable, but of course, before you can find any ideas you need to know the keywords to insert, which is a bit of a catch-22. If you have some vague areas of interest, you can try those combined with 'hot topics in ...' or 'trending topics in ...', or if all else fails, 'current topics in finance' or 'current topics in accounting'. Hopefully, you will find something among the lists on the websites generated that excites you.

A word of warning, though. If you type 'research project ideas in accounting' (or the same for finance), the top hits are all supplied by essay mills encouraging students to plagiarise their entire dissertation (see chapter 4). They provide services to write projects for students alongside a list of very vague and unhelpful titles.

Ask your supervisor, another academic or a PhD student

These ideas speak for themselves! Your supervisor might be willing to suggest some ideas around the investigations on which they have been working. Start by asking them about their research, though, before turning the conversation to trying to extract their ideas for your project.

Read a financial newspaper or look on a finance website

All of the financial media have websites, and many of them also have news apps that can be downloaded onto your phone or other device (CNBC, Yahoo!, MarketWatch, Bloomberg, etc.) The content on these can be accessed for free (although you might have to register) and contain a vast amount of current financial news on various topics updated frequently. However, as above, it will be important to consider such topics from an academic perspective and newsworthy subjects do not always make good research project material.

---

[11] https://moneyforums.citywire.co.uk

[12] https://wilmott.com/

[13] https://www.accountantforums.com

[14] https://www.proformative.com/questions

[15] https://www.accountingweb.com/community-voice

Videos

Podcasts and YouTube videos can also be useful as an entertaining way to generate ideas. A surprisingly large number of intellectually grounded presentations are available in this way, including 'TED-style' talks, which are short performances from expert speakers on a vast range of topics. These can be found on subjects that you are interested in via a keyword search.

Reflect on your skills and interests

An alternative approach to selecting a topic would be to think rationally about your interests and areas of expertise. Before formally specifying the subject of your project, it is worth considering your skills and interests and what you hope to get out of the process (aside from a superb mark):

- How good is your maths and do you like algebra? You may feel very confident at the quantitative end of finance, pricing assets or estimating models, for example. Still, you may not feel comfortable with qualitative analysis where you are asked to give an opinion on particular issues (e.g., 'should financial markets be more regulated?'). In that case, a highly technical piece of work may be appropriate.
- Are you good at data analysis with statistics?
- Can you write code (e.g., in Python, R, C++ or Visual Basic)?
- Do you enjoy writing long, detailed arguments, or would you prefer to focus more on numbers and models?
- Do you like manually collecting data (e.g., through surveys or interviews), or would you prefer just to download it from a website?
- Are you aiming at a particular career path and would like to study something supporting that objective?

Your responses to all of these questions will help steer you towards certain types of research and favour specific approaches to research over others, although they might not help with choosing the precise topic.

Many students find maths and statistics both problematic and uninteresting. Such students may be better suited to more qualitative topics or subjects that involve only elementary statistics, but where the rigour and value-added come from some other aspect of the problem. A case-study approach that is not based on any quantitative analysis may be worth considering. Indeed, an examination of a set of carefully selected case studies may be more appropriate than advanced quants for addressing particular problems, especially in situations where hard data are not readily available, or where each entity is distinct so that generalising from a model estimated on one set of data may be inadvisable. Case studies are useful when the case itself is unusual or unique or when each entity under investigation is very heterogeneous. They involve more depth of study than quantitative approaches. Methodological choices are discussed in detail in chapter 8.

Some students are under the misapprehension that more technical work will always garner higher marks than a discursive piece, but this is a fallacy. Highly mathematical work with little relevance and which has been applied inappropriately may be much weaker than a well-constructed and carefully analysed case study and would be marked accordingly. Consequently, the quality of the work will be far more important than its level of quantitative sophistication in determining the final grade awarded to the project.

Relatedly, a project where the outcome will merely be a number or set of numbers derived from a calculation will probably not constitute a good, scholarly piece of work. For instance, calculating the cost of capital for a group of biotechnology firms or evaluating whether taxi firms would make more profit if they switched to electric cars would both be worthwhile activities from a practical perspective and could generate considerable media interest. But from an academic viewpoint, neither would address any exciting questions. Intellectually, these are not deep and challenging issues, and so would not make good dissertations.

A different way to generate new research ideas is to start with one or two articles (they could be published in journals or working papers, but practitioner pieces or magazine articles might still be suitable) that you enjoyed reading, and you thought were quite inspiring. Then try to identify ways that the research methods in those studies could be varied. For example, the sample period covered or country focus could be changed (e.g., if the research applied a new model to US data, you could use UK data). Or the models employed could be altered or compared with some alternatives.

Although this type of approach might not lead to an inspiring outcome because it would be very much based on something already written, it is a safe option that is more likely than others to lead to a solid piece of work. Here, you would be following in the footsteps of an established and successfully completed study, which can be used as a template to guide all the stages of your research.

3.3   Other issues regarding topic selection

This section discusses several other interesting issues concerning topic choice that have not already been covered.

3.3.1   A controversial subject or something from the news?

When selecting a topic, it is probably advisable to avoid a highly controversial area, such as investigating financial fraud, market manipulation, or auditing failures. While these are all fascinating and important subjects in need of scholarly inquiry, they are likely to be extremely challenging for new researchers with particular difficulties to obtain sensitive and confidential information. There would be much more scope for something to go wrong, leaving you with very little to write about.

You may gain some inspiring ideas based on current events that are taking place in the financial markets or the wider economy. However, choosing to work on something that is currently very newsworthy and popular also involves some additional issues. Such a project might well generate significant initial interest, but it is also likely to date quickly. For example, any research related to covid-19 (covid-19 and stock returns; covid-19 and dividend pay-outs; the impact of culture and wealth on the spread of covid-19, etc.) is very much in vogue at the time of writing this book (spring 2021). But such research will probably be of considerably less interest in a year or two's time, and there might even be a backlash where people are bored with the subject and it is considered largely pointless.

It might also be more challenging to frame the research aims of a news-generated topic within an existing scholarly paradigm than a more conventional and less currently fashionable topic; there will likely be less existing evidence to review and upon which to base your investigation. The risk is then that your work is more likely to end up as something akin to a descriptive report rather than an academic study, and the former would attract a lower mark than the latter.

3.3.2 Interdisciplinary research

You might have ideas from other fields (such as maths, history, psychology, or operations research) that you have studied as part of your current or previous degree programme. You could bring these ideas to your project in accounting or finance, which would be a so-called transdisciplinary or interdisciplinary approach.

Exciting research can emerge if concepts and approaches implemented in other fields are taken and and applied to accounting or finance, although they can be challenging to identify and carry through to completion as this sort of research by definition does not involve continuing an established 'formula-following' path. It is possible that you could find inspiration from the modules that you studied from a different field as part of your previous or current degree programme or that you have read about. Behavioural finance is an excellent example of this, where ideas and concepts drawn from psychology (such as the impacts of personality and emotions on investment decision-making) are employed to good effect for addressing relevant problems in finance.

While finance has increasingly taken ideas from psychology in the development of the fashionable field of behavioural finance, the same has not occurred in accounting, which has instead tended to adopt concepts and theories from sociology.

3.3.3 Does a research project need to be 'useful'?

Your research does not have to have an apparent practical outcome. Often, the work that scholars consider as having the most merit has no immediate usage outside the academy, but instead, it develops new concepts or methods or pushes forward the way they think about a particular topic. It might be that you would prefer your research to have implications for policy or practice and for it to be useful to some external group (practitioners, regulators, policymakers, retail investors, etc.). But this is not usually a requirement for a student dissertation, and you need to be aware that there might be a trade-off if you sacrifice rigour or originality to make your work practical and accessible.

Selecting a topic with high practical relevance, or one motivated by a practitioner problem, could lead to a thrilling and novel project, but it will not hit the academic target and be awarded a high grade if it does not pose intellectually challenging as well as real-world-relevant questions. Making it a credible piece of academic work can be quite a task to achieve since it is sometimes the case that the nature of real-world research is hard to squeeze into a scholarly framework.

3.3.4   Narrowing a broad idea to a manageable topic

Once you have selected a general subject area, the next stage is to transform this broad direction into a workably sized topic that can be tackled within the constraints laid down by the institution. It is crucial to ensure that the research aims are not so broad or substantive that the questions cannot be addressed within the constraints on available time and word limits. The project should not be aiming to solve the entire world's accounting or financial puzzles but rather to form and address a manageably small problem.

If your idea originated from an examination of the literature or other relevant media (a 'bottom-up' approach), you would already be aware of some of the existing work on the topic, and it is then a matter of honing and refining the suggestions.

But if your idea was presented to you by someone else or came to you without examining any of the existing research that came before it, you will need to 'back-fill' this aspect before you can write and submit a proposal as discussed in the next chapter. For instance, you will need to consider:

- How much work has already been done on this topic? Is it a mature area with numerous studies dating back decades or a relatively recent or specialised research focus? What are the pivotal studies on this subject?
- What did existing authors conclude about this topic? What data and methods did they use? What were their research aims or questions?
- Given your response to the previous question, are you aiming to do something a little different, or is it the case that a very similar study has already been completed? If so, it would be worthwhile to consider modifying it somewhat to differentiate your plans from what was previously done.

More discussion of these issues will be presented in the following chapter.

3.3.5   Does a research project need to be original?

Depending on the dissertation's academic level (undergraduate versus master's) and its extent (i.e., how many credits are allocated to it), there might be a requirement to have an element of original contribution in the work. In other words, a need to investigate something different to what has gone before – even if the extent of originality is very modest.

Sources of originality can come from many angles. This can involve using established techniques but applying them to a different country, market or asset.

Alternatively, the novelty could come from the methods themselves, where the student develops a new approach. The following are examples of situations where an original contribution can arise:

1. Testing a new theory or idea
2. Using a different dataset to test existing theories
3. Using a different empirical model to test an existing theory
4. Taking a concept or approach used in other fields and applying it in a different domain (transdisciplinary research)

Although your thinking and writing will be framed by what you have read, you will need to develop and demonstrate your own ideas, rather than just producing a 'rehash' of someone else's work. In that sense, any good dissertation will have an element of originality, i.e., a 'contribution to knowledge'. It would add, probably a tiny piece, to the overall picture in that subject area so that the body of knowledge is larger at the end than before the project was started.

As well as studying a new phenomenon, or a different market to those examined in existing research, another way to make a novel contribution is to re-examine an established problem that was previously not tackled well. Most commonly, a research study can be compromised by an inappropriate or flawed methodology. This issue could be pretty fundamental, such as using secondary data where there was a need to get out and ask people questions directly, or it could be that less-than-ideal models or datasets have been used, rendering the findings tenuous. You might spot this either from the descriptions of the methods used in the papers or where the results simply don't look right. In such cases, your research could follow broadly the same path as the existing study, but fixing what was done wrong and examining the extent to which the findings differ.

3.3.6 What is a replication study, and would it make a good project?

A replication study, as the name suggests, is one aiming to recreate the analysis already undertaken by existing research with a view to confirming or refuting the previous findings. While a pure replication, where a new piece of work aims to do precisely something that has been done already, is a useful starting point for a research project, it would be dull and probably insufficient if it constituted the entire dissertation.

However, there is an asymmetry: if you were able to demonstrate that an existing study (especially a widely cited piece by a well-respected author) contained systematic errors, and you were able to identify the source of those errors, it could be a fascinating and valuable exercise. But the more likely outcomes are that either your results will match those of the original authors, or they will not match because you (not the other author) made a technical error in the implementation. These eventualities are evidently less desirable. Such a project would then be unoriginal and uninspiring if you had 'copied' the design and methods, even if the writing was all in your own words.

Many empirical research projects begin with replication but then extend it somehow – for instance, by updating the sample period or applying the same approach to a new country or asset market or adding a new variable into a regression model. This strategy is reasonably low risk and often a sensible one that can form the basis of a good piece of work. But if you are considering such a project, it is worth checking with your supervisor about whether it is permitted and likely to be well received or not.

3.4   What can go wrong with a choice of topic?

Once you submit your proposal document (see chapter 5) and you are allocated a supervisor, there should be an opportunity to receive feedback on it before commencing any further work. This early critique will avoid wasting additional time if the idea that you have focused on is somehow inappropriate. Naturally, things can and do go wrong in many different ways, but there are several particularly common pitfalls to avoid when selecting a topic. It is more probable that you will run into difficulties further down the line where your initial idea is:

- Too vague and thus not feasible
- Clever but cannot be implemented due to lack of data
- Really a method rather than a research topic
- Journalistic or populist and not appropriate for a scholarly study
- Too broad in scope to be completed in the available time
- Too sophisticated or in too distant a field for you to have a reasonable chance to achieve it in the available time given your background and prior education
- A replica of an existing study

Although there is much more work to be done before any data you collect are analysed, it is crucial to think before doing anything further about what data are required to complete the project. Many interesting and sensible ideas for projects fall flat owing to a lack of availability of relevant data. For example, the data required may be confidential, available only at a considerable financial cost, or too time-consuming to collect from many different paper sources. Before finally deciding on a particular topic, make sure that the data or any other required resources will be available.

Similarly, ensure that the methods you propose to use are feasible within the timescale and your budget. For instance, it would be impressive but challenging to learn a new programming language from scratch or implement a national-scale survey. Are you sure you can achieve that? If you have doubts, discuss them with your supervisor or the person responsible for the research project module before submitting the proposal, who will be able to advise on whether you need to scale back your ambitions. If you aim too high but find it impossible to complete the work by the deadline, it could be a disaster.

After you have an initial topic for the project, be confident in sharing it with others to get feedback at this earliest possible stage. Even if the idea is not fully developed at this juncture, or you are concerned that it would not make such a great project, your supervisor, their academic colleagues, and other students will have suggestions on how to improve it. Even if the response is that the conception is not workable into a valid project, it is much better to be aware of its infeasibility at this stage before expending any further effort on it so that you have time to consider something else.

3.4.1 After selecting a topic, can you change it?

If you want to make a minor change to your dissertation's focus, it should be fine just to go ahead and do so. Almost all dissertations change direction slightly during the course of their completion as the student learns more about the topic, collects the data, and works through the investigation.

But suppose you wanted to change the topic substantively – for example, from how intra-company pricing transfer values are determined to how international bodies can ensure that companies make consistent carbon disclosures across countries. That would represent a complete change of direction rather than a slight adjustment of emphasis. In that case, you should seek your supervisor's approval first.

The department will have records documenting your initial choice (such as from your submitted proposal) and be expecting the final project to be on that topic. At the least, your supervisor might be somewhat irritated that you hadn't bothered to communicate with them on such a substantive issue. Worse, when students commit severe acts of plagiarism or purchase their entire dissertation from an essay mill, it is sometimes difficult to get a project 'made to order' on precisely the desired topic, so rather than follow through with their proposal specialism, they take whatever is on offer in an entirely different area. Hence an unexpected and radical shift of topic at a later stage might arouse considerable suspicion that the work is not yours.

Chapter takeaways – top tips for success

* ⊛ Reflect on your skills and interests to help you select an appropriate topic
* ⊛ Choose your topic carefully – a poor choice will lead you to numerous issues later down the line
* ⊛ Ensure that your research idea is challenging and sufficiently well-defined to be feasible
* ⊛ Your research project does not have to cover something directly useful to practitioners
* ⊛ The best projects include an element of original contribution and do some research that nobody else has done before
* ⊛ Be aware that it is likely you will be able to change your topic later (with approval from your supervisor)

4. ETHICAL ISSUES

Learning outcomes: this chapter covers

✓ What are ethics
✓ Why ethics are important in research
✓ How to apply for ethics approval
✓ What is plagiarism
✓ How plagiarism is detected
✓ How to avoid plagiarism
✓ What is the fabrication of data or results
✓ Mitigating conflicts of interest

4.1   What are ethics, and how do they relate to research?

When research is conducted, it will have a direct or indirect influence on other people. Ethical considerations are about reflecting on and preventing any adverse effects that your research could have on others. 'Ethics' is an inclusive term that encompasses various aspects of behaviour when conducting research work, writing it up, and publishing it. Ethics refer to a set of moral principles and a level of integrity that should be adhered to in the process of doing research, incorporating a set of actions that researchers should take and a corresponding set of things they should not do. Honesty and objectivity in all aspects of the research process are viewed as essential.

All academic work should conform to specific standards of conduct, and as someone at the start of their research journey, it is worthwhile for you to be aware of these debates and rules and get into good habits. Given that the outputs from their endeavours are usually made public, researchers have several responsibilities that include ensuring their results are accurate and can be trusted by others.

Consequently, although when I initially began to map out this book, the ethics material was in chapter 7, I moved it so that it is now positioned here before readers start any of their investigative work or writing (even the proposal).

Although there is a moral aspect to behaving with integrity in research, there are also important practicalities to consider since falling foul of the rules can lead to severe problems. Ethics is not pure science, and different people will hold different ethical standards in several of the 'grey areas', with some researchers believing that a particular practice is acceptable while others strongly consider it unacceptable. Yet there is also a common set of beliefs that most researchers hold about what is tolerable and what is clearly not. This chapter will now flesh out some of these issues and discuss the ethical problems and dilemmas that can arise in various aspects of the process of conducting and writing up research.

There are typically fewer ethical considerations in accounting and finance than in other fields within business and management owing to the predominant use of secondary data, which will become apparent below. But there are nonetheless some key areas where ethical issues can arise – specifically, if:

- Your research could harm someone – for example, if participants are made to feel embarrassed or stressed
- Someone is unexpectedly deceived in the course of your research
- Someone's right to privacy has been breached
- Someone has been involved with your research without their consent
- Someone's information has been used in a way that they did not agree to
- You are dishonest in reporting the methods or results
- You face and do not mitigate any conflicts of interest that arise
- You do not properly treat copyrighted materials and data

It would be impossible never to bump up against any of the principles listed above in the course of conducting and writing up research. For example, it would be a legitimate topic to examine how investors' trading behaviours alter during times of market volatility and whether women are better at handling the resulting stress than men. In the process of setting up an experiment to test this, it would be impossible to achieve the aims without putting participants in a stressful environment to see how they react. While making people feel stressed, especially if it is deliberate, would usually be considered wrong, it would be impossible to achieve the research aims without doing so. In this case, it would be important to mitigate the effects as much as possible, to make people aware of what could happen during the research so that they are able to make an informed judgement about whether to participate or not, and to have a clear plan to support any participant who became excessively traumatised.

This example illustrates that there are few absolutes when dealing with ethics, and there should always be a careful consideration of whether the ends justify the means and how the potential for harm, along with any risks, can be minimised.

The use of deception in research studies requires particularly careful consideration, and is specifically mentioned in the list above and on ethics approval forms for several reasons. First, sometimes if a participant in an experiment is aware of precisely what the researcher is testing and looking for, it will influence the way that the former acts, thus damaging the validity of the findings. Therefore, in order to have the potential of obtaining valuable findings, it is necessary to be at least somewhat economical with the truth. Second, if a participant is deceived and later finds out that this was the case, they may feel hurt in a way that would affect their willingness to participate in any future experimental studies. Even if they consent to participate a second time, the previous deceit may influence the way that they perform next time, making them behave warily and viewing the researcher with suspicion, even if there is no deception involved in the second study.

Having a set of guiding principles and rules on ethics for research programmes, enforcing them, and educating students about them is vital because unethical research can cause harm to others in numerous ways. It is obvious to see how damage could be done by the examples in the list above, but more subtle instances of unethical research practices can still be detrimental to others and thus should be avoided. For example, if one researcher is dishonest in reporting their findings, other scholars (including students) could waste precious time following the original researcher's methods. It is also possible that practitioners or policymakers seeing the published findings might make decisions based upon them that, had the results been stated accurately, they would not have done. Following the conclusions or guidance from flawed research could lead to lost revenues, unnecessary risks, inappropriate policies, and so on. Everyone needs to have confidence in the veracity of what is written in the scholarly research literature so that it can be relied upon and used without the need to question it, and for that reason, amongst many others, all researchers must take the responsibility to behave ethically.

Beyond the academy, behaving ethically and demonstrating that rigorous standards are in place are viewed as increasingly important in both accounting and the financial services sector. The majority of professional qualifications in accounting and finance (ACCA, CFA, etc.) will include at least one module on ethics, and this material will include a discussion of research ethics. The requirement to formally demonstrate that these issues are covered on the syllabus has arisen as a result of the reputational damage that was done to firms, and indeed to the entire industry, as a result of high-profile cases of accounting fraud, including Enron in the US and Tesco in the UK, amongst many others, and financial scandals involving money laundering and LIBOR rigging at big banks.

The likely consequences within the university of being caught behaving unethically are discussed below. But it is also important to note that a potentially even more disastrous outcome for you in the most serious cases can occur where a form of unethical behaviour is noted on your student record. If this happened, it might make it harder for you to obtain a position in an accounting firm or a bank, particularly if the academic staff member writing your reference feels compelled to point it out. If there is any mention of improper behaviour, many firms would not want to take the risk of hiring that person, and they would have plenty of other candidates from which to choose in today's highly competitive recruitment market. Therefore, the most serious unethical practices could result in lost job opportunities as well as lost marks or even a lost degree.

4.2   The ethics approval process

Since dealing with these issues is tricky, especially for new and inexperienced researchers, with the possibility for significant damage if things go wrong, all universities are required to have a robust process in place to ensure that research is conducted ethically. Usually, there will be a formal university-level committee charged with the responsibility for ensuring that all research undertaken at the institution (whether by staff or students) upholds high standards of ethics. But day-to-day matters concerning ethics will frequently be delegated to a school- or department-level committee. This committee's primary responsibility will be to ensure the 'ethical propriety' of any research that uses 'human subjects or human personal data', in other words, research based on people or individual, identifiable data about people. Additional checks are required for medical topics, but these will not be relevant for the vast majority of researchers in business schools or social science faculties and so are not considered further here.

Naturally, ethics approval processes fall most heavily on areas where the potential for harm to participants is the greatest. Such fields include medical research, where the most egregious examples where research has been argued to have been unethical include situations where ill patients have been deliberately discouraged from seeking treatments (see Dooley, 1995, for examples).

The approval process would usually be that any students (or staff members) considering conducting research that uses human subjects or personal data would be required to complete a form that explains how they will collect, store, and use the data. Any research that will use, for example, surveys or interviews, will usually need to go through this process. The committee will have the discretion to disallow the proposed research from taking place or require modifications in its design before the study can begin. These safeguards are in place to protect the reputation of the university and the researcher.

In the worst-case scenario, unethical or very badly designed research could cause severe embarrassment to a participant in the project, such as if some of their personal information was (either deliberately or accidentally) made publicly available. The harmed person would then have grounds to take legal action against the university (and possibly against the individual researcher).

When proposed research projects go before a committee such as this, they will want to be reassured that the research will be conducted in a way that minimises the scope for any problems to occur. For example, when a survey will be performed, the committee will want to see evidence that:

- Survey participants will have given their consent to participate, using a form of the type below
- Participants will have the right to withdraw at any point during the survey, and then any information they had given up to that point would be deleted
- All data will be stored securely; only you or your supervisor would have access to it
- The data will only be retained for as long as it is required and then destroyed
- The nature of your investigation will not offend or cause worry among survey participants
- Only information required for the research will be collected
- The information will be stored, and the results presented, in a manner that protects the privacy of individuals (e.g., in an anonymised or aggregate format)

Vulnerable groups, such as children or people in hospitals, have additional protections. Including them in an interview, questionnaire, or experimental design is likely to require additional layers of scrutiny and possibly even a police check to ensure that you are not banned from working with such people. This is known as a Disclosure and Barring Service (DBS) check in the UK. Given the onerous, time-consuming and costly (there is a fee) nature of these authorisations, it is best to stick to using non-vulnerable adults as subjects in your investigation, if you are using 'live subjects' at all; for student project research in accounting or finance, doing otherwise is hardly worth the risk or hassle.

It is crucial not to begin any primary data collection using surveys or interviews until you have gone through the ethical approval procedure and been given the go-ahead by your supervisor. If there are any issues with your approach or the questions you ask, it could land you in big trouble if you have not been through the due process to obtain authorisation to proceed.

However, research that uses only secondary data will probably not need such scrutiny because it is either at an aggregate level (e.g., for a whole market) or is anonymised from the outset. Therefore, there is nothing sensitive or personal about the information, and there would be no potential harm to individuals if the data were leaked or lost. If, on the other hand, your research methods involve undertaking surveys, interviews, or experiments, then ethical approval will probably be required.

Usually, to obtain ethics approval will require the researcher to complete a form and submit it to a designated person who might have the authority to make a decision if the case is straightforward, or they might refer the document to a committee, who will then consider it at their next meeting. Sometimes, obtaining ethics approval can take several weeks, and therefore you should discuss this with your supervisor at the earliest possible opportunity to ensure that your progress is not held up in waiting for this process to occur. A sample of the kind of form that you might have to complete

Figure 4.1: Sample ethics approval form

Research Ethics Approval Form

Name of Student:
Title and level of the student's degree programme:
Title of project:

Brief summary of the project aims and methods (c.150-300 words)

Is the research externally funded? If so, please provide details:

How many participants do you intend to recruit, and through what channels?

Please confirm that each of the following issues has been considered (tick the boxes)
Security of storage of research data
Confidentiality of research participants
The disposal of data upon completion of the research
Assuring participants of the right to withdraw from the research at any point
Whether participants will be reimbursed their expenses
Whether participants will be paid for their time or receive any other benefits
Whether participants will be permitted access to the research findings
Whether any aspects are likely to cause offence or concern among participants
The signing of consent forms for all participants
To the best of your knowledge, participants will have the capacity to give free and informed consent because they are under 18 years of age or in the sense of the Mental Capacity Act 2005
Whether any participants have a special relationship with the researcher that could affect their ability freely to give informed consent
Whether any aspects of the research could compromise the personal safety of the researcher or participants

Please outline any further ethical issues that may arise in the course of your research and how you will deal with them:

Will the research involve any deliberate deception? If so, please provide details and explain why it is necessary:

- I confirm that I have completed this form honestly and made all known and relevant information available to the Research Ethics Committee. I also confirm to keep the Committee updated if any changes to the above take place after approval has been given.
- I understand that it is a statutory requirement that any researcher who will be working with children or vulnerable adults undertakes a Disclosure and Barring Service check prior to commencement of the research.

Signature: Date:

is given in Figure 4.1.

Consent forms

If you are conducting surveys, interviews or experiments, as well as obtaining ethics approval from your department, you will need to ensure that all participants complete a consent form. This document constitutes written proof that respondents are fully aware of the nature of the research, what their information will be used for, how it will be stored, and who will have access to it. This is known as giving 'informed consent', whereby participants not only agree to be involved, but they are given full information that allows them to choose between participating in the research or not in possession of all the facts. These documents need to be signed (either in hard copy or electronically) and then stored until the project has been completed and marked, at which point they should be destroyed along with any other sensitive information. A sample consent form is given in Figure 4.2.

Legal risk

A further ethical consideration is that you do not expose any of your participants to 'legal risk'. In other words, you must design your survey or interviews so that you are not asking any questions that could encourage respondents to reveal that they had engaged in any unlawful actions, such as taking payments in cash to evade tax or overstating damage in an insurance claim to enhance the pay-out. Doing so could put them and you at risk. If you became aware of such illegal activity, would you have a duty to report it to the authorities? And if you felt that you had no choice but to report the person, how could you reconcile that with the promise you had made to all survey participants that their information would remain confidential to you and your supervisor? The best way to avoid such a situation is to design surveys and interviews carefully to ensure that participants are never asked any questions that would relate to illegal activities.

Anonymity

If you are conducting case studies or interviews, you should offer your participants a guarantee of anonymity and take care that they cannot be identified from the way that you report their roles or other characteristics. For example, if you attributed a quotation to 'the CEO of an accountancy software firm based in Reading and established in 2008 with an annual turnover of £5m', it could make it reasonably straightforward for readers to identify whom you are talking about. This could cause embarrassment or worse if the CEO had said something in confidence that could cast them or their company in a bad light.

If you have any doubts about the integrity of what you are doing and whether it could contravene any rules on confidentiality or data protection, for example, then do not continue until you have sought guidance from your supervisor or another staff member experienced in similar kinds of research and the ethical issues it can lead to.

Figure 4.2: Sample consent form

Consent to Participate in Research

I am a master's student in the accounting department at the University of the Skies. I am conducting a study of how management accountants in manufacturing firms feel about environmental disclosure requirements. This research has been given consent to proceed by the University's ethics approval process. Your signing of this form confirms your willingness to participate.

Sharing your honest opinions will provide me with the best chance of conducting a valuable study. The survey is anonymous, and no individuals will be identified. I will not collect your name, e-mail address or any personal details about you. Individual results will be kept confidential between myself and my supervisor. Demographic questions (for example, your age and marital status) are asked where it is helpful for the study to analyse this information. The raw data will be kept in files that are password protected; these will not be shared with third parties.

Your participation in this survey is entirely voluntary. You are free to exit the survey at any point, and you do not have to answer any questions that you do not want to. However, please note that incomplete survey data will not be used for analysis, and once you click 'submit', your responses will be entered into the database without identifiers, and it will not be possible to withdraw them.

Once you have completed the survey, you will not be required to do anything else, and you will not be contacted again. If you wish to receive further information about the project at any stage, you may contact me by e-mail at <Your e-mail address>.

Thank you for your participation.

Name: Signature: Date:

4.2.1   The Data Protection and Freedom of Information Acts

The Data Protection Act (DPA) 1998 and Freedom of Information Act (FOIA) 2000 are two pieces of legislation that apply to the way that data are handled and who has access to information. Although these are both laws that apply in the UK, similar regulations hold in many other countries. The DPA was amended in 2018 to reflect a pan-European set of common rules (General Data Protection Regulation, GDPR) that has been in place since then. Following the UK's departure from the European Union at the end of January 2020, there have been further, minor changes in the legislation, but the core principles remain the same. The technicalities of the current modifications are quite complex but nicely summarised in a document by the ICAEW.[1]

The DPA requires all those dealing with personal information to comply with certain principles regarding how the data are collected, stored and disposed of. Hence, the rules relate to the same issues that ethics committees are concerned with, which

---

[1] https://www.icaew.com/insights/viewpoints-on-the-news/2021/jan-2021/data-protection-now-the-uk-has-left-the-eu-january-2021-update

is why the Act is discussed here.

The DPA stipulates that any information relating to individuals is used only for the specific purposes it was collected for and that it is only used where necessary. If the information is going to be stored for a prolonged period, it should be updated, and once it is no longer required, it should be destroyed. The data must also be stored securely to prevent possible access by anyone who does not have permission to do so and to protect the information from theft or misuse. Sensitive data such as health status or sexual orientation is treated even more seriously, and there can be severe penalties for a 'data breach' where such delicate information is accessed by those without authorisation.

The Act also grants individuals the right to know of and see any information held about them in computerised and some hard copy records. Individuals can additionally require data held about them to be corrected or deleted. Once an individual makes a request to see this data, they must be provided with it, and a request for it to be deleted must be actioned within a specific timeframe.

The FOIA is another relevant piece of UK law that it is valuable to be aware of. The DPA relates to all organisations, whereas FOIA relates only to organisations in the public sector (e.g., national or local government, universities, schools, hospitals, the police, etc.). The FOIA requires these organisations in the UK to supply upon request any information they hold, not just relating to specific individuals but regarding any of the organisation's activities. The idea behind establishing this law was to engender more transparency and trust in the public sector and increase accountability through openness about the organisations' activities. For example, it might make it easier for any unnecessary waste or poor performance to be brought to light and then challenged if outsiders were given the right to demand access to information that the organisation holds.

Public sector institutions can refuse to comply with an FOIA request in certain circumstances. For example, if the request would take an excessive amount of time to process, if supplying the information would breach someone's right to privacy, or if the data requested would damage a commercial interest. But the default position is that all information demanded should be supplied.

Knowledge of the DPA is useful because if you will be handling individual data (e.g., from surveys or interviews), you will need to comply with the legislation, although doing so will be built into your university's ethics approval process. The FOIA is probably not a piece of law that will apply to you; rather, it might be something you would want to make use of if, for example, you were interested in university or government finances. Making FOI requests can be a valuable source of data that are not publicly available, providing essential input to case studies written about public sector bodies. A substantial amount of detail about the FOIA is available directly from the Information Commissioner's Office.[2]

---

[2]https://ico.org.uk/for-organisations/guide-to-freedom-of-information/what-is-the-foi-act/

4.3   Plagiarism

4.3.1   What is plagiarism?

Even when researchers conduct all of their investigations using secondary data and do not need to seek approval from an ethics committee, there is still one crucial area where they need to consider ethical principles. That is how to handle copyrighted material, how to include ideas and wording from existing studies, and more specifically, how to avoid committing plagiarism.

In essence, plagiarism refers to the act of attempting to pass off another person's work as your own. The term plagiarism covers a whole spectrum of offences, right from copying a few phrases or sentences upwards to something far more serious. The most egregious example I have ever seen was where a student took an academic working paper from the internet, replaced the name on the front with their name and submitted it – so literally, the entire piece was a direct copy from just one source. The student's first name and surname were the only two words they had written themself! Other severe cases involve taking large slabs of text from various sources and splicing them together.

It does not matter whether the source of the material is published work, an unpublished working paper, a letter, or a blog. If you copy some of someone else's words or ideas without acknowledgement that they are not yours, then that is plagiarism.

It is also plagiarism if you get another person to write some or all of your project for you, and you do not acknowledge in writing that they did those parts of the work. This is true if a friend does the job for you or if you pay an on-line 'essay mill' to do it. An essay mill is an essay- and project-writing service where, for a fee, the company will employ someone to produce a fully completed piece of coursework for you to your specification. This can be anything from a short essay to a full thesis, priced according to the level and amount of work involved. The company will hire many writers, covering a range of subjects, and who could be based in any location.

If you use an essay mill, you run the risk that the person who wrote your project for you might commit plagiarism and then what would your defence be? That you didn't realise because you did not write it? Supervisors can often identify that something 'smells fishy' about a project if written by someone else since they will be aware of their students' skills and backgrounds. In particular, it will be easy to spot if the project covers a topic from a different perspective than that taught on the course or is written in pristine English, yet the student who allegedly wrote it struggles to write e-mails fluently. Of course, there could be a perfectly reasonable explanation for any anomalous or unexpected features of the work. But if you have cheated in this way and then some irregularities have been detected, it will be a very tricky situation from which to escape.

Equally as worrying, the quality of the work arising from essay mills comes with no guarantees, and you have no idea whether the person who penned it is really a subject expert who can write well in English. Given the illicit nature of the transaction, if they do a lousy job and you receive a low mark, you will not have any comeback. Not only is this dishonest, unethical, and perhaps the most severe form of cheating, conducting a student research project is a valuable learning experience, and by merely buying the finished product, you will learn nothing.

The chances of being caught out are high since your supervisor will expect to see you and your progressing work periodically, and so will be surprised in the extreme when you appear to go from zero to a finished product overnight. Even if your supervisor does not know you personally, they will be fully aware of your background – both in terms of whether you are a native English speaker and the modules you have taken and what you would be expected to know. Finally, even though they rarely exercise it, universities usually have the right to call students for a *viva voce* (oral exam) in situations where they have cause to believe that something is amiss. If you had bought your dissertation on the internet, it would become very quickly apparent to those asking the questions in a *viva voce* that you had no clue what was in it.

Note that it is not only wrong to copy someone else's writing without attribution, it would also be considered plagiarism if you used someone else's ideas written in your own words, but you gave your reader the misleading impression that the ideas were yours. Of course, it is fine to use prior studies when developing your own research – after all, that is how humanity makes progress, and the body of knowledge grows. But this must be done while at the same time acknowledging existing authors whose work shaped your own.

Plagiarism can be deliberate, where the researcher knows that they are copying someone else's material or ideas without attribution, but they do it anyway. Plagiarism can also be accidental: inadvertent plagiarism can occur if you read an existing piece of work and then later draft a section in the dissertation, including that information. As you are writing, you believe that you are making up new sentences, but you are actually transcribing your recollection from what you had read. In that case, you did not intend to copy someone else's work, and you did not even realise you were doing it.

4.3.2   The consequences of plagiarism

When universities uncover plagiarism by their students, the consequences can be severe. Plagiarism is dishonest; it is cheating and will, if detected, result in a severe breakdown of trust between a student and their supervisor, with the former's reputation in the department permanently tarnished. The practice is viewed extremely dimly, and it dramatically damages the credibility of the researcher.

It could also be viewed as a breach of copyright and an act of fraud because the perpetrator is implicitly claiming to own the copyright to some ideas or writing, which in fact, they don't. Consequently, in theory, a plagiarist could be subject to legal action by the person whose work they have plagiarised, although this is unlikely unless the former was making money from it.

As a result, it is treated as a severe offence and will usually result in disciplinary action. The penalties for plagiarism are likely to vary depending on the extent of it in the work. There will probably be a mark deduction of the order of 5-20 percentage points for relatively minor cases. In more extreme situations where large amounts have been copied, the work is likely to be awarded a mark of zero with or without the right to submit a replacement piece. In its most severe form for a serial plagiarist who has done so and been caught several times, the result could be that they are required to leave the university altogether with no qualification awarded.

Even in the unlikely event that you get away with intentional and substantial plagiarism in the course of your studies, it could come back to haunt you later in life, particularly if you become famous. There are numerous examples of high-profile figures who were stripped of their qualifications when allegations of plagiarism were made against them, sometimes many years after their degrees were awarded. In most cases, they were fired or forced to resign from their roles. Some interesting examples are listed on the City University New York website.[3] There are some particularly notable cases:

- Annette Schavan, formerly German Minister for Education, was stripped of her doctorate when accused of plagiarism by Heinrich Heine University in 2013.[4]
- Ursula von der Leyen, who was at the time German Defence Minister, was accused of plagiarism in her doctoral thesis in 2015, again reported in a BBC article.[5]
- Tony Antoniou was Dean of Durham Business School in the UK when he was accused of having plagiarised his DPhil Thesis at York, even though the alleged incident had happened almost two decades previously, as reported in an article in the Financial Times.[6]

4.3.3 Some spurious excuses for plagiarism

Given that the potential penalties for those who plagiarise and get caught are so severe, with modern software routinely in use at universities making detection highly likely, (see the next section) why do students still plagiarise work? There are various reasons that students might give, none of which justifies the act:

'I don't know what plagiarism is as nobody explained it to me'

Students often argue that they lack an understanding of what plagiarism is. But this is extremely unlikely to be accepted as an argument since all universities now go to great lengths to explain it – not just in the research project but probably also in the student handbook and in every piece of coursework from the beginning of course registration. Even if you never bothered to look at your department's student

---

[3]https://www.baruch.cuny.edu/rio/research_misconduct_examples.htm
[4]https://www.bbc.co.uk/news/world-europe-21395102
[5]https://www.bbc.co.uk/news/world-europe-34376563
[6]https://www.ft.com/content/bb122680-87d0-11dc-9464-0000779fd2ac

handbook or their dissertation guide, for sure, there will be sections on plagiarism in both. Ignorance is no excuse.

'I want to use my own words but I am not a native English speaker'

The whole point of doing a degree in English is to learn how to write in the language, and this is a valuable skill that, once learned, you would have for life. Dissertation markers are well used to reading work written by non-native speakers and will be sympathetic to their genuine efforts to write original text. Any penalty for poor grammar (if applied at all) is likely to be much less severe than that for plagiarism. It is wrong to believe that you would be better off to copy someone else than to miswrite it yourself. Besides, as I will discuss below, it is perfectly acceptable to employ a proof-reader to go through your work at the end to fix up the grammar. Modern software such as ProWritingAid and Grammarly is handy in helping to improve the standard of written English too, particularly if your level is already reasonable, although if the drafting is very poor, these apps will struggle to make it better. In the latter case, using a proof-reader (a person rather than a package) would be recommended.

'I left everything until the last minute, so I just copied it'

If you left the project because you were ill, or you had too many pieces of work due, it is not legitimate to suggest that you didn't have the time to write in your own words. If you were genuinely sick or there was an exogenous reason why you could not do the work, your school is bound to have a process where you can put in a claim to get more time due to extenuating circumstances.

It is also likely that your programme would have been organised to ensure that deadlines do not bunch together. There is no doubt that you would have had at least a couple of months to complete the dissertation and probably even longer, so leaving it until the last minute and then running out of time is not an excuse to plagiarise.

4.3.4 Plagiarism detection

Just as the scope for plagiarism and the ease with which it can be undertaken have grown with the development of the internet, so too has the capacity for identifying the places where it has occurred. Turnitin[7] is a piece of software that detects plagiarism. It is used ubiquitously in UK universities and has also been adopted in many other countries. It claims to be 'the world's most effective plagiarism detection solution.' The software incorporates a vast database containing electronically available books, web pages (both current and older), newspapers, and journal articles. It also retains all of the essays and projects written by students that have previously been uploaded into the system. Of course, it does not contain literally every source globally, and its coverage of older content that is only available in hard copy format is very patchy, but overall, the database is incredibly comprehensive. Therefore, whenever you

---

[7]https://www.turnitin.com

lift material from published sources, working papers, or previous student work, the chances of being discovered are exceptionally high.

The software works by producing a 'similarity report' that gives an overall match of the current work to all existing sources in the database (e.g., 12%), which is then broken down into the percentage attributable to each source. When the software is producing a similarity report, it is useful to exclude both quotations and the reference list, for these can sometimes provide spurious matches that considerably increase the recorded similarity without actually constituting plagiarism. Also, tiny matches, or where there are technical terms that are hard to rephrase or prevalent phrases, should be ignored. For instance, 'I will now proceed to examine the results' or 'Engle (1982) developed the autoregressive conditional heteroscedasticity model,' have probably been written thousands of times and saying that again is not plagiarism.

Some schools will establish a threshold for the overall similarity index (e.g., 15% or 20%) with anything below deemed acceptable and anything above needing further investigation. Nevertheless, the marker needs to read through the report and see whether the matches are predominantly from short, randomly located groups of words or concentrated on one or two big blocks. The latter would usually be considered to be much more likely to constitute plagiarism than the former.

If students have lifted chunks from an existing source without quoting them directly, but this is interspersed with some of their own writing, this is sometimes known as 'paragraph plagiarism' or 'paraplagiarism'. Although arguably less serious than copying entire pages or sections, this would nonetheless be viewed as breaking the rules and penalised accordingly. You have still committed plagiarism if you copy someone else's phrases, whether intentionally or unintentionally, even if some of the material is yours.

It is essential to cite the sources of all ideas, even when you successfully paraphrase the work into your own words. Failure to add a citation and include that paper in the reference list at the back of the dissertation is still plagiarism. While this sort of plagiarism where ideas are taken is less likely to be detected by the software than reusing someone else's words, it could still be spotted by your project marker.

Some people try to cheat the software – for example, by playing with the characters so that the letter 'a' is replaced by a foreign language character that looks very similar but is not. They hope that the software then cannot read any of the words, and so no matches will be recorded even in cases of severe copying. Superficially, this might work, but the perpetrator will be in big trouble if the marker spots the attempt at deceit, and a matching score that is too low (0% or 1%, say) will be very suspicious. Genuine pieces of work that students have written themselves will never have similarity scores of zero since the program will always identify some phrases that match by chance with those written before by someone else. Therefore, a score of, say, 2%-8% is normal and usually of no concern.

Should students use plagiarism checking software?

An interesting question is whether students should be permitted to use the software themselves to pre-check their projects or whether it should be reserved exclusively for universities to employ after the work has been submitted. Some people might argue that it is inappropriate to let students use the software as a way to learn how to paraphrase by doing it wrong and then making the minimum amount of modification required to fix the issue, continually putting marginally changed drafts into the software until a version emerges that passes the plagiarism test.

However, others would argue that looking at the similarity report is the best way for students to identify any plagiarism, even if inadvertent, in their work. By doing so, they would learn how to improve, thereby reducing the likelihood of a formally submitted project failing the plagiarism detection test. This argument seems to trump any philosophical objections, so most universities now allow students to submit an early version of their project to the Turnitin site and examine the similarity report. You should, therefore, always take up this opportunity if it is permitted in your department, even if you are confident that your dissertation is free from plagiarism.

The Premium versions of Grammarly[8] and ProWritingAid[9] also embody plagiarism checkers. Although they are less comprehensive than Turnitin since they do not include previously submitted student work, they would be better than nothing to use for pre-checking if Turnitin is not available. There are also other plagiarism checking sites such as Quetext,[10] which has a free version that allows the user to upload a short essay and a 'pro' version that allows much longer documents to be tested for a monthly fee.

4.3.5   How to prevent plagiarism

It almost goes without stating that serious and intentional acts of plagiarism can be easily avoided by simply redrafting the material in your own words and including a citation. However, unintentional and less severe cases are more likely to occur and should still be avoided since even minor plagiarism could lead to a lower mark than you would otherwise have obtained or other issues, including losing your supervisor's confidence and goodwill. Frequently, students are concerned that they might inadvertently commit plagiarism in their projects, but provided that you follow the reasonably straightforward guidance below, it is extremely unlikely to happen.

Obviously, the crucial point is to ensure that all the dissertation material is written in your own words unless it is in quotation marks. In essence, this means paraphrasing existing authors' arguments, and doing so successfully requires skill and practice as it must be done manually for every piece of text. It is fine to use a thesaurus to search for synonyms, but you need to stay in control and decide where to use them and replacing a few words at random with substitutes is not sufficient to

---

[8]https://www.grammarly.com
[9]https://prowritingaid.com/
[10]https://www.quetext.com/pricing

avoid plagiarism.

There are now on-line paraphrasing websites that will produce a reworded version for you when you enter a block of text. Using one of these is probably still plagiarism unless you state that a paraphrasing site created this aspect of your draft since the modified version will still not be written in your words, albeit it is also not in the original author's words. I tried inserting a paragraph from a paper I had written into such a website, and the outcome was incoherent. It was almost comically bad, which gave me considerable reassurance that as a writer I cannot yet be replaced by a robot. Therefore, I strongly recommend against using an automated paraphraser.

Making careful notes from existing sources is vital, and in particular, ensuring that you record any material that you note down directly without alteration and which parts you have already put into your own words so that there is no subsequent confusion. Also, make your summaries on each study not too long after reading them when the author's phraseology is relatively fresh in your mind. In that case, if you are in any doubt about whether what you have written is too close to the original source, you can always check since you know where it came from.

A minor rearrangement of a piece of text with the replacement of a handful of terms with their synonyms is not sufficient to avoid committing plagiarism, even if you cite the source of the ideas. Paraphrasing successfully requires making your version of the information considerably different from the original. To be able to do so will also demonstrate an understanding of the material since a non-expert would find this hard to achieve.

Ensure that you use appropriate referencing and quotation marks throughout for material copied from any source, published or not. Referencing has two primary purposes: first, to give credit to the originator of ideas and knowledge, and second, to ensure that other researchers can identify and follow up on the sources of those ideas to learn more about them. Any ideas taken from existing work should refer to that source unless they are already 'common knowledge'. If you are in any doubt about your ability to avoid plagiarising or the issue concerns you, ask your supervisor.

4.3.6   Avoiding plagiarism: an illustration

Here is a sample of text from a paper that I co-authored (Brooks, Fenton, Schopohl and Walker, 2019), taken directly from the original source:

> 'The two worlds of scholarly finance and of financial market finance have never been closely linked. It is therefore interesting that the legitimacy of finance as an academic discipline and indeed its apparent intellectual strength, which we document in this section of the paper, have been able to develop over the past two decades despite its tenuous connections with real world financial markets. Moreover, as we discuss further in section 5, the advent of the global financial crisis barely dented the self-image of finance academics or raised questions concerning the validity of finance as a scholarly field of enquiry. This has arisen as a result of the separate

socially constructed environments in which academic finance and the financial services sector operate, with the former gaining and retaining its legitimacy from internally generated metrics such as "elite" journal publishing and citation factors.' (p.27).

Now I will present three different redrafts of this, but it should be noted that there are, of course, many ways that the work could be summarised effectively, and so the illustrations below are by no means unique.

Version 1

'Academic finance and financial market finances have always been closely connected. It is consequently fascinating that the validity of finance as a scholastic field and moreover its seeming intellectual vigour have grown over the past 20 years in spite of its weak linkages with the actual financial world. Also, the onset of the global financial crisis hardly made a difference to the self-image of finance scholars or made them reflect on the legitimacy of finance as an academic subject. This situation was caused by academic finance and the financial services sector being in distinct, socially constructed environments. Academic finance gets and keeps its validity from inward-looking performance measures, including publication in the top journals and citations.'

This version has managed to undertake some paraphrasing, but there are still several serious issues. The first and most important problem is that there is no reference to Brooks et al. (2019) as the source of the original ideas. Second, the structures of the original version and this paraphrased one are too similar, with the ordering of the material being retained. The simple substitutions of one set of words for some synonyms are not sufficient to avoid plagiarism or for the writer to demonstrate their understanding of the material.

Version 2

'Brooks et al. (2019) suggest that academic finance and the financial services sector have both grown over the past 20 years but independently of one another. They further argue that "the advent of the global financial crisis barely dented the self-image of finance academics or raised questions concerning the validity of finance as a scholarly field of enquiry. This has arisen as a result of the separate socially constructed environments in which academic finance and the financial services sector operate" (p.27) because academics and practitioners focus on different objectives, with the former being pre-occupied with getting published in the top journals. '

This version is not plagiarised since it has been significantly rewritten from the original version except for the part in quotation marks, and it is clear that this part is attributed accurately to the original authors. However, to have such a long quotation in a relatively short summary is probably not ideal and might be considered 'excessively derivative'. It would have been better for the writer to have redrafted this aspect into their own words.

Version 3

> 'Brooks et al. (2019) suggest that academic finance and the financial services sector have both grown over the past 20 years but independently of one another. They further argue that the global financial crisis did not affect how academic researchers felt about the strength of their discipline, which appeared to remain strong, because academics and practitioners focus on different objectives, with the former being pre-occupied with getting published in the top journals. '

This version is an accurate and succinct summary of the original passage that is free from plagiarism.

A few additional anti-plagiarism resources

A wealth of resources is available on the internet, too (although beware that some websites sell plagiarism checks at high prices, which is not worthwhile if you have university access to Turnitin) – including:

- A useful introductory treatment at Wix[11]
- A description with video and examples at Scribbr[12]
- A suite of interesting videos on a site sponsored by Turnitin[13]
- Finally, numerous other videos on YouTube can be found by searching using keywords such as 'how to avoid plagiarism.'

4.3.7   Self-plagiarism

As the name suggests, self-plagiarism occurs when an author recycles some material they wrote previously and uses it again somewhere else without attribution to their prior work. Unfortunately, experienced academics are sometimes guilty of this too. A typical scenario is when they publish a paper that applies a particular method or model, and they then use the same model elsewhere but using a different market or context, copying and pasting the description of the methods and using a very similar template and literature review for the study.

Although considered less grave than copying someone else's words, self-plagiarism is still often taken seriously by university departments. In research projects, it occurs when students include material that they have already submitted for another assignment, albeit a considerably expanded version. Self-plagiarism is fairly easy to catch since it is likely that the earlier assignment will now be in the Turnitin database, and so the new work will find a significant match to it.

If you elect to study a different topic for your project than anything else you have done before, even accidental self-plagiarism will be impossible; if not, then be

---

[11] https://www.wix.com/wordsmatter/blog/2020/02/ways-to-avoid-plagiarism/
[12] https://www.scribbr.com/plagiarism/how-to-avoid-plagiarism/
[13] https://www.plagiarism.org/collection/videos

careful to use entirely different wording for the two pieces of work. Treat your own previous work as if it was written by someone else and paraphrase from it rather than copying directly. Most universities will have a rule, either explicit or implicit, that the same piece of work, or parts of that work, cannot be submitted for more than one assessment. This can also apply to work that you completed at a previous institution, and copying from that could be detected if your former university put the essay or project into the Turnitin database, where the new work could identify a match with your old piece.

4.4   Falsification of data or results

Alongside plagiarism, the fabrication (also known as falsification) of results is considered another serious academic malpractice that could apply equally in accounting and finance as in the sciences. Falsification essentially means making up or modifying your results to fit better what you wanted to find or so that the findings are easier to explain using an existing theory.

For instance, you might be criticised if your survey sample size was small because you could not persuade many people to complete it. So, to get around this, you might write that you had 123 participants instead of the real figure, which was 23. Or you had expected a negative relationship between two variables in a regression model because this is what previous studies had found, so you simply change the sign on your parameter estimate from positive (which it actually was) to negative.

Both of these are examples of falsification of results, which is terrible scholarship and not acting with the integrity expected of researchers. Not only is it cheating, but it also defeats the purpose of all the effort that you had put in to get the results in the first place. More practically, making up results is hard to do thoroughly and systematically, opening up the possibility for inconsistencies that lead your supervisor to become suspicious because things don't look right. There are many ways that made-up data or results could be spotted, including when:

- The results look just too good to be true
- The results appear inconsistent with each other
- The proportions of each data type look wrong (e.g., you appear to have more large firms in your sample than exist in that country or market)
- It is infeasible for a student with that background to have conducted such a comprehensive or sophisticated analysis in the time available
- The results presented could not have been generated by the models described in the methods section

As discussed above, plagiarism is extremely likely to be detected as automated software has such a comprehensive database. But while detection is somewhat more challenging for falsification since to do so would require a keen eye and some detective work on the part of the reader, you might still be caught out. If that happened, the consequences would be dire, perhaps even more so than plagiarism, depending on how egregious it was.

Universities tend to treat plagiarism or falsification cases harshly because their reputation is at stake as well as yours. They would not want someone who had cheated in that way to complete their programme and obtain a transcript or degree certificate giving the misleading impression to the outside world that the student had successfully mastered all the skills required to undertake a high-quality piece of scholarly research.

Students falsifying data or plagiarising their projects will disappoint their supervisors and family or friends if they found out, but more high-profile misdemeanours will have a more significant and wide-reaching impact. Unethical or otherwise poor-quality research eats away at the respect that people both inside and outside the academy have for it. Most famously, a paper published in the *The Lancet* (a top medical journal) by Wakefield *et al.* (1998) claimed to have found a link between the measles-mumps-rubella (MMR) vaccine and autism. Yet, it was later reported in the national newspapers in the UK that the study's data had been falsified. The journal subsequently retracted the study, and Wakefield was struck off the medical register – see, for example, Deer (2011), for a discussion of some of the issues involved. The publicity surrounding the original research was so considerable that it damaged confidence in the vaccine and cast doubt in many people's minds about the veracity of other scholarly research findings, in some ways bringing the entire academy into disrepute.

The lesson here is to avoid falsifying data, don't misrepresent your findings, and don't draw firm conclusions when the results do not warrant it. Even though you are unlikely to be vilified in the way that Wakefield and his co-workers were, it would be the first step on a slippery slope that could nonetheless have severe consequences for your academic progress.

4.5   Other ethical issues

Although the MMR vaccine data falsification seems shocking and evidently wrong, representing a serious fraud, many ethical dilemmas are more subtle than this, with the choice to do or not to do it being less clear-cut. Here are a few examples to reflect upon.

1. Suppose you have a new theory for explaining the cross-sectional variation in asset returns. You collect data for the period 1960-2019, but you find by chance that the approach only works for the period 1960-2015 and then it breaks down. Do you report all the results or just those for the sub-sample where you obtain good results? If you report all the findings, in essence, your project will be proposing a novel model that appears not to work. On the other hand, if you report the earlier sub-sample results only, they will appear much more potent (although the information will look dated if it stopped in 2015). But are the improved findings worth the deceit?

The situation is arguably less serious than a falsification of results since the findings for the period to 2015 are genuine. However, it would still constitute dishonesty by omission rather than commission, meaning that you did not make up the results, but they are nonetheless misleading if presented on their own.

A model only working for part of the sample (either for a specific time only or for certain firms and not others or certain countries and not others) is a common occurrence, and therefore this is a situation many researchers face. One approach, and arguably the best one, would be to present both sets of results and then supply a reassuring explanation (backed with evidence) as to why that is the case.

Understanding why a model works in some instances but not others is a significant contribution to knowledge but challenging to achieve, causing many researchers to take what they believe to be the easy route, which is to bury the bad results and only present the good ones. Hiding some data or results just because they are inconvenient is unethical.

2. More generally, you should always be transparent in the way you write up what you have done. Failure to report certain aspects of your methods is a questionable research practice. Being transparent means both stating all the steps you took (even if they might appear 'dodgy') and not stating you did something when you didn't do it. For instance, if your raw data included several outliers (e.g., where prices were zero or where something had gone demonstrably wrong with the recording process and you had to make some adjustments), then explain that. If both the reason for the problem and the way that you dealt with it are justifiable and make sense, then the perceived quality of your work will not be adversely affected. Indeed, it might be the case that previous researchers had already documented the issues that you are now facing, and so it would a sign that something was suspicious if you had not also encountered them.

   If, ideally, you would have cross-checked something but you did not get the opportunity to do it, do not be tempted to pretend that you had. Do not make up any missing results (although it is acceptable to interpolate or extrapolate to cover missing data points if that is necessary and provided that you explain clearly what you have done and why). Making up results (even some of them) would constitute falsification of information.

3. Deliberately failing to state the assumptions you needed to make to conduct your analysis or deliberately using inferior or invalid techniques because they are more straightforward to implement would also be dishonest. It could bias the results or present a misleading picture of the findings to unwary readers.

4.5.1 Accuracy and careful investigation

Another crucial aspect of the research process is that the investigator should be careful throughout, paying attention to detail and doing everything possible to ensure accuracy. Some of the most severe problems that can arise if researchers deliberately falsify or misrepresent their findings have been described above, but troubling issues can still occur if researchers make accidental errors due to sloppy procedures or a lack of care.

Research findings must be reliable and trustworthy, so you should try to get into the good habit of double-checking every step, engaging in robustness examinations wherever possible. Accuracy extends beyond any empirical work to also cover how your project is written, so you should take care to ensure that the statements you make throughout the draft are clear and unambiguous. Your supervisor or other readers of your drafts should be able to look for unclear or poorly worded explanations.

4.5.2 Conflicts of interest

Conflicts of interest may result when a student has 'multiple relationships' with a person or organisation. They can occur in research where the participants are friends or family members of the researcher, for example, and so cannot be expected to provide entirely unbiased, independent responses.

Conflicts of interest can also sometimes arise in sponsored research, such as if a bank were to fund research on competition in the UK customer lending market. This funding could give rise to a conflict of interest because a bank would probably prefer to see the findings come down on one side of the debate (that competition in banking is already working well and that no further regulatory intervention is required). Similarly, drug companies often fund research into tests of the side effects of newly developed medicines in the context that if such side-effects are found and documented, the new drug will probably never be utilised, and the vast sums spent on its development up to that point could be wasted.

Within the academy, a journal editor would face a conflict of interest when one of their PhD students submits a paper for possible publication there or when a Head of Department works as a consultant for a company that develops learning materials that the academic's department purchases. Another example of a conflict that could arise is when the admissions tutor for a particular academic programme is a family friend of one of the applicants.

In all of these examples, the person or organisation conducting the research or making the decision has more than one interest in the outcome, which could affect their judgement at various points in the research's progress or in making other choices.

Conflicts of interest are dangerous in research since they could encourage the investigator to design the study or present the findings in a particular, biased way in order to satisfy another party. In other situations, a resolution would be to separate the conflicted individual from the decision-making process, (e.g., the admissions tutor passing responsibility for assessing the family applicant to another member of staff).

Evidently, however, you cannot be isolated from your own research. Therefore, you should reflect on any conflicts of interest that you might face in conducting your research and writing it up and, if they arise, how they could be mitigated. For an unsponsored student project, these are likely to be minimal, but where they exist, they should be discussed with your supervisor and stated in the ethics approval form in the interests of transparency. This step is called 'disclosure' of a conflict. Some useful resources to learn more about conflicts of interest and how to manage and avoid them:

- The National Academic Press has a helpful article on conflicts in the context of medical research, where such issues most commonly arise[14]
- A further discussion with examples at the US Office of Research Integrity[15]
- A detailed and more general discussion by Curzer and Santillanes (2012) is available from Research Gate[16]

This section has presented several ethical dilemmas that project students may face, and in deciding how to act, the critical question is always, 'do the ends justify the means and is behaving underhandedly worth it and would you take the risk?' In each case, behaving unethically can have severe consequences, and it is essential to know where such actions can arise and how to avoid them.

Further reading

- All books on conducting project research and dissertations will include one or more chapters on research ethics, but there are also more specialist texts entirely devoted to this topic, including Hammersley and Traianou (2012), who discuss some of the debates and dilemmas involved in conducting research
- If you are particularly concerned about plagiarism, two short books focused on this issue and explain ways to avoid it and how to reference correctly are by Williams and Davis (2017) and Lancaster (2019).

Chapter takeaways – top tips for success

- ⊛ Be aware of how important it is to conduct research ethically
- ⊛ Consider whether your project will require formal ethics approval and if so, apply as early as possible
- ⊛ Know the Data Protection Act 1998 (if you are in the UK, but similar legislation will be in place in most countries) and reflect on whether it has implications for your research

---

[14] https://www.nap.edu/read/1821/chapter/7

[15] https://ori.hhs.gov/education/products/ucla/chapter4/Chapter4.pdf

[16] https://www.researchgate.net/publication/
225294925_Managing_Conflict_of_Interest_in_Research_Some_Suggestions_for_Investigators

Chapter takeaways – continued

⊛ Understand what plagiarism is and how to prevent it
⊛ Be familiar with plagiarism checking software such as Turnitin, and use it to check your work prior to submission if permissible
⊛ Try to minimise or mitigate against any conflicts of interest that could arise in your research
⊛ Ensure that your investigative research is carefully and accurately conducted, with no data or results falsified

5. THE RESEARCH PROPOSAL

Learning outcomes: this chapter covers

✓ What a research proposal is
✓ How to draft a research proposal
✓ The elements of a good proposal
✓ How to design a Gantt chart or project timeline

5.1   What is a research proposal?

The research proposal is a brief (typically between one and six pages) document that shows your department what you intend to write your project on, how you will do it, in what sequence and over what timescale. It could be thought of as a pitch or a project bid for what you plan to work on. The proposal will include information on the project's scope, the methods and data you will employ, and possibly some discussion of risks to successful completion or ethical issues that need to be considered.

Although much shorter than the final project, the proposal still needs to be written in a formal, scholarly style. It needs to have a clear, logical structure, be of the appropriate length, and including all of the required information. The purpose of this chapter is to discuss all aspects of the proposal writing process, including tips to make it as strong and effective a document as possible.

A first consideration is in terms of the approach you should use to drafting the document regarding the appropriate level of technical detail and the level of knowledge assumed of the reader. On this issue, it is usually best to write it for an 'intelligent non-specialist.' In other words, draft the proposal for someone who knows the field (broadly defined) but not the precise topic. If, for example, you are writing a dissertation on responsible tax, you can assume that the reader is also an accountant of sorts, but not that they are a tax specialist. A single academic member of staff will likely be sifting through all the proposals and allocating them. Once you have written the proposal, you will be assigned a supervisor who is hopefully knowledgeable about the narrower topic that you have chosen to study, but you should not assume at the outset that the proposal reader will be.

Requirements regarding the research proposal vary substantially from one university to another. It might be the case that you are not required to draft one at all, in which case you may usefully skip this chapter. On the other hand, there might not only be a requirement to prepare a proposal, but it might also be formally assessed and constitute a small part of the project's overall mark. Even if that is not the case, the proposal is an important document and putting in the time to draft a good one will lay the groundwork for a smoother ride through the rest of the process. It is also likely that the proposal will be the first point of contact between you and your supervisor, and if it is incomplete or evidently hastily written, it will create a poor initial impression.

The research proposal allows the department to have an early view of whether your project is likely to meet the required standards. The academic staff can then provide suggestions on how to get it up to scratch (or, indeed, they might recommend trying again with another idea). The document will allow your supervisor to ensure that your project idea is feasible to complete within the timescale and given the resources that you have available and what you have learned so far on your degree programme. The proposal should also demonstrate that you have considered whether any ethical issues are likely to arise in your research and, if so, how you will deal with them.

Writing proposals is useful not only because it is usually a formal step in the process of completing the research project but also because the act of writing it will make you:

- Read and summarise a little of the existing literature carefully
- Think about the novelty of your idea and how it fits into the body of previous research
- Assess the plausibility of the proposed methodology
- Think about where the data will come from
- Determine whether the idea is too big, too small, or of just the right size given the time you have available
- Consider whether there are likely to be any ethical issues to be concerned with
- Establish a timetable to completion and think carefully about how long each stage is likely to take

A further benefit of having to write and submit a proposal is that it imposes some initial structure on the process and forces you to start thinking about the project from a very early stage. Otherwise, you might have been tempted not even to begin working on it until a lot of time has already elapsed. There might be a particular form that you must complete, or more likely, you will be expected to draft your own document within a pre-defined set of parameters.

Once you submit your proposal, the allocation of a supervisor will likely be based on your chosen topic. If you subsequently make a radical switch to an entirely different area, then your designated supervisor may no longer be the most appropriate subject expert. Yet changing to another supervisor might not be permitted, and it would cause significant confusion and disorder if many students similarly changed their minds and tried to switch supervisors. Hence, the best strategy is to choose carefully from the outset and to put as much effort and information into the proposal as you can. It is often the case that the proposal, if detailed, will transform naturally into the project document since the structure is quite similar. It's as if the proposal forms the skeleton for the entire project.

You will likely receive detailed feedback on the document to guide you going forwards. The more developed the proposal's content, the more effective can be that feedback, which will give you a stronger foundation to progress the work. But even if you have not been able to develop your ideas very far by the time the proposal is due, it is better to submit something incomplete than nothing at all. Even jotting down a title will provide a way for your department to point you in the right direction and can be the starting point in a conversation.

The proposal should be tailored to the audience and the word limit, so you should find out straight away what the requirements are and work within them. If it is a struggle to write the proposal, this is a bad sign that the research ideas are not sufficiently sharp, and it might be that you need to do more reading and thinking before having another go at it. The motivation and intended contribution are probably the most important parts of the proposal and should be given sufficient time and space accordingly. Students sometimes get too focused on the technical details (e.g., where they will get the data from, or even including a mathematical derivation of the quantitative model that they are going to use); this is not necessary at this stage and should be left for the main project.

If the proposal is being formally assessed as part of the project module mark, it is worth seeing if you are permitted to obtain comments on it before submission. You can then incorporate the feedback to improve the document's quality and, therefore, the mark obtained.

The key attribute of a good proposal is to start with a good research idea, and once you have this straightened out, you can draft the rest of the proposal fairly quickly. As discussed in detail in chapter 3, some students will already have the core idea from the outset, but in other cases, it will only emerge slowly after a long period of reading and discussion. In some ways, students who take longer to get their research idea are in a stronger position from then on as they will have done quite a lot of digging and will consequently have become familiar with the topic and the existing literature. On the other hand, those who had their research idea 'handed to them on a plate' or where it arrived in a flash of inspiration will need to catch up with what is already written on the topic.

5.2   What should the proposal contain?

Schools will vary enormously in their requirements here, so read the rubric and deliver what is requested. But in general, provided that there is sufficient space, all good proposals should include several key elements:

- A descriptive title
- An executive summary or abstract
- A general motivation section – why is the general area attractive?
- A brief review of the relevant existing literature with enough detail to demonstrate your familiarity with the core material
- A clear statement of the objectives and the research questions or hypotheses
- A brief description of the methodological approach to be employed (e.g., quantitative analysis of data, development of a conceptual model, conducting experiments) and of the data sources if relevant
- A statement confirming that you have considered any ethical issues and whether the investigative work will need ethics committee approval or not (see the previous chapter)
- A discussion of any anticipated risks to successful completion
- A brief timeline of significant milestones and when they are expected to be completed
- A list of references cited in the literature review part or elsewhere in the proposal

A suggestion for possible lengths for each section is given in Table 5.1 for examples of proposals that are three pages and eight pages long. Of course, these are just general guidelines, and an excellent proposal could nonetheless depart significantly from these suggestions. I will now discuss each of the sections required of the proposal in a bit more detail.

5.2.1   The title

You need to select a working title for the proposal – this might not be the title of your final project, but it should nonetheless provide a reasonable idea of what you are planning to do. It should be concise – perhaps a maximum of 12 words or a shorter title followed by a sub-title totalling not more than around 15 words – and explain what the project is about. Although a well-considered title might remain relevant for the final document, you would not be required to stick rigidly to it. It is not worth agonising at this stage as your research could move in any number of directions that

Table 5.1: Possible research proposal lengths for each section

Element	Short proposal (pages)	Long proposal (pages)
Summary	–	$\frac{1}{3}$
Introduction	$\frac{1}{2}$	1
Literature review	$\frac{1}{2}$	2
Research objectives and questions	$\frac{1}{2}$	1
Methodology and data sources	$\frac{1}{2}$	2
Ethical issues	$\frac{1}{3}$	$\frac{1}{3}$
Risk assessment	–	$\frac{1}{3}$
Timescale	$\frac{1}{3}$	$\frac{1}{2}$
References	$\frac{1}{3}$	$\frac{1}{2}$
Total	3	8

you cannot predict when writing the proposal. Just draft a title that makes sense given the ideas that you have now.

5.2.2 The summary

This section would be a single paragraph of around 100-150 words that gives the reader the gist of your ideas - including the topic, the research questions, the methodological approach you will use, the geographical coverage or period covered (if relevant), any data or resource requirements, and what you are expecting to find. For a shorter proposal, this section would usually be omitted altogether as the entire piece is essentially a precis so that the abstract would be a summary of a summary.

5.2.3 The introduction

This section will first set the scene for the topic to contextualise the material you will discuss below. You would then cover the motivation, which is a statement of why the study is needed. This will usually involve establishing the background and then identifying a gap in existing knowledge that your research will fill. You would then explain what you want to do (only in broad terms at this stage), why it is exciting and what is the significance of it and for whom. Will your work be mainly aimed at other academics, developing new knowledge that other researchers could take forwards, or will it be directed predominantly at practitioners or policymakers? What is the need for the research you intend to produce? This section needs to persuade the assessor that the project will be relevant, exciting, and worthwhile.

5.2.4   The literature review

The review does not have to be exhaustive at this stage, covering everything already written on the topic. It just needs to be suggestive and sufficient to convince the reader that you can see where your ideas will fit within the knowledge base and that you are reasonably confident that you are not merely repeating work that is already out there. Note that many (most?) research proposals are 'review heavy' – that is, they contain too much review and background information with not enough space devoted to the actual research that will be conducted and how. The latter is the core of the proposal (and will be the core of the project) – the literature review is just context setting, albeit necessary background.

Even if you have done a lot of reading, focus on the most important and relevant articles in the review part of your proposal. If your literature review is more than around a third of the proposal, you should consider cutting it down to include only the most pertinent sources or discussing each piece in less detail. The rest of the material is not wasted because it can be saved for discussion in the literature review of the actual project, where you will have considerably more space to devote to it.

While the review does not need to be extensive at this stage, the more legwork you do now to see what is out there, the less will be remaining to do once you start on the actual project. And the better position you would be in to hit the deck running with the investigative part at an early stage rather than spending a great deal of additional time later on review work, which many students find the least interesting aspect of the research process. Conducting a thorough review from the outset also diminishes the chances that you (or worse, your marker) discover an existing paper that already does exactly what you have done.

5.2.5   The research objectives

This section is at the heart of the whole proposal and outlines what you aim to study and achieve from the work. Be succinct and clear on what these aims are. Although your research objectives will likely change as you get deeper into the project, thinking carefully about them now will help you clarify the methods and data aspects and ensure that these parts of the proposal are coherent. You will need to identify a way to explain your ideas for the investigation. This can be in one of several ways, or a combination of them, where you provide:

- A set of statements about what you plan to do, or research aims and objectives
- A set of research questions
- A set of hypotheses

Any of these are acceptable, and they can be viewed as equivalent ways of expressing the same ideas. It usually works best to have multiple research questions, aims or hypotheses. Even if you have one core aim, try to break it down into a set of sub-aims, which will make the task of addressing it more manageable, even though you probably do not have each part of the core aim fully worked through at this stage. Having several aims will also make the purpose appear more substantive and facilitate having separate pieces of analysis that collectively make enough to constitute a dissertation. Perhaps 2-4 aims is about the right number; more than that would seem excessive and infeasible to address in detail given the time constraints and limited space in the proposal document. Using a fictional example to illustrate, you could write the part outlining your research objectives as follows:

> 'The overall aim of my project is to investigate the impact of the tone of earnings announcements on UK companies' share prices. I will analyse the relationship between the sentiment expressed in the reports and changes in the share price within a window from 20 trading days before to 20 days after the announcement. I will also examine the impact on the volatility of stock returns and trading volume during the event window. I will draw out the implications of the findings for the way in which companies can express their earnings reports to encourage particular market reactions.'

When expressing your aims in writing, there are many key verbs that you can use to describe what you wish to do (and if you have several aims, try not to use the same word repeatedly but make use of its synonyms), for example: assess, calculate, compare, compute, contrast, determine, evaluate, explain, explore, identify, investigate, summarise, propose, understand.

Ideally, the aims will cover all aspects of the investigative work from the initial part to the conclusions where you would draw together the findings and propose policy recommendations. So the first aim could use words such as describe, summarise, or understand (with regards to the data or phenomenon under study). The second aim or aims could use words such as: explain, assess, or investigate, as this is the part where you would be trying to understand why something happened using causal relationships. The final aims could then relate to the broader implications of your findings, such as identifying recommendations for firms or regulators or investors, and so on. Note that there is no need to include general aims that would apply to every project irrespective of the subject matter (e.g., 'I will review the literature', or 'I will summarise my findings'). Of course you will do that since all projects do, and these are requirements, so there is no need to list them.

In principle, a researcher following a positivist scientific approach should specify the research aims first and then proceed to collect the data and analyse it, as discussed in section 2.3. However, in practice, many researchers get some data, play around with it, see if they can generate some impressive results, and then try to 'retro-fit' a set of aims or a theoretical model that can explain what they observe. Although, strictly, such an ordering of the steps can lead to issues around data mining, finding spurious relationships, and misattributing the causes, it is probably acceptable at the student project level. And realistically, provided that your drafting is careful, nobody will know when reading your work that the output was generated first and the aims were written after. Therefore, in reality, you will be able to modify your research aims at a later stage when you have had the opportunity to dig deeper into the literature, collect your data and begin the investigative work.

5.2.6 The methodology and data section

This section will probably be brief and merely outline the approach you will use at a high level. You only need to present enough detail to show the reader that you have thought about how you will attack your research questions and to inspire sufficient confidence that you are knowledgeable about your chosen methods. These will probably be tentative at this stage to be updated and refined as you read more and start the investigative work later. As for the aims and title, you will not be forced to stick rigidly to the methodological approach and data sources you specified in the proposal. Returning to the example used above, the kind of structure you could use here is as follows:

> 'I will obtain daily share price and trading volume data over the past five years on all listed stocks that are or were members of the FTSE100 using Bloomberg. I will estimate the daily returns to each stock use a rolling window to calculate the standard deviations of returns as a measure of volatility. I will download the earnings announcements from the Dow Jones Newswire database. The sentiment analysis will use a dictionary of positive and negative words based on the approach developed by Loughran and McDonald (2011). The sample will be split into sub-groups based on whether the sentiment is positive, negative or neutral. An event study will then be used with a 40-day window centred on the announcement with the abnormal returns examined and compared for each group.'

Note that unless your proposal is very short (a page or two), you would need to provide more detail than this on your methods and data collection. The amount you write on this aspect should be proportionate to the overall length of the proposal along the lines of the suggestions in Table 5.1 above.

5.2.7 The timeline

This part needs to demonstrate to your prospective supervisor that you have thought about the feasibility of the work in terms of how long each stage is likely to take and in what order you expect to undertake the steps. It is useful to be compelled to think about this, and although your supervisor won't hold you to meeting the exact dates for each section, it will help establish a framework so that you can gauge your progress as you proceed through each stage of the project. Think about the tasks to be done for the timeline, which could comprise the following list:

1. Draft proposal
2. Meet with supervisor to discuss submitted proposal and assess any training needs
3. Discuss whether ethical approval is needed and, if so, complete and submit the form
4. Begin detailed literature gathering
5. Commence the first draft of the literature review
6. Complete the draft of the literature review and submit it to the supervisor for

Table 5.2: Sample timeline for a research project

Task	Time period	Time taken (weeks)	Detailed summary of the step
Literature review	March-June	12	Gather reference list; detailed reading; draft review
Develop methods	June	4	Set up spreadsheets and check Python code works; write methods section
Collect data	July	4	Download data from Bloomberg and Dow Jones; write data section
Data analysis	July-August	8	Clean and organise data; run the programs; obtain results; analyse and write them up
Completing and refining the draft	September	4	Write introductory and concluding sections and then the abstract; complete first draft; proof-read and get feedback from supervisor and friends; make final changes and checks

     comment (if permitted)

7. (Re)formulate research aims or hypotheses
8. Determine methods to be used
9. Consider data requirements
10. Check data access and availability
11. Download data or conduct survey (including the pilot), interviews or experiments
12. Conduct preliminary data analysis and produce descriptive summaries
13. Conduct principal data analysis and create results tables
14. Write the first draft of the entire project document
15. Send draft to supervisor and others; modify in the light of the comments
16. Undertake final checking, polishing and submission of the draft

Personalising this list and adding indicative dates to each item is a significant step forwards, and you can tick off each task as you complete it.

There are several ways to construct a timeline, which could be anything from a brief and straightforward list to a formal flow diagram or Gantt chart. To offer an illustration, suppose that you begin your project in March 2020 and need to submit it at the end of September in the same year. So you have seven months altogether, but you will have more time from July to September once the taught modules and exams are out of the way. A basic list-type structure (including only the primary headings) would be as depicted in Table 5.2 assuming that you work a few hours per week in March-June and almost full-time from July-September.

A Gantt chart (named after its inventor, Henry Gantt) is simply a chart

Table 5.3: Sample basic Gantt chart for a research project

Task	Mar	Apr	May	Jun	Jul	Aug	Sep
Literature review	■	■	■	■			
Develop methods				■			
Collect data					■		
Data analysis					■	■	
Completing and refining the draft							■

demonstrating how a project will be structured and the timescale over which it is expected to progress. It shows the same information as the table above but in a slightly different format, and an example of the chart is given in Table 5.3.

Things will likely go wrong at some point, and therefore it is advisable to build some slack into each stage. Producing a Gantt chart is quite a useful exercise even if you are not formally required to submit it, since it encourages you to think about how long you expect each aspect of the project to take and in what order to carry out each task. Once you have completed the project, you can then compare the chart you produced before starting with the outturn; I would guess that every aspect will have taken longer than you had anticipated.

5.2.8 Other sections

While the list above probably covers everything that the majority of proposals would include, there are several other aspects to consider writing something about:

- Can you identify (albeit you are at a preliminary stage) any practical issues that you might face in progressing the research (e.g., difficulties in getting respondents to engage with a survey) and note them down to get early suggestions on how to avoid or mitigate these problems? This is a forward-looking risk assessment demonstrating that you have considered potential hitches you may face, although, of course, many different things can go wrong and hence it is impossible to predict most of them.

- Will you need to undertake any specific training or development to achieve what you want to – for example, learning a new quantitative or interview technique? Again, noting this down will maximise the chances that you are pointed in the right direction to receive the support required, and it will create a favourable impression that you have carefully considered all of the issues from the outset.

- Will you need ethics approval, if so, for which parts of the work and why? If you are using only secondary data from a third-party website (e.g., downloaded from FAME or Bloomberg), then a simple statement that you have considered any ethical issues that may arise and you believe that no ethics committee approval will be necessary would be sufficient.

5.2.9 What can go wrong with a proposal?

Proposals tend to vary much more in terms of their quality than the final projects, simply because students treat the former with a wider variation in seriousness, owing to them usually not being assessed.

Some students put a minimal amount of effort into their proposals, barely writing a few lines off the tops of their heads, while others agonise for weeks and produce a detailed and polished document. However, when students put in the work to draft a proposal but which is nonetheless still weak, it is usually one of the issues in the following list that applies.

- Weak structure or poor writing style
- No originality in the idea or no imagination
- The project idea is either trivial or too all-encompassing and thus not feasible
- The idea is highly practical but not amenable to scholarly study
- Too much literature review or the review is out of date
- No consideration at all given to data collection and whether this is likely to be too costly or time-consuming
- A requirement to obtain confidential information or 'buy-in' from interview participants who will have no incentives to be involved
- Too much detail on the models to be used, including derivations and pages of algebra
- The writing is rambling and repetitive
- Failure to cite fundamental studies or inaccurately reporting them
- Too many or too few references

Some of these problems relate to the structure or style of the proposal document while others track back to the research aims or choice of topic. Evidently, a high quality proposal can only be constructed on the basis of clear research aims and issues with writing the document can reveal more fundamental problems with the underpinning research ideas that need to be addressed.

Until you finally get the go-ahead from your supervisor to begin working on a specific topic, it is worth having a 'plan B'. As well as your fully worked up proposal that you have spent the time to craft into the required format and level of detail, you should also have a back-up idea that you could turn into a workable proposal fairly quickly if plan A falls flat for some reason (e.g., your supervisor suggests abandoning it, you cannot get the required data, or you realise it will be too arduous given the constraints). That way, although you would lose some time when having to work up the second idea to the development stage of the first, all will not be lost.

However, if you encounter difficulties with your primary choice of topic, in the first instance, it is worth considering whether you can modify rather than abandon it. Changing the idea slightly implies that most of the reading you have already done will continue to be relevant. Beginning with something totally different is a more drastic action meaning that much of your previous work may have been needless, setting you back and wasting valuable time investigating another idea.

Further reading

Many specialist texts exist on writing research proposals, but most are aimed at established academics who need to apply for funding rather than students. Those written for the latter include O'Leary (2018), which provides a straightforward introduction, and the more comprehensive books by Denscombe (2019) and Punch (2016).

Chapter takeaways – top tips for success

⊛ If you are required to submit a research proposal, investigate what is needed in terms of the length and level of detail

⊛ Ensure that your proposal is not 'review-heavy' where the literature review part swamps your own ideas and proposed methods

⊛ The most important part of the proposal is the statement of research aims, questions or hypotheses

⊛ Make preliminary decisions on the methods and sources of data that you will employ

⊛ Draw up a timeline or Gantt chart. Even if this is not formally required, it will be helpful as a way for you to establish informal deadlines and determine whether you are on target or not

⊛ Ensure that your proposal is as detailed, well-thought-out and polished as possible since it can be used as a template from which to begin the actual project

The investigative part

6. FINDING THE LITERATURE

Learning outcomes: this chapter covers

✓ What a literature review is
✓ Why you should review the literature
✓ The types of material that can be examined
✓ Where to look for possible sources of material
✓ How to read an academic paper

6.1 What is a literature review?

A literature review may be defined as a document that presents a thorough examination and organisation of the existing knowledge that has arisen from established researchers' work in the field of interest. By writing a literature review, you will learn to find and recognise the information relevant to your topic, identify the most important contributions and learn how to evaluate the quality of each piece of research.

You will also 'synthesise' the body of knowledge. Synthesising means that you can work across the existing studies, classify them, draw out the common threads, and put them into a framework. By synthesising the literature, you will be making a new contribution by combining studies to create new interpretations of existing research and possibly viewing it from a different perspective than the original authors. Notice the difference between a summary and a synthesis. A summary is just a shortened version of the original piece, albeit written in different words. It will not provide a novel insight compared with the existing work. A synthesis, on the other hand, will use more than one source to generate fresh ideas. In conclusion, a literature review is not merely a list of papers or a collection of summaries; it is much more than that.

In years gone by, taught modules would often require students to delve into the primary literature (i.e., journal articles and research books) but nowadays, courses increasingly rely solely on textbooks and other standardised materials. This teaching approach means that their research project will be the first time many students are exposed to the research literature. This brings with it numerous challenges – tasks are all covered, in order, in this chapter or the next:

1. Deciding what kind of material you need to read and on what subjects
2. Where to find the material, ensuring that you uncover any relevant sources but not wasting time looking at studies that are not germane
3. Trying to decipher the language used in the studies to get a grip on what the authors are writing about and how it relates to your project
4. Organising the material and crafting it into a well-written and well-structured literature review of an appropriate length
5. Ensuring that the referencing is done correctly and producing the reference list in a suitable format

When you first begin to search through the sources, the sheer volume of material can appear overwhelming, but much of it will either be irrelevant or part of a parallel stream of work with little incremental value so that it can be skipped over or read cursorily. With experience, you will be able to rapidly identify the sources that you need to note the existence of, those that need to be read thoroughly, and those that can be ignored. The review task then becomes not quite as daunting as it might have first appeared, and you could make rapid progress.

Doing the searches to find the relevant work, reading it and then writing the review are all time-consuming activities that might take, perhaps, a fifth of all of the time available to complete the project. It needs to be done thoroughly, of course, but on the other hand, don't spend so long seeking, reading and summarising the literature that you leave insufficient time for your investigative work.

With some thought and thorough planning, the review can be completed successfully without too much stress, but there are broadly two primary ways that it can go wrong. First, if you do not search in a sufficiently systematic fashion, and you end up missing key studies relevant to your research. Not spotting these will be a problem if you end up needlessly repeating what others have done or said, especially if your project markers are aware of these other pieces. Second, if your exploration is so broad that you cannot identify the crucial studies to incorporate so that you include too many and your review drifts, lacking focus. Reading this chapter thoroughly should help you avoid those issues and many others of a more minor nature.

6.1.1 Could the entire project be a literature review?

Yes, in theory, this ought to usually be possible within the rules at most institutions since writing a detailed and insightful review that synthesises the literature is quite a challenge and would be a contribution to knowledge. If you really wanted to write a 12,000-word review and nothing else because you enjoy reading and summarising existing studies so much and you don't want to do any empirical work, then check with your supervisor that it would constitute an acceptable dissertation.

However, it is tricky to do this well, and the project would be required to go considerably beyond presenting a summary of the existing research on a particular topic. You would need to provide a new taxonomy of the work – classifying it in a novel and exciting way or providing unique insight about what is known, what is not yet known and proposing a new agenda for future work in the area. Most students enjoy the literature review aspect of a dissertation the least, and hence unsurprisingly, it is not a popular choice for an entire project. Given that it is an arduous task to draft it to the standard required to constitute a whole piece, it is also a risky choice compared with the more common empirical model testing approach.

6.2 Why should you review the literature?

A primary objective behind getting students to write a literature review is that they should demonstrate their understanding of and ability to synthesise a specific branch of existing work *in depth* (note the emphasis here). Therefore, you should avoid covering such a breadth of material that you have no time, energy or words remaining when it comes to the part of the literature relating to precisely your chosen topic so that you only skim over the surface. Although the literature review might begin very broadly, it needs to quite rapidly narrow down to the specifics of the research matter directly covered in the investigative part of the dissertation.

Prior to beginning the investigative part of your project, it is vital to examine the extant literature thoroughly. As you will have spotted, every research article in a journal or research monograph will contain a literature review aspect. Likewise, all student projects need to incorporate such a review, which can provide inspiration for the current research and establish an appropriate context. It might also serve as an early warning for possible issues that might be faced. You cannot identify where the gaps are in the body of knowledge until you have read much of it in that area.

The primary reason researchers (both students and staff members) always begin a new project by reviewing existing studies is to inform their work and to help them sharpen the research questions they want to consider. It allows them to see where their research aims fit within the range of work that has already been done. A second key reason is to ensure that their ideas have not already been employed by someone else and that the current research project is not a partial (albeit unintended) rehash of a prior study.

As you are reading for the literature review, it will lead you to develop lots of new ideas, and it might even encourage you to question whether the subject in your proposal is still the right one to pursue. If, upon digging deeper into the literature, you want to change your research aims or even the whole topic, should you do so? This is a tricky question since you will be learning fast as you become more immersed in the body of knowledge, and, naturally, the information obtained will help you refine your aims and polish your ideas.

But it is usually advisable not to drift too far from the original topic – your department may not allow it, and you don't want to be in the position of unnecessarily throwing away all of the study that you have done so far. If you have already gathered data or code, will that have to be scrapped too? Will the ethical approval you have sought still be valid, or would that have to be resubmitted? These are delicate issues that have to be weighed carefully when considering any non-trivial revisions to your original proposal topic.

In addition to the content of each study that you read, another aspect to reflect upon is the style that the authors have used, both in terms of the structuring and flow of material and how arguments have been phrased. Think about which literary techniques you feel work best, are easiest to follow and most pleasant to read, since this will help you make decisions about how to organise your writing throughout the project when you get to that stage.

Even if the ideas you have for your research are highly practical and motivated by a real-world problem, it is nonetheless vital that you embed your work in the existing literature. You will therefore need to reflect on which parts of the literature best fit with your research area and try to identify and explain the linkages. Failure to achieve this is likely to result in a poor quality review that appears disjointed from your investigative work. This could lead to a low mark, even if the other aspects of the study are strong.

Conducting a thorough examination of existing papers will make sure that you use contemporary approaches incorporating the latest thinking in the research area since carefully reading through existing studies will help you identify the methodologies that other authors have most commonly used to tackle their research questions. You will be able to assess the approaches that worked best and those that were less successful, which will support you when you subsequently come to begin your investigative work.

6.3   What should you read?

The review should cover not just empirical applications in your topic area but also discuss the theoretical frameworks that have been adopted in the relevant literature and the methods used to test them. Conducting the literature review will provide you with suggestions for these aspects of your project too. In order to conduct a thorough review, you will need to examine a range of different kinds of sources, including both published and unpublished material. The former will comprise journal articles, books and book chapters, while the latter might include lecture materials, websites,

PhD theses, blogsites and working papers. Each of these sources will be discussed, but first, the following sub-section reflects on how readers can evaluate the quality of what they read – in particular relying on the peer-review mechanism.

6.3.1 Checking the validity of your reading material

Ensuring the validity of what you read and cite is vital for several reasons. First, and at the most basic level, poorly written articles or books will waste a considerable amount of your precious time trying to decipher and understand what the author means. Second, even if the authors of the work had no idea what they were writing about, your supervisor will, and so if you quote in your project studies that contain errors, it is plausible that these will be spotted by the person marking it. Third, if you follow a method that an existing author inappropriately or incorrectly applied, you will inadvertently make the same error as they did.

With time, you could develop the skills needed to make your own judgements about the quality and integrity of the material you are reading, but in the meantime, there are several proxies that you can use – these are 'gold seals' that can usually be taken as implying that the work is at least of reasonable quality:

- Use the author's credentials as a proxy for quality assurance. If the author is well established, has written on the topic before and is affiliated with a reputable university, that usually implies that the work should be of at least an acceptable standard. Naturally, even the world's leading scholars make errors, but their output should nonetheless be more reliable than something posted by an unknown individual on a website.
- Use the publisher as a proxy for quality assurance – for books, publishers usually put proposals and draft manuscripts through an extensive review process before accepting them for print, and hopefully, any that were not of a sufficient standard would have been rejected
- Use the journal's prestige as a proxy for quality assurance – as for books, the majority of journals have rigorous refereeing processes where articles are 'peer-reviewed' by acknowledged experts in the field
- Use the style and presentation as a proxy for quality assurance. If the work is poorly organised, poorly written, or the presentation is very unprofessional, that can be a sign that it is not a solid piece and it should be read with caution. Poorly written work with grammatical or spelling errors, or where the structure is bad, should probably be discarded
- On the other hand, a shiny pamphlet report is a sign of a high marketing budget and not necessarily good underpinning research. Therefore, don't be duped by a glitzy presentation either; instead, focus on what has been written
- If an author uses numerous citations from relevant and acknowledged sources, that is a good sign regarding the likely standard of their work, albeit not a guarantee; equally, a small number of poor-quality sources is indicative of inferior research

- Check a range of sources: if many authors are independently making the same point or find the same result, it is more likely to be valid. It is, unfortunately, the case that sometimes an entire research area goes down the wrong track when one researcher makes an error that other scholars then repeat following the original erroneous approach. In that case, the subsequent studies cannot be considered independent from the first one. Eventually, other researchers will come to realise the issue, and they will write about it and correct it, but this may take a considerable time to occur
- Use the age of the work as a proxy for its validity. Following on from the previous point, although not always the case, we expect the literature to progress towards 'the truth' so that newer findings build upon older research and hence the former should supersede the latter. The progress of a research literature over time does not imply that older work is necessarily flawed, but instead that newer studies are likely to be more reliable. There has also been a greater emphasis on rigour and robustness in published academic work over the past decade or so than there was previously

Peer-review

For most journals, the publication process involves an in-built quality seal known as peer-review. What happens is that each academic author selects a journal to which to submit a paper that they have been working on, and once submitted, the journal editor will usually send the work out to a reviewer (also sometimes known as a referee). This is the peer-review process, where the work is evaluated by the peers of the submitting author (i.e., other, established academics who have published previously on the same topic). Here, one or more scholars independent of the author(s) of the work (the referee(s), also known as reviewers) evaluate it and make comments for improvement before recommending whether the journal accepts the paper for publication or rejects it. Such a process ought to imply that, once the work has jumped over this hurdle, the research is sufficiently reliable that the contents can be taken at face value and the findings and conclusions assumed to be justified.

The peer-review system for journals is better than nothing but far from a perfect way to ensure that all published work is free from errors, inaccuracies or biases. In particular, the refereeing quality will depend upon the skills, experience, and knowledge of the reviewers. Many leading journals use only one referee for each submitted paper, meaning that there could easily be flaws in the work that the reviewer misses. Referees are usually unpaid, and therefore the incentives for being very thorough are limited to professional pride and a belief in scholarship.

What this means for readers of articles is that, ideally, you should always be sceptical of everything written, never taking what a book or article says at face value, even if published in the most respected journals. If the same argument is made or the same result emerges in several independent studies, it can probably be accepted as a genuine finding. Nonetheless, I will end this point by stating that while there can be flaws in the articles published in peer-reviewed journals, these are nevertheless far more reliable than non-refereed outlets such as blogs, webpages, newspaper articles and pieces in popular magazines.

6.3.2 Lecture notes and textbooks

Lecture notes and textbooks are often a great place to start reading on a particular topic because they usually provide a more accessible and logically ordered treatment of the material than articles. Notes and books typically begin right from the beginning and use a consistent notation and terminology throughout that are easy to pick up rapidly. On the other hand, space is at a premium for journal articles, and as a result, there is a tendency to cut straight to the methods and models used in the paper, assuming that the reader is already familiar with a set of other studies that had previously been published on the topic. Different journal articles might also use varying ways of writing the same phrases or equations, and the differences in terminology can cause considerable confusion for someone new to the research area. Textbooks often contain many references to the original research literature, enabling you to build your bibliography in key areas rapidly.

It is perfectly acceptable to include material from your lecture notes in your dissertation, and in most cases, it can be considered 'common knowledge' and hence included without crediting the lecturer as the source. However, like all secondary material that you incorporate, you should write it in your own words to avoid plagiarism. It is vital not to rely exclusively on lecture notes, though, and you should combine them with the other reading you have done.

However, while textbooks and course materials are indeed a good starting point, they should not be the only or predominant source that you use since they tend to date fairly quickly, and so they might not contain the latest thinking in more recent issues of the leading field journals. Textbooks might be too basic or too broad and lacking in detail concerning the specific subject you are working on. They can be the starting place of your literature search journey, but they should not be the end point. If your reference list contains many texts, especially if they are aimed at the introductory level, it will make your work appear rather amateurish.

Alongside textbooks, research monographs should also be mentioned here. Unlike texts, they will likely contain original research material that the author has chosen to publish in a book format rather than as a (series of) journal article(s). Research monographs are ubiquitous in the arts and humanities but less common in accounting and finance, and they are harder (and often more costly) to get hold of than journal articles. Accessing research books will be discussed in the next chapter.

6.3.3 Journal articles

Journals, or periodicals as they are sometimes known, are published at regular intervals, typically quarterly but sometimes monthly or at another frequency. They contain several articles (typically 6–12) in each issue, each of around 10–30 pages in length. The articles will comprise the research of (predominantly) academics working in the field, which has been submitted to that journal. The issues are usually published both in-print and on-line, although the latter is now the primary mode of access.

Each journal tends to have a specialisation in terms of the type of work published there (empirical work, informed opinion pieces, theoretical models with a lot of maths, review papers, etc.). Journals also vary systematically in terms of the articles' style and length, and sometimes the viewpoint (such as being pro-auditor or pro-regulation in the tax avoidance debate) expressed in the journal so that other perspectives are rarely if ever presented in that outlet.

Periodicals with 'Letters' in the title publish short articles (e.g., *Economics Letters, Finance Research Letters*), which provide a brief and, therefore, quick-to-read treatment for the reader. However, the lack of words means that they cannot develop their arguments with the same depth as regular journals, limiting their use as sources for student projects.

In accounting and finance, most scholars consider publication in the leading journals to be more prestigious and valuable for their careers than writing books (even research monographs) and therefore, they draft all of their best ideas into journal papers. Fortunately, most journal articles are easy for students to obtain electronically and free of charge, provided that their university library subscribes to that journal, either by purchasing it individually or through a 'bundle' deal – see section section 6.5 below. The other feature of journal articles is that, at 6,000–12,000 words, typically, they are mercifully short and so can be read relatively rapidly compared with books (which are likely to be of the order 80,000-150,000 words).

Journal articles will probably constitute the principal source of material for your literature review, although this will depend on the topic to some extent. If you are working on a very current subject, such as fintech or cryptocurrencies, most studies will be so recent that they may not yet have been published. Also, given the practical nature of the topic, much of the research will have been conducted by practitioners who tend not to publish their work in journals.

Why do some papers become popular?

Some papers in the literature are considered 'seminal'. These are influential studies that almost everyone working on the topic refers to in their research. Such work will have changed how people have thought about a problem (so-called 'pivotal' studies) or have had a significant impact on industry or government. The researcher might have been introducing a new idea or at least one unique to that subject area. Literature reviews should always mention any seminal papers in the area.

Occasionally, it is hard to identify the seminal studies when you are new to a research area. But if you notice that many recent authors are citing a particular study, it is probably worth you finding, reading and referencing the work too since this indicates its importance.

Sometimes journal articles become widely cited not because they are seminal but rather since the work is published in a top-rated journal or because the authors are already famous or from 'elite' institutions. In such cases, the paper will get much more publicity and exposure than comparable work conducted by less well-known writers from less prestigious universities. Readers of these publications will take the author or journal's 'brand value' as a proxy for the quality. Researchers also tend to cite easily accessible papers, and they tend to mention the same work that other researchers in the area are referencing. This citation pattern results in the distribution of citations being heavily skewed towards a few mega-hits while many academic studies receive almost no citations at all.

An interesting illustration of this is the so-called 'GARCH'-model which became extremely popular in the 1990s for capturing and forecasting volatility in finance. Two researchers independently developed and published ostensibly the same model in 1986: Stephen Taylor, who presented the model in his book, *Modelling Financial Time Series* (Wiley, New York, NY); and Tim Bollerslev, who published it in the *Journal of Econometrics*, a leading outlet. At the time of writing this book, Bollerslev's paper has 28,521 citations according to Google Scholar, while Taylor's equivalent work in his book has just a seventh of that number, 3,821.

From time to time, papers become widely cited not because they are the first to present a new idea but rather because they popularise an existing one, for example, by making it more accessible to a particular audience. Perhaps the previous study in the area that did not gain widespread acclaim arrived too early when the research community was not ready to consider it seriously, or it was initially published in an obscure outlet that most scholars do not look at. In such cases, both the famous paper and the original study should be mentioned in your review.

6.3.4 Should your literature review focus only on the 'best' journals?

Whether your review should only incorporate materials from the highest rated journals is a relevant question, and if you decided to restrict your reading in that way, how could you identify the top outlets? The numbers of journals in accounting and finance are vast, but, as for all fields of study, there is a handful of journals considered to be the most prestigious of all. These outlets are highly competitive for authors to get into, and as a result, they usually reject the overwhelming majority of articles submitted there for possible publication. Many of the papers that become the most widely cited in accounting and finance are published in these journals, and they tend to have very high standards of refereeing and a requirement that, to be accepted, work must make a significant contribution to knowledge.

The Chartered Association of Business Schools (CABS) is a professional body representing business schools in the UK. Among other activities, they produce the Academic Journal Guide (AJG), formerly known as the 'ABS List', which provides a rating of many journals across 22 business and management areas, including accounting and finance (which are considered as two separate fields). The journals included in the list are rated on a four-point scale, with the very highest-rated few of these in the top category further designated as 'Journals of Distinction' (JoDs).

Table 6.1: *Journals of Distinction* in the Academic Journal Guide

Accounting	Finance
Accounting Review	Journal of Finance
Accounting, Organizations and Society	Journal of Financial Economics
Journal of Accounting and Economics	Review of Financial Studies
Journal of Accounting Research	

In the most recent version of the AJG at the time of writing (refined in 2018), in accounting and finance, the JoDs are given in Table 6.1.

The entire AJG can be accessed freely, but to do so you would need to register first. [1] The Guide contains around 90 journals in accounting and 110 in finance, each rated on the scale described above.

However, while many academics might consider the work published in JoDs to be leading the field, it is frequently not the most accessible material for students new to research, and these journals often contain a large proportion of theoretical or conceptual pieces. More straightforward applications of models that can be employed as a template for a student project can usually be found in lower-ranked journals. Therefore, it would not be appropriate to limit a literature search to only work published in these top-rated journals, which would likely miss a considerable amount of relevant and readable material. While less esteemed than those in the short table above, many other journals publish original and high-quality articles across a much broader range of topics.

Should papers from very low-ranking or unknown (even unrefereed) outlets, badly written or technically weak pieces, and so on be incorporated into the literature review? You might suggest that the obvious answer is 'no', but this is a difficult balance in reality. In general, you probably would not want to include them for the reason discussed above because their findings could be unreliable and the conclusions misleading. As you become more experienced in reading papers and evaluating research quality, you will be able to make up your own mind whether a flawed paper in an unrefereed journal is nonetheless worth citing.

Journals where the articles are not peer-reviewed (refereed) or where the authors pay to place their work in the outlets (so-called 'vanity publishing') are sometimes best avoided as the quality of the articles contained within them may be weak in many senses – poorly written, biased, shoddy empirical work, inappropriate conclusions, etc. You can generally tell if journals are refereed by looking at their webpages. Usually, journals organised by the major publishers, with prestigious editorial boards, having available impact factors (a measure of how much the work in the journal is cited that is compared to other outlets, which allows them to be ranked) or that are in the AJG, are likely to be refereed.

It would, however, be worth incorporating even weak studies if they are directly

---

[1] https://charteredabs.org/academic-journal-guide-2018/

relevant to your topic (especially if they are more relevant than better quality studies). But be sure to highlight the weaknesses of such studies and warn the reader that, while you are citing the work due to its applicability to your research, it should not be taken at face value due to its flaws.

You should also try to ensure that your outlook is sufficiently broad that you are able to capture research on your topic that is published in journals outside of its discipline. For instance, I have published finance research in management, economics and accounting journals. So if, for instance, you are working on a topic in accounting, it would be inappropriate to restrict your searches to only those journals with accounting in the title. If you do so, there is a danger that you could miss relevant studies, and those published in outside-of-field outlets are more likely to take an interdisciplinary perspective or to use a different methodological approach compared with papers published in the core journals. This feature often makes the work refreshingly different and inspiring, and therefore definitely worth seeking out and reading.

6.3.5 Review papers

Drafting a literature review is simplified if there is a survey paper (sometimes known as a review paper) on a nearby topic. Survey papers are in essence published literature reviews on a specific, narrowly defined field of research. They were traditionally written by 'heavyweight' academics in the field, and journals would only accept them if the authors were exceptionally renowned and well established in the area, but that is probably no longer the case.

Finding one or more of these articles will make your job much more manageable and will provide you with a rapid and handy overview of the state of knowledge on a particular topic at the point in time that the review was written. They can be an excellent place to start before you delve deeper into the literature since they will usually provide a broad-based but possibly shallow introduction to that topic, which will enable you to identify the order in which you should read the other studies. Review papers will also provide you with a ready-made bibliography of further research to read.

There are particular journals in each field that publish numerous survey papers, and indeed, it might be all that they publish, such as the *International Journal of Management Reviews*; *Journal of Economic Surveys*; *Transport Reviews*. The *Journal of Economic Literature* provides excellent survey articles in economics (occasionally also covering finance topics), and likewise, the *Journal of Accounting Literature* publishes reviews in its field, although there is currently no directly comparable journal specialised in finance.

A quick word of warning, though – just because a journal has the word 'review' in the title does not necessarily imply that it specialises in, or even accepts, review articles. For instance, the 'Review' in the titles of the *American Economic Review* and the *Financial Review* are misnomers in that they are both generalist journals rather than publishing literature reviews. Survey papers are found alongside regular articles in (most) other journals, so you have to search for them. Editors increasingly like review papers because they tend to become more widely cited than new investigative work and therefore increase the impact factor and hence the stature of the journal.

If you are fortunate enough to find a survey paper on your dissertation topic, it might be tempting simply to copy (or paraphrase from) it, but there are several reasons why this would be highly inadvisable:

- Your topic may not map precisely onto the review, in which case the latter will not provide a complete treatment of all of the sources you need to examine
- Unless it was written within the past year or so, it is likely to miss out on the latest research, and your literature summary may appear dated if you do not incorporate the latest thinking on the topic
- It might be that you want to cover a slightly different topic and have a more or less comprehensive perspective than the review. For instance, the review may focus only on arguments in favour of something and ignoring viewpoints against it while you wish to provide a more balanced discussion
- The review might plausibly be 10,000 words long, whereas you perhaps have only that number for your entire dissertation, and therefore you will have to be much briefer

6.3.6   PhD Theses

Although undergraduate and master's dissertations are seldom made publicly available, PhD theses often are nowadays. Ethos, part of the British Library website,[2] has electronic access to more than half a million PhDs produced by students at UK universities.

You need to register to access the full text of the theses directly from Ethos, although there is frequently an option to download it without registering from the university repository where the PhD student studied. This repository is an incredible resource with a vast amount of free and almost instantly accessible information. For example, I typed *tax + accounting* and obtained 252 hits; *asset pricing* yielded 808 hits; even *fintech* returned three theses.

PhDs will be considerably longer than the dissertation on a taught programme, with higher expectations regarding the study's depth and originality. However, they are usually also more penetrable than journal articles, providing detailed literature reviews and a thorough discussion of any empirical procedures and data handling details. Doctoral theses are typically 60,000–90,000 words long and do not struggle with the word limits applied to journal articles. Hence it is worth logging onto the Ethos site and using the keyword search facility to see whether there are any theses available covering your topic.

Only final versions of 'accepted' theses will be posted on the website, and so whilst this does not guarantee that the work will be free of inconsistencies or even

---

[2]https://ethos.bl.uk/Home.do

errors, it will have, at least, been subject to an examinations process and reached the standard required to award a PhD degree at that university where the candidate studied.

6.3.7   Blogsites, websites and newspaper or magazine articles

While blogs or unsubstantiated opinion pieces do not fit well in a scholarly literature review, they may nonetheless provide useful ideas for writing the introduction to the research project. In the introductory chapter, writers would usually step back from the specifics of the academic research to motivate the ideas and models discussed by explaining them in general terms or showing that they are relevant in a broader context.

It is straightforward to obtain information from the internet, including on blogsites, personal webpages and elsewhere, but how can you be assured that a particular piece you are reading is of sufficient quality that you can rely on the information it contains? Experienced scholars will be able to identify quickly whether a piece of work looks solid but evaluating the worth of an article or book is much more challenging for novice researchers.

Blogsites and magazine-type articles will not be 'refereed', so the validity of the claims made usually cannot be verified, and the pieces are typically short, lacking in depth or findings backed by data with analysis. Just when the author of such an article starts to get into the core of the arguments, the study is finished. A discussion of some of the issues that this raises is given in the next section.

6.3.8   Working papers

Should you read and cite all relevant work or impose a limit to only studies that have been published? In my view, it is essential to seek out not only published work but also working papers, which represent the latest research that has more recently been completed. The scholarly publication process is slow, and it might typically be a year and possibly even two or more years from when an author completes the first draft of a new piece of work until the point where it is published. Usually, on-line versions of work accepted for publication become available well before the print versions come out. Sometimes working papers are, alongside other unpublished reports by companies or government bodies, conference proceedings, etc., known as the 'grey literature'.

However, the danger of examining unpublished work, such as a working paper, is that it has not been subject to any peer-review. For unpublished papers, you have to make a leap of faith that the researchers who conducted the study and wrote it up have been competent and honest in all aspects. An experienced scholar ought to be able to read a piece of unpublished research and evaluate its quality, but being able to make such a judgement requires a skill that can only be learned with experience (and ideally some training). The best approach is always to be sceptical, and if in doubt, be tentative in the way that you write about a specific author's claims, particularly if the study has not been peer-reviewed.

6.3.9   Determining the scope of your literature search

When determining what to read, you need to think about the scope of your search – both geographically in terms of which countries and markets you will cover, but also over what time period. A common presumption is that older work has been subsumed in what is written more recently so that there is less requirement to read the former, although you should nonetheless cite the classic studies in the area that formed the foundations of subsequent thinking on the topic.

On the other hand, try to ensure that you examine the most current sources, not just focusing on the classical references on a particular topic. As a rough measure, skim through your reference list as it develops, and if it is contemporary enough, it ought to contain a sufficient sprinkling of work published in the last few years, particularly if you are working in an active research area. If you are unable to locate much work over this time period despite having conducted an extensive search, it might be an indication that the topic is not currently fashionable in the academy. That is not necessarily a problem or a reason to choose something else to study, and it means that you are less likely to discover part-way through that someone has already done what you wanted to do. But it does mean that you might find less interest in your work than would have been the case if you had chosen something more contemporary.

In terms of the sequence in which to read a large volume of papers, when I start working in a new area, I sometimes find it useful to order the research studies I have gathered chronologically and begin by reading the oldest. This ordering can be helpful because each new study on a particular theme usually builds on previous research, skimming only very briefly over this, and assuming that the reader is familiar with much of it. If you read papers out of chronological order, it can be confusing when the authors have assumed that you are familiar with prior studies. Reading papers in date order allows you to chart the development of the literature over time to see how (or if) it has progressed and whether the trends in the focus of research have changed.

6.4   How to focus if there is too much to read

Suppose that you're working on a topic where there is already a large body of research. In that case, you will need to be selective in what you read and what you write about as there will be simply too much existing literature for you to be able to cover all of it in the available time and words. For example, if your topic is empirical tests of the capital asset pricing model (CAPM), economic value added versus cash value added (EVA versus CVA), or fair value accounting, there will be thousands of potentially relevant studies. In this situation, how do you decide what to read and what to include in your review? I would suggest focusing on three sets of studies:

1. The 'seminal' papers in the area – these will be the few core studies that everyone else cites in their work and are likely to represent the major breakthroughs in the subject area.
2. The most relevant work in the area, narrowly defined. So, more precisely, your topic might be 'Testing the four-moment CAPM in emerging markets.' Then you would probably want to look at as many studies as you can get hold of on higher-moment models and tests of the CAPM while ignoring any work broader types of tests of other variants of the CAPM. If that still yields an unmanageable volume of existing literature, then the search could be further narrowed, for example, to 'higher-moment CAPM models and tests applied in the context of emerging markets,' and so on.
3. The latest research on the topic so that your review is fully up to date.

In this sort of situation, the most important aspect is that you have covered the topic's key elements, not that you have covered every paper.

When you are swamped with potentially relevant material, there are some types of studies that might be best avoided. Given that your time is highly limited, don't waste it reading:

- Work that is of low quality – poorly written, unreliable findings, insufficient or inadequate data, weak methodology, etc. If a paper is highly relevant and contains exciting or new ideas but has some flaws in the execution, then cite it and point out the problems – this is all part and parcel of drafting a critical literature review
- Work that merely replicates the findings of existing studies or applies them identically to a new data set (unless your work involves using precisely that data set)
- Purely mathematical work (unless your topic involves developing a mathematical model)

As well as knowing where to seek out the relevant literature, another essential aspect is being aware of when to stop looking. There will come the point when you have uncovered (almost) all of the most pertinent studies – the ones that everyone else is citing and some more specialist pieces on precisely your topic. As discussed above, it is also crucial to examine the working paper repositories to become aware of the most recent additions to the literature, but once you have done that, it is time to stop looking and start consolidating what you have found. If you continue to search in ever more opaque locations that are hard to reach (for example, seeking papers written in other languages), they will almost certainly be much less relevant and not worth your time to find or examine. Incorporating obscure studies will also make your review document longer and less focused than it needs to be, with fewer words left for your investigative work.

6.5 Where to find the literature

Once you are aware of the various outlets, as presented in the previous section, where research – both published and unpublished – can be found, the next stage is to begin the process of searching for the material. Some authors suggest that a literature review search should be 'systematic', and in some fields such as health studies, this seems to be an absolute requirement for an acceptable dissertation. But my view is that there is no such thing, for it could only be systematic if you knew exactly what you were looking for, in which order, and where you were going to find it. Your search can be extensive and perhaps even almost exhaustive so that you have searched as hard for relevant existing work as could reasonably be expected of a student, and in virtually all cases that will be sufficient.

Fortunately, there are several key (virtual) locations to identify and obtain the material you need to read for your review, making the process of searching comprehensively relatively straightforward. Although in the past I spent many productive (and enjoyable!) hours in university libraries 'browsing the stacks', nowadays it is improbable that you will have to set foot in the building when gathering the literature for your project unless you are doing work that requires specific historical documents or old books that are not available electronically. Everything you need will almost certainly be available through the internet.

If you are totally unsure where to start looking for relevant literature, even after following the suggestions below, your university library is bound to run courses – either on-line or in-person – that will start right from the beginning and will explain in detail all of the resources that are available to you.

Gathering the reading material required for your review is a two-stage process. The first step involves getting together a list of bibliometric data pertaining to the items you require. This means you need to identify the author(s), article or book title, date, and journal information (the title, volume number, issue number and page number) if the piece is a journal article or publisher and place of publication if it is a book. The second step comprises using the data you obtained at the first step to find and download the article or book.

For the first stage, you will probably use a search engine, a database, or the reference list from your course material or articles you are already aware of. I will now discuss each of these sources.

6.5.1 Using search engines

These are the obvious places to start when gathering the information to do a literature review. Hence, the initial phase to collecting the research articles will be to think about and note down a set of keywords that encapsulate the essence of the mass of work you are interested in tapping into. Examining the first few search results will probably suggest further, or more refined, keywords.

Usually, a search engine linked with a database of journals or working papers will only look for matches in the title, abstract and author-selected keywords, and

Figure 6.1: Screenshot from Google Scholar

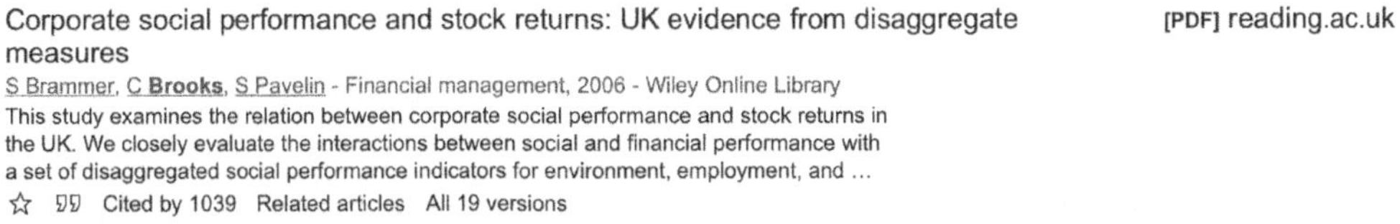

Corporate social performance and stock returns: UK evidence from disaggregate   [PDF] reading.ac.uk
measures
S Brammer, C **Brooks**, S Pavelin - Financial management, 2006 - Wiley Online Library
This study examines the relation between corporate social performance and stock returns in
the UK. We closely evaluate the interactions between social and financial performance with
a set of disaggregated social performance indicators for environment, employment, and ...
☆ 〝〞 Cited by 1039   Related articles   All 19 versions

not the main body of the article. This limitation is unfortunate since it might be that a particular methodological detail you are interested in is only discussed in that section of the paper and not in the abstract. Other search engines such as Google that look inside pdf files will examine the entire document, not differentiating between sections, which might be more useful in that sense.

If the search terms you enter into the engine are too vague, you will obtain too many hits, making it a tiresome job to trawl through them all, a lot of which will be irrelevant. On the other hand, if your terms are too specific, you will get few hits, and there is a danger that you will miss some useful material.

In order to ensure that your searches include the most relevant material possible (and exclude irrelevant hits), use 'and', which in this context is known as a Boolean (logic) operator, with your search terms in quotation marks. For example, typing 'four-moment capm emerging markets' will lead to over 500,000 hits on Google, although the most relevant matches appearing at the top are right on topic. By default, engines will list results containing any of the search terms (in essence, implicitly using 'or' between the search words). However, it will probably list the web pages containing the highest number of matching words, which will be the most useful hits, at the top. On the other hand, a search by typing four-moment 'capm' and 'emerging markets' yields a little over 800 hits, all of which look highly relevant. Note that, in general, search engines are not case sensitive, so there is no need to use any capitals.

6.5.2 Google Scholar

It is also worth using Google Scholar[3] rather than Google since the former is focused purely on scholarly output and will yield a list of relevant material focused predominantly on academic articles rather than newspapers or blogsites. For example, Figure 6.1 shows one such output from Google Scholar, which provides information on the title, authors, journal or other publication outlet, abstract, and how many times it has been cited. It also shows, on the right-hand side, a clickable link to a place where the paper can be downloaded. In this case, the paper is one that I co-authored, which appeared in the journal *Financial Management*. A pre-publication version of the paper is available free of charge without registration from the University of Reading repository.

If you are specifically interested in books rather than working papers or journal

_____
[3] https://scholar.google.com

Figure 6.2: Citation downloads from Google Scholar

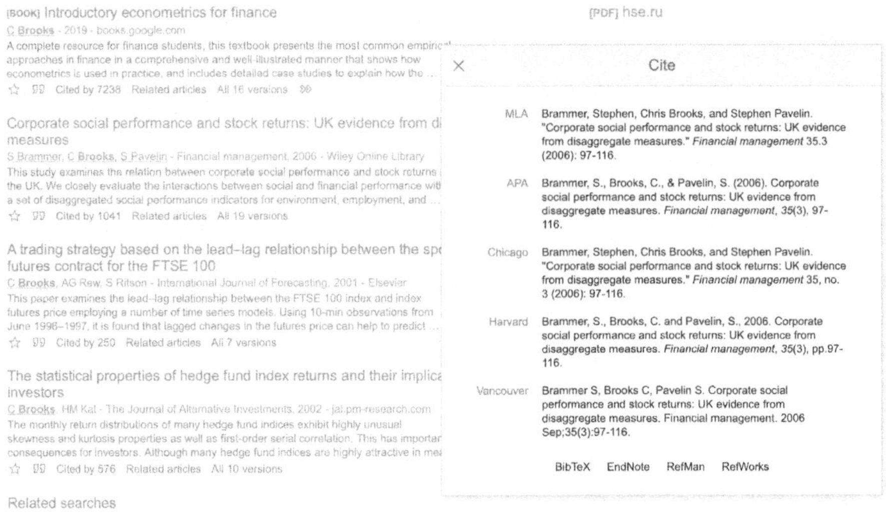

articles, then search using Google Books. Another benefit of using Google Scholar is that it is possible to download a citation by clicking on the quotation mark. When you do, the screen will appear as in Figure 6.2. It is also possible to download this information in several different formats to be dropped straight into reference management software such as EndNote, ProCite or BibTeX. This consistency not only saves time but will also ensure a standard of consistency and accuracy that would be hard to achieve when typing the references manually.

6.5.3   Your university library catalogue

An essential source of material will be your university library's electronic catalogue. Several searchable databases can probably be accessed from the library's webpages. The web links below provide general information about the databases but obtaining articles can only go through your institution:

- Ingenta (formerly BIDS) is a repository for journal articles[4]
- Web of Science (which was formerly known as the Web of Knowledge) provides access to large numbers of journals, particularly in the natural and physical sciences[5]
- JStor is an on-line repository for over 2,000 journals and 90,000 e-books and other media[6]
- Ebsco (Business Source Ultimate) is a repository containing the full text of over 2,500 journals spanning much of business and management, including

---

[4]https://www.ingentaconnect.com
[5]https://www.webofknowledge.com
[6]https://www.jstor.com

accounting, economics and finance[7]
- Sciences Direct is the publisher Elsevier's portal and repository for its extensive collection of journals across the sciences, arts and humanities, and social sciences[8]
- ProQuest Central is a database and archive containing large numbers of journals, books, theses, and newspapers[9]

Most universities subscribe to bundles of journals from all of the leading scholarly publishers (Cambridge University Press, Elsevier, Oxford University Press, Palgrave, Wiley, etc.), and so you should have access to a broad range of titles. But in general, the library catalogue can only be used to search for journal and book titles and not for individual articles within each title. So you need to know precisely which items (and the names and volume/issue/page numbers or books you need) before you start.

How to find a known journal article using a university library catalogue

Each library will have a slightly different system, but the approach in each case will be broadly the same:

1. Go to your university's main website, and from there, find the library pages (possibly via the student portal)
2. Find the link to 'e-resources' or 'e-journals'
3. Type the title of the journal or book (or part of it) in the search bar and hit enter. For example, I typed 'British Accounting Review' and got the output in Figure 6.3
4. Click on the link to the date range that the paper you want to download falls within. You will probably now be asked to enter your university IT system login details. You might have to go through 'OpenAthens', a system for managing journal access used by most universities. Even if this is the case, you would still use your usual university login username and password, which will automatically link with your university's server to verify the details
5. Find the journal volume and issue number in which the paper is located, then click on and download a pdf of the article

As the screenshot shows, all articles going right back to 1988 are available to University of Reading researchers for this journal. All of the major publishers have similar bundle deals with universities to make their content available electronically, so if the article you need is published in a reputable journal, it will probably be available through your university's library catalogue. When you click through to a journal article, you will usually be given access options, and it is often possible to enter your university's name, followed by your IT Services username and password. If your institution subscribes to the journal, access will be free and should lead you straight through to a pdf of the article. Not only that, but the e-journal finder will

[7] https://www.ebsco.com/products/research-databases/business-source-ultimate
[8] https://www.sciencedirect.com/browse/journals-and-books?subject=business-management-and-accounting
[9] https://www.proquest.com

Figure 6.3: Screenshot from ejournal search

Showing results 1 to 1 of 1
for the search: Title begins with "British Accounting Review"

Note Alternative titles may have matched your search terms. Remove alternate titles

Limit by: Peer Reviewed | Open Access

The British accounting review   Terms of Use
Alternate Title: *British accounting review*
ISSN: 0890-8389
Look up Article
Peer Reviewed

1988 to 1994 in Elsevier Business, Management and Accounting Archive inc. supplement For off-campus access, select "Sign In" in
          the top right of the screen, then click the 'sign in via your institution' option. Search for the University of Reading. Click
          'Sign in via your Institution' again and then log in as normal.
01.03.1995 to Present in Elsevier:Jisc Collections:ScienceDirect Freedom Collection:2017-2021 For off-campus access, select "Sign
          In" in the top right of the screen, then select "Other Institution" and search for University of Reading. Click
          this and then log in as normal.
1996 to 1999 in IngentaConnect

allow you to click straight through to access it.

Other places to find specific journal articles

But what if the article you need is located in a journal that is not part of a bundle (e.g., a journal published by a learned society that your university does not subscribe to)? If the material is peripheral to your core research topic or you were investigating it primarily out of curiosity, you might elect to ignore that piece and concentrate on more easily accessible sources. However, if it was an essential reference, there are several other places you could look for the paper:

1. See whether the work is available through Google Scholar, as discussed above.
2. Most universities have repositories where they store all of their staff members' published articles. These are made available free of charge to everyone without registration once a publisher-determined embargo period after initial publication (usually 1–3 years) has passed. Try to find the authors' university repositories and see if the work is in there
3. Many authors (including me) put all of their work on the Social Sciences Research Network (SSRN) when it is completed in working paper form prior to publication and then leave it there indefinitely where it can be downloaded freely and without registration[10]
4. Similar to 3, many authors use Research Gate as a repository for their work,

---

[10]https://www.ssrn.com/index.cfm/en/

although you may have to register to access the papers stored there[11]

5. If all else fails, you could e-mail one of the authors directly for a particular paper, tell them how interested you are to read their work, and politely request that they send you an electronic copy of the document. In almost all cases, they will oblige

If an essential reference is a book rather than a journal, it is often trickier to obtain it electronically. It is still worth going through your university library catalogue to see if you can get an e-book copy as they often have versions that they can loan out electronically. As for journals, some publishers now have bundle deals allowing unlimited access to a wide range of books from their collections. Be aware, though, that unlike journal articles that can be downloaded as pdf files and printed, e-books usually have tight digital rights management (DRM) protection, which means that they cannot be printed, and it might not even be possible to download them, so they have to be read directly on-line.

Google Books, Amazon Kindle Books and Apple iBooks also have a comprehensive coverage of recent books. Although most of them must be purchased or rented for a fee, the electronic versions tend to be significantly cheaper than their print equivalents.

6.5.4 Working papers and literature on the internet

Unfortunately, the lag between a paper being written and published in a journal is often two years (and increasing fast), so that research in even the most recent issues of the printed journals will be somewhat dated. Additionally, many securities firms, accountants and central banks worldwide produce high-quality research output in report form, which they often do not bother to try to publish in journals. Much of this is now available on the internet, so it is worth conducting searches with keywords using readily available web search engines. A few suggestions for places to start are given below.

Searchable sources for unpublished articles and working papers

Besides general search engines, including Google Scholar, there are other, more specialist databases that can be used for keyword searches. These include:

- SSRN is an incredibly vast repository of close to a million working papers across a range of relevant fields in the social sciences, including accounting, economics, and finance. It is keyword searchable, and the documents can be downloaded freely and without registration[12]
- ResearchGate is, like SSRN, a large, searchable repository of working papers but not limited to the social sciences[13]

---

[11] https://www.researchgate.net

[12] https://www.ssrn.com/index.cfm/en/

[13] https://www.researchgate.net

- IDEAS is a vast database and repository of articles and working papers in economics[14]
- The National Bureau of Economic Research (NBER) holds a vast database of discussion papers and links including data sources[15]

Universities

Almost all universities around the world now make copies of their discussion papers available electronically. Two examples from leading accounting and finance departments, although of course there are many more, are:
- Department of Finance, Stern School, New York University[16]
- Wharton Financial Institutions Center, University of Pennsylvania[17]

Central banks

The US Federal Reserve Banks and the Bank of England also have sets of working papers and other resources:
- Bank of England containing their working papers, news and discussion[18]
- Federal Reserve Bank of Atlanta including information on economic and research data and publications[19]
- Federal Reserve Board of Governors International Finance Discussion Papers[20]
- Federal Reserve Bank of New York discussion papers[21]

International bodies

- International Accounting Standards Board (IASB) discussion papers[22]
- International Monetary Fund (IMF) World Economic Outlook Report, Global Financial Stability Report, Fiscal Monitor Report and their discussion papers[23]
- World Bank working papers in finance[24]
- Organisation for Economic Cooperation and Development (OECD) working papers[25]

Professional associations and learned societies in accounting and finance

Professional associations represent the industry and its participants and employees, while learned societies represent academic staff. Professional associations are usually

[14]https://ideas.repec.org
[15]https://www.nber.org
[16]https://www.stern.nyu.edu/experience-stern/about/departments-centers-initiatives/academic-departments/finance/research/working-papers
[17]https://fic.wharton.upenn.edu/working-papers/
[18]https://www.bankofengland.co.uk/research
[19]https://www.frbatlanta.org
[20]https://www.federalreserve.gov/econres.htm
[21]https://www.newyorkfed.org/research
[22]https://www.iasplus.com/en/resources/ifrsf/due-process/iasb-discussion-papers
[23]https://www.imf.org/en/Research
[24]https://www.worldbank.org/en/research
[25]https://www.oecd-ilibrary.org

responsible for setting professional standards in that sector, and they provide training, education and examinations that lead to industry qualifications. The education aspect means that they can often be a valuable source of materials for dissertation research. Professional Association websites sometimes host blogs or opinion pieces regarding new field issues, which can help generate ideas and drive awareness of the current problems of particular interest in the industry. The relevant bodies, which can easily be searched, are:

Professional Associations
- Association of Chartered Certified Accountants (ACCA)
- Chartered Institute of Management Accountants (CIMA)
- UK Finance (including what was formerly the British Bankers Association)
- Chartered Institute of Public Finance and Accountancy
- Chartered Institute of Taxation
- Institute of Chartered Accountants in England and Wales (ICAEW)
- Institute of Chartered Accountants in Scotland (ICAS)

Learned societies
- American Accounting Association (AAA)
- American Finance Association (AFA)
- British Accounting and Finance Association (BAFA)
- European Accounting Association (EAA)
- European Finance Association (EFA)

The learned societies are usually responsible for publishing one or more of the leading field journals. For example, BAFA is responsible for the *British Accounting Review,* published by Elsevier.

6.6   How to read an academic paper

Knowing how to read a research article is another skill that takes some time and practice to develop. In particular, you need to know:
- What to look for in the work
- How to determine where the paper fits into the broader literature and how it is related to previous studies
- How to summarise the key points in a few lines
- How to identify any weaknesses or omissions (as well as the strengths of the piece), and, more generally, how to evaluate the study critically

Clearly, when you decide to read a particular piece, you will start with the presumption that the work has some relevance for your project. Sometimes, upon reading the abstract, doubts might already begin to creep in that perhaps the paper is not so useful after all. That being the case, it is still worth very briefly skimming the rest of the article to check that, indeed, the apparently irrelevant contents of the summary did not hide a gem. Try to look for keywords or phrases that link with your topic.

When the work is not relevant, discard it; if it is only peripherally relevant, it is worth just making some brief notes, and you could always return to it subsequently if necessary. If, upon a quick skim, it is evident that the paper is related to your project, you would continue to read it in depth.

If you are very short of time, you might need to focus your reading, and in such eventualities, you might consider examining only the abstract, introduction and conclusions in cases where the work has some relevance, but you would not consider it a primary reference for what you are doing. In some ways, these are the most important sections – the introduction will explain the motivation for the work and will probably provide a more detailed summary than the abstract, while the conclusions will again discuss what was found and how it fits into the wider literature. For some studies, you will need to review the core methodology employed carefully and the results obtained, especially if the conceptual approach is similar to the one that you will use.

Particularly when you first begin the detailed reading for your review, there will surely be large numbers of specialist or technical words and acronyms that are unfamiliar, and this will impede your understanding. But if you persevere, using search engines or an on-line glossary to establish their meaning where necessary, it will become much more straightforward with experience, and you will be able to go through each paper faster and increasingly effectively. When you come across unfamiliar technical terms, there are several useful, specialist on-line glossaries available that can be used to find the meaning of specialist words, including:

In accounting
- The Accounting Dictionary at My Accounting Course[26]
- The Accounting Tools Dictionary of Accounting Topics (which has very detailed information)[27]
- The Accounting Coach Dictionary of Accounting Terms[28]

In finance
- The Dictionary by Farlex[29]
- Investopedia[30]

Making and organising notes

Make notes on each paper as you go along – try to record the gist of the information in the study. It is common for students to gather an extensive collection of research

---

[26]https://www.myaccountingcourse.com/accounting-dictionary

[27]https://www.accountingtools.com/dictionary

[28]https://www.accountingcoach.com/terms

[29]https://financial-dictionary.thefreedictionary.com

[30]https://www.investopedia.com/financial-term-dictionary-4769738

articles – either photocopies or pdf files – and then to feel somehow that a significant part of their work is done. But just having possession of an article does not mean that you have absorbed the contents, let alone understood them. Only by reading the articles and, crucially, making notes, will you be able to say that you have reviewed the literature. Unfortunately, reading the papers and then organising your notes and ideas into the review chapter are the time-consuming steps. Identifying and gathering the material is usually the relatively quick and easy part.

Going through the pile of papers and making brief notes on each one is not in itself sufficient: you need to have some understanding of the work and be able to remember and articulate the key points from each study. Later, you will also need to be able to classify and compare them, drawing out the similarities and differences, but this is discussed in the next chapter. Be careful to use your own words from the outset and make it clear in your notes if you are quoting directly, which will avoid inadvertent plagiarism. Although some people prefer to make hand-written notes and only type things up at the end, it will save a lot of time if you keep everything electronically from the outset.

While different research articles will vary substantially in their length, structure and writing style, several key aspects will be common that you should be able to identify and make a mental note of:

- The research questions
- The key investigative methods used
- The nature of the data – sources, coverage, timespan, etc.
- The main findings
- Is there anything particularly new, inspiring or different about this study compared with others on this theme?

Sometimes you will need to read a particular passage or whole section several times before it begins to make sense. Don't be concerned as this is entirely normal. It might be that you are new to this subject, and so you have less background knowledge about it than the author had assumed. It is also true that some authors are better communicators than others, and your lack of understanding might be a result of a poorly drafted article and a confusing writing style.

Also, try to identify which aspect of the writing you don't understand – is it the language, because the proportion of unfamiliar words is too great, so the meaning is obscured? Or do you know the terms but not how they are being used so that you cannot see what the author is trying to say? In that case, perhaps it is the methods or models that are not clear, or maybe you understand how the author is using the techniques, but you cannot see why or to what end?

If the terminology is the source of confusion, a dictionary (or a glossary of technical terms) might be useful. Or you could try a different piece on the same topic by another writer who uses a more accessible language; in the latter situation described in the previous paragraph where you cannot grasp why the steps in the paper are being taken, move back down the chain to an article published earlier or a textbook treatment where (perhaps) more will be explained. Once you have strengthened your background knowledge on that precise subject, you can return to the research literature and see if you then understand it better.

When reading an article, it is possible to make notes concurrently, but it is usually better to read a whole piece of text first, then to summarise it from memory, which will give you a better overview, enabling you to better extract the essence of the work rather than just paraphrasing directly from what is written. But equally, don't leave it too long after reading a piece before you write a summary of it; otherwise, there is a danger that the details will become fuzzy and you would have to reread it. Or worse, several studies might merge in your mind and you mix up the elements from one paper with another, leading to an inaccurate review and a mis-attribution of ideas.

Make it clear in your notes which parts you have paraphrased into your own words and which you are quoting directly. Making careful notes in this way is essential for several reasons. First, it will help you remember the most important aspects of the work to ensure that you don't waste time rereading it. Second, it should help to avoid errors later where you inadvertently plagiarise from a source because you thought you had written it into your own words as you were going along, but you had not. If you identify particular sentences that you might want to quote directly in your project, copy them down accurately with full bibliometric details. Also, remember to update your reference list at this stage, including all of the details of the source – this will make it much easier at the end than trying to create the list from scratch.

A particular difficulty when you initially begin the reading is that you will be unsure of which parts of each paper are the most relevant to make notes on. Sometimes it will just be the core findings or interpretation that is relevant to you, but for other studies it might be the detailed data and methods that are of interest. Ideally, you would read several studies first, get a feel for the subject area as a whole, and then go back to the first studies you read and re-examine them.

Remember that since you will be working on the project for some weeks or months, your notes will need to be clear and detailed. The summaries still need to make sense to you later when, for example, you come to write your conclusions, and you had forgotten the details of the papers you had read when you were drafting your literature review.

You should retain all of your notes, whether they are in electronic or paper form, until after you submit the project document as you might need to refer to them later or require them as evidence that you had done this groundwork in case you are accused of any malpractice (see chapter 4).

As well as just making notes, you will need to decide at an early stage about how you will organise them. Without doing so, you will have two enormous tasks: one identifying the relevant literature and reading it, and the other to make sense of your mass of summaries and try to work out how to get them into any kind of continuous narrative. The better quality, more accurate and organised are the notes you make as you are reading now, the quicker you will be able to pull the literature review document together later.

It is worth pointing out that different people remember and interpret information in varying ways, and this will determine the best way for them to develop their notes. I prefer a linear summary written in words in a single colour since, in my case, it is the words and phrases that stick out rather than the way that they look on the page. But many people find that it helps them visualise the threads between the studies better and extract the key messages by using different colours, spider diagrams, or concept maps. You could also arrange the summaries chronologically if you are working on a topic where the literature developed steadily over time.

Keeping all your notes electronically will make them much easier to work with, move around, and incorporate directly than if you write them on paper. It will also make them much easier to back up. If you haven't already, experiment with different approaches to note-taking and organisation until you find a style that works well for you.

Be a sceptical reader and a persuasive writer

Always be on the lookout for a 'sales job' and in such cases be sceptical of the veracity of the arguments being made. You need to be able to distinguish between three things:

1. Widely accepted fact
2. Supported perspective based on evidence
3. Unsubstantiated opinion

The first type will be entirely objective and the last entirely subjective, while the middle one may contain elements of both objectivity and subjectivity (for instance, if the evidence is weak or the researcher applies their own interpretation to ambiguous results). It is fine to quote and discuss all three writing types in your dissertation, but you need to make it clear to your readers which category a particular piece falls within.

Also, employ a degree of scepticism when looking at the statistical output in a study: don't assume that because there is quantitative work, it is necessarily correct. The author may have made errors in conducting the analysis, and even if the work has been carried out competently, they might have deliberately misrepresented the findings to emphasise the stronger aspects and hide any anomalous results. In general, the more sophisticated the techniques used, the harder it is for readers to understand and challenge the results, but the more likely it is that something will have gone wrong.

In a large number of situations, the writing style used has to be persuasive. Although you are not selling a product, you are nonetheless trying to sell your ideas – why your topic is interesting, why the methods you chose are the most appropriate, why your data are relevant, why your results are robust, and why your findings might be useful to a wider audience. To persuade people that your arguments are valid, you need to make them in a logical structure and using language that is precise and will resonate with your audience. You need to use evidence, either from your own empirical work or by citing a paper from the existing literature, for every point you make that would not be considered 'common knowledge'.

Equally, you should be aware that other authors will be using their writing intending to persuade their readers (including you) that their methods, data and analysis are not only correct but better in some senses than those employed in previous studies. The use of persuasive language makes critical thinking and always being on the lookout for flaws in empirical design and implementation all the more important. Each time you read a study, there are several questions that it helps to hold in the back of your mind:

- Does the paper present new findings or new insights that make it worth reading and citing? Or is it merely recycling old ideas?
- Does the work have implications for end users, such as practitioners or regulators? Or does it contribute to scholars' understanding of a particular problem or phenomenon?
- What information has the writer omitted from their argument or description of what they did?
- On which aspects of the results in the tables or figures did the writer not comment?
- Is the sample used sufficiently large and representative to justify the writer's conclusions?
- Were there other methods or models that could have been more appropriate to achieve the writer's empirical aims? For example, did the author select a quantitative study when a series of interviews would have addressed the research questions more effectively?
- Is the dataset employed appropriate and of a sufficient size? How was it chosen: because of its relevance or for convenience (possibly resulting in a so-called easy data bias
- Has all of the relevant work that was available at the time of writing been cited? Or is the literature review in the paper deficient?
- Is there a disconnect between the theory presented and the empirical implementation of it?
- Is there a lack of theory leading to the potential for spurious findings?
- Are the author's analyses and the findings stated the only plausible interpretations, or are there other, equally valid inferences?
- Are all of the conclusions justified by the evidence that the author (or previous authors) has (had) presented, or are some speculative?

It is vital that you read and include in the review studies that take a different position in their arguments to yours; if nothing else, it demonstrates that you are aware of such studies and citing them will enable you to demolish their lines of reasoning. For example, if you are arguing that 'the CAPM beta is dead', you should also refer to other studies suggesting that it is still valid and useful.

6.7 Reading rapidly

Learning how to read effectively but rapidly is a useful skill to master. You need to be willing to put in many hours of reading to become knowledgeable enough about the subject to produce a solid literature review. But if you learn to be selective and identify what is likely to be worth delving deeper into, and you can develop the skill to go through the papers quickly, you can save a lot of time.

For instance, speed readers can group blocks of several words together rather than reading each word individually, meaning that their eyes can scan over the page far more quickly. Another aspect of reading quickly is scanning for relevant keywords, which means that the sentences involving them are reviewed more thoroughly, and sentences omitting them can be skipped over. You might also be able to recognise groups of words that tend to go together so that you know how a sentence will finish without reading it closely, in the same way as autocomplete functions in e-mail and text message software. Of course, there are dangers with this approach if you go into autopilot and sacrifice understanding for rapidity. Reading a paragraph twice quickly might take longer than if you had gone through it more slowly and thoroughly in the first instance, but if you can effectively scan over documents, you could save a significant amount of time.

Reading quickly can also be supported by good eyesight, good lighting, clear printing or a good screen, an appropriate font size, a lack of distractions, and not being drowsy. Therefore, to make the quickest possible progress with your literature mountain climb:

- Use reading glasses if you need them, and have an eye test if you think your short distance vision is less than perfect
- Invest in a desk lamp and position yourself near a window where possible
- Ensure that the printer has enough ink and that the font size is sufficiently large; don't be tempted to save paper to the extent that the output is hard to read. Some of my colleagues shrink two A4 pages to fit onto one, which I find almost impossible to examine
- Minimise or remove distractions (see chapter 1)
- Get a good night's sleep before working, and plan your reading to take place at times when you are at your most alert
- Never read for more than an hour without taking a break, otherwise your concentration level will slip, and your mind will drift even if you don't initially realise it

Skimming has the same objective as speed reading, but in the latter case, you would aim to read every word in an article, just faster than usual, getting through the material much quicker but still obtaining a good understanding of the material.

Scan reading for a literature review is hard because you don't know precisely what you are looking for, you only have a general idea. Using a handful of keywords and entirely excluding everything else would likely lead to missing many relevant, perhaps even vital, pieces of information. Skimming successfully is a skill that takes time to cultivate but one that is nonetheless worth acquiring. There are some interesting resources on how to speed read that might be fun to follow up and try:

- An extended article on the BBC website that is a useful place to start[31]
- Several articles with links to other pieces on Speedreadingtechniques.org[32]
- The SpeedReadGuide channel on YouTube[33]

As with learning to touch-type, becoming an effective speed reader would be worthwhile, but it will take a lot of time and practice to develop. Initially, while learning to touch-type, it would take longer to key in a block of text than doing it the more conventional way. I never invested the time to learn to touch-type and still do so with two fingers, which causes enormous amusement to people who see it. Similarly, you might decide that you do not have the time to invest in learning to speed read, but if you do, it will be a skill that you would be able to draw on throughout life.

6.7.1 What you should read in detail and what to skim

Do not merely rely on article or book titles to decide what to read in detail, what to skim read, and what to ignore. Titles can be extremely misleading as authors often select idioms or well-known catchphrases to grab attention; titles also contain so few words that it is hard to cover all aspects of the study.

There are broadly two approaches to skim reading: covering virtually the entire article or reading only some individual sections but more thoroughly. Either way, the abstract is, of course, the place to start and should provide a strong indication of whether the paper is likely to be worth reading further or not. But, like the title, the number of words in the abstract is strictly constrained and consequently, unless the author is exceptionally skilled in maximising the amount of information provided in a tiny space, there will be numerous details that will not come across from reading the abstract alone.

If you choose to skim read the whole piece, you will scan through, paragraph-by-paragraph, looking for keywords or specific phrases relevant to your topic, skipping over the rest of the text. At the same time, you would be aiming to get the essence of what is being written so that, if you were asked to, you could provide someone with a brief summary of the main point of the article.

A further suggestion is to link the speed and detail of your reading with the material you are covering. Background and peripheral material can be gone through reasonably quickly, while articles that are core to your objectives or where you are trying to understand the methods so that you can replicate them need a thorough examination.

---

[31] https://www.bbc.com/future/article/20191129-how-to-learn-to-speed-read
[32] https://www.speedreadingtechniques.org/how-to-speed-read
[33] https://www.youtube.com/user/SpeedReadGuide

Skimming books

If some of the material you are reviewing constitutes entire books (as opposed to book chapters, where the same approach as for journal articles can be adopted), you will need to focus your reading on small parts of them, at least initially, as it will be infeasible to read several books in detail in the time available. You can start by using the book's synopsis in place of an article's abstract and the table of contents to identify the most relevant parts.

Skim reading books can be quite challenging, not just because of their sheer length but also because they are usually written so that each chapter builds upon previous chapters, with the author taking for granted that the reader will subsequently recall any definitions and notation already introduced. Hence the chapters are not self-contained, and it might be that if you find chapter Z to be particularly relevant, you need to go back to chapters Z-1, Z-2, etc., to be able to understand it fully.

Books have the additional benefit of an index, which can be used to perform a keyword search. However, frequently, index entries relate to pages in the book where that word gets a mere brief mention with no useful detail and hence an index is usually much less helpful than a table of contents for guiding skim reading.

Ensure that a book is really going to be useful before ordering it from the library or buying it. I have wasted a considerable amount of time and money over the years on books that their blurb appeared to suggest would be just what I needed but caused significant disappointment when they arrived.

To be useful, books need to be pitched at the right level, given your knowledge and understanding at the time you read them, and they need to contain an appropriate amount of detail. Books that are too easy, telling you again what you already knew, or too hard so that you understand nothing, are of little use to you. On balance, it is usually preferable to go for books that challenge you, though, since your level of knowledge will multiply as you read more and get deeper into the investigative work.

6.8 Reflecting on a research area

Once you are in the position of having read and made notes on a reasonable amount of material, you will begin to be able to identify the common threads between the studies and make tentative steps to see the direction the literature on your chosen topic is going and how it is evolving. At that stage, some questions to reflect on are:

1. What are the primary themes that have emerged in this area?
2. Does this topic have a solid theoretical underpinning (if so, from which types of theories), or are the bulk of the studies purely empirical in nature?
3. Are there specific individuals or particular universities leading this research effort, or is it geographically well spread? Have practitioners, research agencies or central banks produced any of this body of work, or is it only of interest to academics?
4. Are there any pivotal studies that changed the research direction on the topic

and that nearly every other study since then has cited?

5. Are the majority of studies using the same methods and data, or is a range of techniques employed?

6. How has this topic developed chronologically? Was there a burst of activity at a specific point in time, or did the research efforts span many years? Is it still being investigated, or has the volume of material waned?

7. Are studies on this topic published mainly in journals (and are they the leading journals), books, or working papers?

8. Is there evidence of a disagreement between authors regarding their findings, or is there a consensus that has emerged?

9. Is there any interdisciplinary work in this area, or is it all within the discipline?

10. Are there any apparent gaps in this body of work where queries that arise to you have not been answered? This question is perhaps the most challenging yet the most important of all: if you can come up with a good response here, you have the basis for your project's investigative work.

Identifying the weaknesses in studies

As I will discuss in detail in the following chapter, a literature review needs to be critical of the studies it is discussing. Therefore, when analysing a paper, try to identify flaws in the arguments being made, which can then form the basis of your critique. For instance:

- Does the study's empirical work lack a theoretical foundation? A common criticism of accounting and finance research is that the investigator throws together a set of variables and writes about any statistically significant relationships without thinking why these items were in the model until after it was estimated.

- Are dubious assumptions being made? These might be implausible, but have they been justified and has the findings' sensitivity to them been examined?

- Are the arguments made in the paper based on false logic?

- Have competing ideas or explanations of the findings been ignored entirely rather than considered and then dismissed based on evidence? In other words, have the authors selected one interpretation of the results which is consistent with the explanation that they wanted to put forward, but where there are also other possible explanations that they have ignored or not discussed? This one-sided perspective is surprisingly common in research studies.

Chapter takeaways – top tips for success

⊛ Be aware of the reasons why researchers conduct literature reviews and the pitfalls that lie in wait if the review is ineffective or incomplete

⊛ It might be advisable to begin your review with basic sources such as lecture materials or textbooks, but the core of the review will likely be drawn from academic journal articles

⊛ Know how to evaluate the quality of your reading material and ensure its validity

⊛ Ensure that you also examine unpublished studies, especially recently produced working papers

⊛ Know where to find relevant literature using search engines, Google Scholar, library-based databases such as JStor, Ebsco and the Web of Science, as well as repositories such as SSRN and ResearchGate

⊛ Ensure that you are aware of what you should be looking for in academic studies and how to identify flaws and limitations of the work

⊛ Reflect on where each article you read fits within its wider genre

7. WRITING THE LITERATURE REVIEW

Learning outcomes: this chapter covers

✓ How to write a literature review
✓ How to make your writing critical
✓ How to structure and format the review
✓ How to incorporate direct quotations
✓ How to correctly reference existing studies

7.1 Writing the review: some preliminary considerations

This section presents some initial questions that will likely arise in your mind as you begin to think about organising your notes and writing the review. Each of those threads is then expanded throughout subsequent sections in this chapter.

7.1.1 How long should the review be?

Determining the length of the review and how many chapters it should span within the project is not as straightforward a matter to resolve as it might appear. There is no definitive response to this issue, and the most appropriate length will vary depending on the subject matter and the volume of existing output on the topic, as well as the total number of words available for the project. In general, the more discursive (less technical) and the greater the extant body of work, the longer your review is likely to be. As stated in chapter 1 of this book, the mark scheme or research project handbook (if there is such a document in your department) might indicate what proportion of the overall project should be allocated to the review. But in general, it should not be more than about a quarter of the entire piece.

The convention, which also seems the optimal choice in most cases, is to make the review exactly one chapter long. A review that spans more than a single chapter is likely to be unwieldy and excessive for a dissertation that is only 10,000-20,000 words long in total. On the other hand, a review that is less than a chapter and combined with something else would not constitute an ideal structure as the review is likely to comprise a different kind of material to the investigative work in your project, and so is better if it is formally separated. Sometimes, the introduction and literature review are combined into a single chapter, but this would only be sensible if both chapters were too short or too interconnected to stand alone.

Inevitably, when you begin writing your literature review, you will have a substantial amount of material in the form of notes, ideas, summaries and articles marked with a highlighter pen. Deciding how to organise the subject matter is an essential step to going from a mess to a coherent draft. But it is often hard to know where to start.

Drafting the literature review to say what you want it to is a skill that usually takes time to perfect. Ideally, the review will set the scene for your investigative work and put your research into a proper context. Just as many research proposals are review-heavy, so too are the dissertations themselves. Although the length of the review will depend on how much material there is to review (for example, if you are writing on accounting standards or the capital asset pricing model, it is not feasible to examine everything), in general, it should not comprise more than about a quarter of the whole draft.

You need to quickly develop a system to classify the literature that you have gathered. This classification will also help you to organise the review. For example, you could arrange it by the methodology used (e.g., descriptive, interviews, quantitative analysis, or by a theoretical vs. empirical approach), by sub-topic covered, chronologically, etc. Organising the review logically is often one of the trickiest parts as you are likely to have a mass of studies and be unsure where to place them, initially having no way to order the material. If you have used a two-dimensional approach to classifying the studies, such as a spider diagram, at some stage, this will need to be transformed into a single-dimensional collation of the material with a storyline that creates a sensible ordering.

You will need to structure the information and relate it to the research questions you are developing. Try to identify the common threads that link research studies together thematically – this could be through their methods, the perspective they take (e.g., for or against a particular viewpoint), data coverage, country or market focus, findings, or when they were written. The work can then be organised in several ways – for instance, by topic, method (the technique used), country or market covered, findings (researchers A, B and C all found evidence in favour of the theory while X,

Y and Z found evidence against it), and so on.

A good way to start is by categorising the material according to the class of models or theories. The classes can then be ordered chronologically (where the earliest developed model class appears first in the draft), or by importance (with the models currently considered most important ordered first), or by the level of sophistication of the model class (beginning with the most straightforward types and gradually increasing in complexity). Then, within each of these categories, you can describe when and how the model or idea was derived, what are its key features and benefits, what were the results of empirical research on it, whether the model or theory has been criticised (and if so, why and how), and what are the alternatives.

Merely summarising the literature is relatively easy but writing an effective literature review takes considerable skill and organisation. The appropriate style of the review will vary slightly depending on the subject matter. For example, if you are covering a highly technical subject such as mathematical finance, you would need to include numerous equations, compared with more discursive material on a topic such as how to account for corporate environmental damage.

The literature review should follow the style of a comprehensive appraisal published in a scholarly journal and should always be critical in nature. It should comment on the relevance, value, advantages and shortcomings of the cited articles. The review should be written in continuous prose and not in note form. It is important to demonstrate an understanding of the work and provide a critical assessment – i.e., to point out key weaknesses in existing studies. Being critical is not always easy and is a delicate balance; the critique's tone should remain polite as further discussed in subsection 10.1.3. The review should synthesise existing work into a summary of what is and is not known and identify trends, gaps and controversies.

Accounting has an extensive and well-established critical stream, with a range of journals publishing critical research, including, most notably: *Critical Perspectives on Accounting*,[1] and the *International Journal of Critical Accounting*,[2] although many other accounting journals also publish some studies of a critical nature such as the *Accounting, Auditing & Accountability Journal*.[3] But this tradition never really established itself in finance where there is only one such journal (the *Critical Finance Review*,[4] which, according to the journal's home page, will 'take more risks to try to attract more controversial and provocative papers'). It should be noted that studies in critical accounting are not just concerned with pointing out the weaknesses in individual studies, which is what all good literature reviews will be doing; rather, they will be highlighting the limitations of entire approaches to theory and practice.

---

[1] https://www.journals.elsevier.com/critical-perspectives-on-accounting/
[2] https://www.inderscience.com/jhome.php?jcode=ijca
[3] https://www.emeraldgrouppublishing.com/journal/aaaj#aims-and-scope
[4] https://www.nowpublishers.com/CFR

7.2 The beginning, middle and end of the review

Just as for a novel or a research project as a whole, a good literature review will have a beginning, a middle, and an end. It will also have a narrative – a flowing story that links together as if there is a single thread running through it from beginning to end.

The opening part of the review should provide a gentle introduction to the problem. It should put the issues you will investigate into a wider context, and it should also explain why the problem or area is interesting and for whom. In the introduction to the literature review, explain how the material you are reviewing links with other related areas. Where does your topic fit into the wider context? The introduction should then provide a brief outline of the rest of the review. The review's main body would then follow, separated into sections as described in section 7.6 below.

The final section of the review should provide a summary of the literature that you have reviewed that leads naturally onto the 'gap' in the body of knowledge that your investigative work helps to fill. When writing the concluding section to the literature review, maintain the focus established in the introduction so that the precis is directed towards your study's topic. The summary should be reasonably short and straightforward – perhaps a couple of paragraphs or so – even if the volume of work you are reviewing is vast and technical.

A good review should lead naturally onto your theoretical or empirical work and should complement it. When you are considering which existing studies to include in your review, think about whether they will add to or detract from what you are trying to achieve overall in your project. You need to incorporate all of the key sources in the area but avoid padding with irrelevant or marginally relevant material that will take up valuable words and make the core material harder for the reader to locate. While you are writing the review, look out for gaps ('lacunae' as they are sometimes called) in the body of work and think about aspects of the subject area that have not been explored. Identifying lacunae will help you to refine your research ideas or to replace them with new suggestions that have more relevance or are more feasible.

Synthesise the results into a summary of what is and is not known. This synthesis will allow you to identify:

- Trends (e.g., 'most researchers used to believe X but now the majority of studies seem to suggest that Y is the reason')
- Gaps (e.g., 'as far as I am aware, nobody has as yet examined ...')
- Controversies (i.e., topics upon which researchers cannot agree and where there are mixed findings)

All of these will help you to develop or refine your research questions.

Don't just include a list of authors and their papers but explain what each study is doing, what is different about it compared with other studies in the area and why it is relevant for your work. When time is limited, it is often better to have a modest number of sources explained in detail, with their relevance and shortcomings shining through, than to have a long list of references with each study given merely a cursory treatment. Your draft needs to include the issues raised by the following questions:

1. What are the main topics of interest in this research area? How do they fit together?
2. How has the research area developed over time?
3. What is the theory or conceptual framework underpinning this area of study?
4. What methods are usually used to tackle the research questions? Is there a good spread of approaches, or are all the papers using the same techniques? Have any interdisciplinary investigations been applied to this topic?
5. What sorts of data are being used? Are developing countries also a focus of the investigation, or is the evidence confined to certain countries, especially the US?
6. Is there consensus across the literature in the answers to the research questions, or are the conclusions disputed?

In terms of style, it is better to vary the way you describe papers rather than starting each sentence with the authors' names, such as: 'Brooks (2008) examines X . . . and finds this. Smith (2013) studies Y . . . and finds that. Jones (2017) develops Smith's ideas to include Z. . . ' This almost reads like a set of notes for each paper that has been unimaginatively spliced together, which is an amateurish approach and is dull for the reader.

7.3 Making your review 'critical'

One of the essential aspects of an effective review is that it should be critical of the studies it cites, which means identifying and pointing out the weaknesses in existing research and the points where it could be improved. Don't merely provide a list of authors and their research or use a style that involves no depth, such as 'X argued this while Y suggested that', which would be a superficial treatment of their work. Instead, you should demonstrate understanding by providing some detail and a critical assessment. Being critical is not always easy to do appropriately – it is a delicate balance to achieve, and the tone should always remain polite and slightly understated.

Sometimes, students find it surprising that they are expected to criticise existing studies. After all, these were produced by established, accredited and sometimes well-known scholars – how can you, as someone near the beginning of their academic journey, find problems with top researchers' work? However, even work conducted by the world's best scholars can be improved upon or does not cover every aspect of a problem. Therefore, you should feel empowered to challenge findings or statements that you disagree with, and your confidence in doing this will grow as you read, learn and understand more about the subject. This is all part of being able to produce a critical literature review.

Most of the time, being critical does not mean identifying fatal errors in the studies; instead, it is about seeking out the limitations or aspects of the research that could be improved. It is rather like those who conduct research on car engines intending to release updated versions. They are not trying to develop a totally new type of engine design, and they are not suggesting that the previous versions were dangerous or likely to break down. Instead, they hope to develop new designs that are more fuel-efficient, faster or quieter, etc.

But the critique is essential to incorporate – after all, if the current work is beyond criticism, then that particular research problem has been solved, and no further study of it is needed. Critical comments should be backed up with evidence from the work being criticised or from other sources as far as possible so that they do not appear as unfair or unsubstantiated accusations.

Finally, note that while your review should have elements of critique, it is not necessary to be critical about every study you cite, and many can be presented as statements about what previous researchers have written using neutral language. All research, even ground-breaking studies published in the leading journals, has some flaws, of course, so when writing a critique, try to focus on the most substantive issues. Don't bother to point out trivial matters such as typos, grammatical mistakes or minor errors in the analysis; focus on sufficiently grave problems that could influence the findings or call them into question.

7.4   The importance of presenting a balanced argument

It is imperative when writing the review that you consider studies taking a different perspective from your own. For example, it is sometimes the case that there are two entirely opposing ways to tackle a particular problem. This might be two different classes of model, or more fundamentally, two methodological paradigms.

To give one illustration of a situation where this may occur, in many sub-fields within business and management, the 'big data' approach based on quantitative analysis and formal mathematical models has become predominant while the alternative way of obtaining findings from qualitative analysis of interviews and non-participant observation is eschewed.

It might be that your review would be richer if it sought out and acknowledged that there is another approach in addition to the one that you are using, although yours will naturally make up the bulk of your review. Of course, it might be a much lower-level difference across studies, such as estimating the efficiency of a particular banking market using nonparametric (data envelopment analysis) or parametric (the stochastic frontier approach) techniques. In that case, your review ought to discuss both parametric and non-parametric approaches, together with their relative strengths and weaknesses, even if you intend to focus on only one of these techniques in your investigation.

Providing another example, in economics, the 'Chicago school' (so-called because it was initially developed by faculty at the University of Chicago) holds a strong philosophical belief in the superiority of free markets for making economic decisions and in the efficiency of financial markets, associated with Eugene Fama amongst many others. An opposing view is held by Robert Shiller, a behavioural economist at Yale University, that markets frequently depart from efficiency and experience speculative bubbles. Sometimes journals will only publish research taking a specific viewpoint, so there are, for example, journals that take an efficient markets perspective and those taking a behavioural view. If you limit your literature search to one set of journals in such circumstances, the work will lack balance. It will not reflect the diversity of opinions and approaches that exist, and you would be implicitly suggesting that there is consensus where, in fact, there is none.

If you are working on a controversial topic – for instance, one with a political dimension or where there is more than one strand to an argument, you also need to be careful of misleading or one-sided statements. This situation is subtly different to the one above – here, it might be the case that the author is an expert on the topic and knows precisely what they are doing, but they deliberately use their writing to try to persuade the reader to accept a particular viewpoint when the truth might be more subtle. Government propaganda fits into this category – while there might be some elements of truth in what is being said, the strength of the evidence is exaggerated to push the individual to act (or not act) in a particular way.

In your project, you will likely need to provide a balanced treatment rather than a biased one, which is more in the spirit of a scholarly investigation. You should also present the information you find that runs against the central perspective you are making or the results you obtain. But put this into context, and say that, on balance, you favour explanation X rather than Y because the weight of evidence supports the former. You can then dismiss the counterevidence or counterargument as being weaker for some specific reasons that you have identified.

If different studies reach conflicting conclusions, this implies that the current state of knowledge cannot solve the puzzle, and your write-up should reflect that, in which case further research is needed to determine which, if any, of the perspectives is correct. It is also an interesting situation when one study seems to yield different findings than all the others on that topic. One possibility is that the outlying piece contains methodological errors that make its conclusions invalid. But it is also plausible that this study simply used a different yet equally acceptable approach, and therefore the consensus in the rest of the literature on that issue is shaky.

7.5 Should the review include quotations?

Including brief quotations from existing studies can be highly valuable in getting a point across. Often, an acknowledged expert would have phrased an argument in a particular way that is profound and encapsulates what you want to say better than you could do so yourself. If that is the case, it is valuable to include the quote. Quotations can also be used as evidence to demonstrate particular points that you want to make.

But in general, avoid quotes longer than, perhaps, three or four lines since incorporating so many of someone else's words diminishes the worth of your review. For something longer than this, you should put it into your own words there will always be numerous different ways to do that. Regarding the appropriate presentational style to adopt for quotations, those which are short should be incorporated directly into the sentence that discusses them. More extensive quotes (e.g., three or four lines or more) should be placed on a separate line in your document and indented from the left-hand margin. An example of this is given in subsection 10.3.6.

It is also best to explain what you are quoting and why, rather than just dropping it in, which might confuse the reader as to its relevance or purpose and disrupt the flow. Relatedly, in terms of the volume of quotes to incorporate, a small number sprinkled into a review can add interest and a strong connection with existing studies. But including too many is detrimental since the whole point of the review is to demonstrate that you have assimilated what you have read and that you can paraphrase it rather than copying it verbatim from an existing source.

Although including quotations (when appropriately cited to make it clear that they are taken from an existing source) is not plagiarism, if you incorporate too many of them, it might be considered that your work is excessively derivative. This means that it is too closely related to what is already published so that you are adding nothing new, even in terms of your writing, let alone the ideas. If your marker concludes that some aspects of your dissertation are excessively derivative, you would likely be penalised. Therefore, there is a delicate balance in the inclusion of quotations in a review: a few short ones enhance and enrich it; quotes that are too long or too numerous damage it.

7.6 Should your literature review include sub-headings?

Sub-headings can help organise a piece of work and will usually make it easier to read, so they are recommended. However, it is also advisable to avoid using too many, which would disrupt the flow and make the document appear amateurish. Each sub-section needs to be substantial, for example comprising roughly between half a page and a few pages; if a sub-section is just four or five lines long, merge it with the one before or after.

It is of less concern whether the sub-sections are numbered, which is a matter of personal preference. It could be that only the main section headings (so-called A-headings) are numbered, for instance, while those of a lower level are not numbered but are simply underlined:

Chapter 1: Introduction and Motivation

    Section 1.1 The development of asset pricing models

        The CAPM
        Arbitrage pricing
        Atheoretical factor models

    Section 1.2 Empirical tests of asset pricing models

        ...

    Section 1.3 Intended contribution of the dissertation

    Section 1.4 Outline of the remainder of the document

It would also be possible to move to even lower hierarchical levels (e.g., Section 1.2.1.4), whether numbered or not, but this always seems like overkill and is not necessary or helpful in a document of the length of a student project. So, in the example above, in my view it is preferable for the sub-headings relating to the CAPM, arbitrage pricing, and so on to remain unnumbered.

7.7 Referencing

Citations have two purposes. First, they show your readers the sources of some of your project's ideas, which gives due credit to those existing authors. Second, they allow readers to follow up those references if they want more detail on what had been done. The latter purpose implies a requirement that the references are complete and accurate; it is annoying and a waste of time trying to track down a piece of work that somebody else had cited only to find that some referencing details are wrong.

There are two general approaches to referencing – putting the details in footnotes on each page with no list at the end of the document and gathering all the references together into a list without full information in footnotes. The former style is typical in the humanities, such as history, but is rare in accounting and finance and so it is safest to have a list. Within this category, there are various referencing styles concerning how the information is displayed, but this is a second-order consideration – the most important aspect is that the details are all there and correct.

In some journals in the natural and physical sciences, the convention is to use a numeric system for references. Here, each reference in the list is given a number, and that number is used as the in-text citation rather than the author surname and year. For instance:

'Finance has been argued to lack the critical stream that has been crucial

in the development of accounting research' [7]

where the number refers to the seventh numbered citation in the list at the end of the document. This convention is rarely used in the social sciences, however, and I suggest avoiding it.

Try to keep full and accurate bibliographic records for all the papers you read – if you do this carefully from the outset, it will save much time and hassle later. Pay attention to names and journal titles since your supervisor will likely be familiar with these, and so any typographical errors here will be spotted and could undermine confidence in more substantive aspects of your work.

If you are in any doubt about how the reference list should look in your dissertation, simply examine the list at the end of almost any published academic paper. Most schools are not overly concerned about the formatting of the references so long as the list is accurate, in a consistent style, and alphabetically ordered by the first author's surname. If no more specific stipulations are made, the 'Harvard style' is standard and works well. Although it has a large number of minor variations, it is broadly the approach that has been used throughout this text and in the reference list at the end of the book.

7.7.1   Latin terms in referencing

Some good Latin terms to know for when you are referencing (or to help your understanding of the referencing style used by others) are:

- *op. cit.* (short for *opere citato*), which is used to refer to a piece that has already been cited but, perhaps, a few sentences or paragraphs ago. For example, 'Brooks and Oikonomou (2018) survey the literature on the link between environmental, social and governance disclosures and firm value. Much of this work builds on stakeholder theory (Freeman, 1983; Jones, 1995) that discusses how firms establish and prioritise relationships with their constituents. Firms may have well-intentioned or cynical reasons for trying to enhance their social performance (Brooks and Oikonomou, *op. cit.*).'

- *et al.* (short for *et alia*), which means 'and other authors.' *et al.* is the most common such abbreviation and is very useful when there are several authors to an article that you are referring to more than once. For example, Brooks, Hoepner, McMillan, Vivian, and Wese Simen (2019) can be shortened to the much more manageable Brooks *et al.* (2019). A standard convention uses the entire list of author names the first time it is referred to in the document before switching to *et al.* in all subsequent citations of the same piece.

- *Ibid.* (short for *ibidem*), which means 'in the same study'. You would use this when the study you have just referred to makes another valid point but perhaps on a different page. So, for example, you might write 'Finance has been argued to lack the critical stream that has been crucial in the development of accounting research (Brooks and Schopohl, 2018, p.615), and it also lacks diversity in the methodological approaches it uses (*ibid.*, p.632).'

Note that Latin terms are usually written in italics, and a full stop should follow any abbreviated words in each case.

7.7.2   Direct and indirect referencing

There are two broad styles of working references into a passage of text, and these are sometimes known as direct and indirect referencing. Examples of each are as follows:

Direct referencing

'Brooks *et al.* (2019) argue that finance scholars have devoted insufficient attention to the study of ethics.'

Indirect referencing

'Insufficient attention has been devoted by finance scholars to the study of ethics (Brooks *et al.*, 2019).'

Notice that in the second case, the parentheses surround the entire reference, and there is no second set of parentheses around the publication year. Either approach is equally acceptable, and using both within the document will vary the style and make it more entertaining to read. References can also be stacked up (usually in alphabetical order by author name or chronologically with the earliest listed first) if more than one study makes a similar point (e.g., Brooks *et al.*, 2019; Persand, 2014).

7.7.3 Secondary references

Ideally, you would read every piece of existing research that you cite. However, this might be too time-consuming in reality, and there might be articles that you feel compelled to mention due to their relevance and importance but which you cannot get hold of (for example, due to their age or limitations in your library's journal subscription bundle). In such cases, there are two options. One is to cite the unread work as if you had read it based on paraphrasing what the study you have examined writes about it. The other possibility is to write it as a 'secondary reference', where you explicitly recognise that you are reporting an idea 'second-hand'. For example, you might write: 'the careers of women in academia have been held back by a lack of senior female role models (Sealy and Singh, 2010, cited in Brooks *et al.*, 2014).'

It is clear here that you have read the paper by Brooks *et al.* but not the one by Sealy and Singh, although it is the latter whose point you are including in your argument.

Neither approach is ideal: if you cite a paper without reading it, you rely on the author whose work you did read having reported accurately the findings of the piece you didn't. On the other hand, while one or two secondary references are acceptable, more than that will make you appear lazy and unprofessional. In that case, your supervisor will question why you didn't make more effort to track down and read the original work yourself. On balance, my preference is to refrain from using any secondary referencing.

7.7.4 Making a list of references

At some point, you will need to construct a reference list. It is much easier to do this as you go along rather than trying to pull it together at the end when you have forgotten the details of where some of your materials came from, and you need to look for them again.

The reference list in the project will just be a list of papers and books. But still, when you are working on the literature review, you might find it helpful to use some software to classify each item using topics, dates, a short summary of the methods and main findings, etc. If you keep a systematic record of what you have read and what are the key papers, this will save you a lot of time constructing the reference list at the end. It will also help ensure that you do not miss anything and avoid inadvertently reading the same work more than once, not realising until you have almost completed it a second time, which I am embarrassed to admit that I have done on several occasions. The most straightforward way to do this is to use a word processor or spreadsheet package with which you are already familiar.

Alternatively, you could use specific software such as EndNote, ProCite or

BibTeX (the latter is for those who use LaTeX to typeset their documents, which was used for this book, rather than Microsoft Word or Apple Pages). The advantage of this automated referencing software is that once you have inputted all of the information into the database, it is possible to search and extract it in various styles, already formatted to drop straight into your dissertation. Using a specialist referencing package is valuable if you will have a large number of references or will be using them for more than one piece of work. But it might not be worth the effort to learn how to use the software if you have a small number of references to be used in only in this research project.

7.7.5   How many references should be on your list?

The primary focus will be on the reference list for the project as a whole rather than for the literature review part alone, and at a later stage, you will need to combine the reference list from your literature review with those from citations across the rest of the document (the introduction, methods, conclusions, etc.).

In general, and as stated in several places in this text, the number of references will depend to a considerable extent on the material being covered. The more discursive and the more mature a subject area, the longer the reference list would be expected to be. Therefore, while it is hard to give a precise figure, if your dissertation has fewer than ten references, it is likely to appear as if the link with existing work is insufficient. You will probably want to include citations in the methods and data sections to other studies that have used a similar approach and compare your findings with those in existing papers or books. Adding such citations will increase the overall reference count, and thus I would typically expect that there would be at least 15-20 citations in the list.

7.8   Problems with a literature review and fixing them

The first and most fundamental reason why a literature review can turn out badly is when the author did not come up with any (or many) relevant studies to write about, so the review has no core and is full of peripheral material from websites on irrelevant topics.

In general, if you can find almost no existing research whatsoever related to your topic, it is probably not an ideal one for you to focus on either as you will have no prior studies to guide you or to help establish a framework. The lack of previous research also indicates that, for some reason, established scholars have not found it to be a topic worthy of investigation and publishing. It might be because the phenomenon is entirely new or due to a lack of data since the main variables of interest are almost impossible to measure. Alternatively, it could be because the subject matter is very practical and populist, so not amenable to academic study.

Aside from being unable to find sufficient relevant research to survey, literature reviews can fail to live up to their potential for several reasons:

1. Important studies have been omitted
2. Recent studies have been omitted so that the review is dated and reads as if it had been written years ago
3. The number of sources is too low
4. The sources are focused primarily on basic internet materials
5. The writing lacks a good structure so that it drifts and is hard to follow
6. The style is repetitive or not engaging
7. The review is descriptive and not critical
8. Too many marginally relevant or unimportant studies are cited, so it is hard to identify what the purpose of the review is
9. The review jumps in too quickly at the beginning, so it takes a long time for the reader to discover what material is going to be covered and why
10. The review 'falls off a cliff' at the end without summarising what has been covered
11. Overall, the review is either too short or too long
12. The referencing style is poor or inaccurate

Any of the above faults will diminish the quality of the work, but none is fatal. They can all be remedied, mostly fairly straightforwardly. The numbers in the list below correspond to those in the list immediately above, and provide some suggestions to fix common problems with the literature review:

1. Ensure from the outset that you identify the pivotal studies on each particular topic. These should become evident fairly quickly since they will be the studies that many other researchers are citing. Make certain that your literature search is as comprehensive as possible, looking at a wide range of the sources described above. Also, use the full range of years during which relevant research was published rather than a narrow time window.
2. This issue follows from the previous one. The most recent work on a particular topic might not yet be published since the lag between papers being written by scholars and published in journals can be as much as two or three years. Consequently, it is vital to examine both published and unpublished sources. Students who rely on paraphrasing from a small number of existing studies with excessive secondary reading and referencing rather than reading widely and drawing information from the individual studies run a higher risk of their reviews being outdated. A project that omits recent studies also has a higher chance of repeating investigations that have already been conducted and of failing to use cutting-edge techniques.
3. A sound literature review needs to cover a sufficient number of sources. As discussed above, while the appropriate number varies depending upon the material and the amount of existing work on the topic, it is clear that three or four sources would be insufficient, and perhaps ten would be a minimum acceptable number.
4. Not only the number of references but also their origin requires some

consideration. The list should not only comprise popular pieces (e.g., blogs or newspaper articles) or basic internet-based sources such as Wikipedia, notwithstanding its value as a starting point. While it is acceptable to include some such sources, at its core, the review needs to delve deep into the academic literature, which means looking at papers published in journals, working papers not yet published, and possibly scholarly books.

5. The structure is almost as important for readability as the writing style. For example, using sub-headings (but not too many and not too many sub-levels) will help the reader avoid getting lost in the flow of the document and mapping out the sections before commencing writing should also help ensure that the structure is clear and works.

6. Developing a fluid writing style is something that takes practice and clear, detailed feedback. But some steps can be taken at an early stage, and which will help enormously. First, a good structure and planning should limit repetition. Second, try to link paragraphs and sections together so that the writing flows naturally rather than being 'bitty' or disjointed. Third, and as discussed above, try to avoid starting too many sentences with 'Bloggs (2009) argued X and then Jones (2012) stated Y.'

7. Again, as discussed above, literature reviews should be critical, not just presenting existing work but also pointing out the limitations, flaws, and what the authors did not do.

8. Literature reviews should be organised around the most important studies on the topic. Dependent on how extensive the body of work is, they should not cover research that is not really at the core of the subject and should not cover work that is of low quality or excessively derivative of prior studies. Such research should only be included at all if the number of studies on your precise topic is minimal and expanding the choice set to include this work is necessary to generate a review of a reasonable length. Also, try to avoid undergoing a sojourn along a blind alley where a self-contained but barely marginally relevant body of work is presented in great detail. Including such material would use up valuable words and detract from the focus of the piece.

9. An effective review should have a beginning and an end, as well as a middle. This means that the start of the review chapter should explain what strand of the literature you will be discussing and why. Perhaps, if space allows, you could provide a mini-roadmap of the structure of the chapter. Ideally, it will be apparent to the reader how the work you are reviewing ties in with your aims and objectives.

10. At the end, the review should not just stop with a discussion of the final existing study that you wish to mention; instead, it should summarise what is known and what is not, providing a lead-in to your investigative work that will begin in the following chapter.

11. The literature review's total length is very much a 'Goldilocks and the Three

Bears' situation – it needs to be just right. If the review is too short, it will give the impression that you did not spend long on it, and it will omit key studies or cover them superficially. On the other hand, if the review is too long, it will swamp the dissertation document, using up valuable words and possibly pushing you over the word limit or making the work less enjoyable to read.

12. Accurate referencing is one of the easiest aspects to get right, and so there are no excuses. Always make sure that you take precise notes about which study said what and when. Also, make sure that there is a 1:1 correspondence between the citations made in the text and the list at the end of the dissertation. Ensure that all of the references are complete, including full titles, journal names, volume and page numbers, etc., and listed in alphabetical order by (first) author surname. Pay particular attention to author names, which might be from an unfamiliar language or be spelt in different ways (e.g., Brooks versus Brookes). It is hard to spot and correct such errors once they have been made, so it is better to get them right the first time.

7.8.1 Final literature review checks

Before submitting the review for comments from your supervisor or putting it on the shelf and starting on the investigative parts of your project, when you complete the first draft of your review, run through the following checklist. You should be able to answer the following questions effortlessly, so if you have any doubts, then reflect on how the work can be improved before you move on. These are all issues that your project's markers will be considering, so if you are unsure about any of the points, think about how you might be able to modify the review to address them.

- Is my topic primarily mathematical or discursive? This will significantly affect the type and style of the review
- What is the scope of my literature review?
- How well have I searched the literature? Will I have uncovered relevant material published in non-core journals and working papers?
- Have I set the perspective appropriately to ensure that I have found any relevant material but excluding anything that is irrelevant?
- Does my review include the latest thinking on the topic, or is it dated?
- Is the material I have reviewed relevant, and does it demonstrably link with my research questions?
- Have I written the review in a critical style, identifying and pinpointing weaknesses?
- Do I merely summarise the studies I review, or do I assess and draw the links between them?
- Is the review balanced, and have I also incorporated studies that take a different perspective to my own?
- Have I set the scene appropriately in the introductory section of the review and summarised the body of work in the conclusions?

• Have I identified any gaps in the field's knowledge about the subject?

Further reading

There are numerous, detailed books on how to survey the literature and write the review. Some popular texts include Booth *et al.* (2016), Ridley (2012), and the very detailed text by Greetham (2020).

Chapter takeaways – top tips for success

⊛ You need to develop a system to organise and classify the literature you have reviewed

⊛ The review should have a beginning, middle and end. It needs to set the scene with context and motivation first before moving onto the main body and then finishing with a summary of what you have covered and what is known and not known on the subject

⊛ Your review should be balanced and include alternative approaches or viewpoints that contradict yours

⊛ Small numbers of judiciously chosen quotes can enliven the review, but don't make them too long or numerous

⊛ Your review should include an appropriate number of sources, which will depend on the nature of the subject matter and the extent of existing research on the topic

⊛ Ensure that your referencing is consistent and precise

8. RESEARCH METHODS

Learning outcomes: this chapter covers

✓ The difference between methodology and methods
✓ How to select your research methods
✓ How theory is used in research
✓ The kinds of theories are relevant for accounting and finance

8.1 Preparing for the investigative part of your project

This part of your project is at the core, and it is the aspect on which the final mark will primarily be based. It is beyond the scope of this book to teach either quantitative or qualitative approaches from scratch, and although many research project textbooks try to do just that, it is usually a disaster with their treatment not having sufficient space to explain the techniques in any detail. Most students will undoubtedly have covered this material in other modules on using quantitative or qualitative methods in much more detail than covered in those books, while readers who have not sat such courses are left confused by the sparse, lighting-speed coverage.

That being the case, at this stage, I will not cover either quantitative or qualitative approaches in detail. I do, however, provide some discussion of survey and interview techniques because, in my experience, undergraduate and master's students of accounting and finance are less likely to have taken modules that cover this already (unlike students of sociology, psychology or management, for example). For readers of this book, the task will be to select the appropriate methodology for your chosen topic and apply it effectively. Consequently, this chapter is partly focused on achieving that objective, with additional information sources provided throughout the chapter.

Both accounting and finance are usually considered social sciences – that is, the 'unit of analysis' is usually people and the outcomes that we observe and measure in both fields are the results of decisions and actions by people. However, unlike sociology, for example, finance in particular but increasingly accounting too, draw methods from the natural and physical sciences. This plurality of approaches provides researchers with an enormous array of possible strategies to tackle their research aims.

As well as examining the existing research on your chosen topic as covered in the previous two chapters of this book, the other area where you are likely to have to do some additional reading is on the methods. Whether you are using an econometric analysis of secondary data, questionnaires or interviews, unfortunately, it is unlikely that you will have covered the approaches in sufficient detail to be able to proceed without further groundwork.

Therefore, even if you have completed the literature review, there is still additional reading to do, albeit more specialised and less in volume. As you begin to pin down the details of the investigative methods to use, you would probably not need to read each article in detail, and it would make sense to skip straight to the methodology section of the paper to see if it employs an approach that you are considering. If so, you might also focus on the results section to see how it worked when that author used those techniques.

Once you have read enough of the subject-specific material to be aware of how researchers usually address their research questions in your topic area, you will need to become more of an expert in that technique yourself. At that point, where do you start? There are essentially three stages in the process. First, you need to identify the most appropriate methods to tackle your research problem. This is covered in the following section of this book.

Second, learn about and implement the chosen method. This is the research design step, which is about establishing a framework to apply the techniques you have chosen and determining how you will use them to answer your questions. It is an essential part of the process that must be nailed down before the investigative work begins. Having a weak or ill-conceived design will lead to problems later down the line and has been likened to building a house without any plans to guide the construction. If you determine how you will go about the investigation on the hoof, it will show through in the final draft, so map out how you will gather the data and how you will analyse them before you start.

The third stage is to interpret and analyse the results. Whatever means you use to collect the data (download, survey or interview), don't get so carried away with it that there is insufficient time remaining to conduct the analysis and writing. These latter aspects are at least as important, and to do a good job might take longer than you expected. Getting the results into tables and graphs, describing them, explaining what they mean, how they relate to your research aims or hypotheses, and comparing them to other studies' findings all require time. So try to stick to the schedule that you established at the beginning and spread your time accordingly.

8.1.1 Are 'methodology' and 'method' the same?

Strictly, no, the two are different, although the two terms are frequently used interchangeably in accounting and finance. Here are more accurate working definitions of the two terms that explain their differences.

Method

'Method' is a somewhat lower level and straightforward concept that refers to the systematic, concrete process used to obtain and analyse investigative data. The method is the tool you use on a practical level: an interview, survey, regression analysis of secondary data, and so on.

Methodology

'Methodology', on the other hand, is the high-level strategy for generating knowledge and the rationale for the approach taken to research – in some ways, it is an analysis of methods and, for example, why one method is chosen over another.

In essence, given how the term is usually used loosely in accounting and finance, the methodology involves determining the best approach to answer your research questions or hypotheses. For instance, you might have a reason to believe that firms with more diversity in their management boards will perform better on environmental issues than those with less variety or that younger investors are more risk-tolerant than those who are older. How will you assess each of these suggestions? The testing approach you use can be thought of as the methodological choice.

8.2 Choosing your research methods

8.2.1 The research design and strategy

The starting point for selecting the project's investigative methods will be your research strategy, which is the overall approach that you will use based on the objectives you have set for the research. The strategy relates to the highest-level decisions that you need to make when determining how to do your research, including the scale and scope of the investigation and what you intend to achieve. It will also involve the choice between the use of quantitative or qualitative techniques. The strategy will then lead to a research design, which is the methodological framework that you will use to address your research aims, including selecting the investigative approach and methods, the types of data you will collect, and how you will analyse them.

You might need to justify your research strategy, particularly if the method you use is not the most commonly applied to that topic. For example, suppose you are examining the link between the characteristics of chief executive officers (CEOs) and the operational performance of the companies they run using a panel regression. In that case, you probably do not need to take time to explain why that is the best approach to use since, after all, this is what almost all existing studies will have done. But if instead, you decided that you would try to address the question by in-depth interviews of a small group of CEOs, that would benefit from some justification and explanation about how you would achieve your aims. Some discussion would be valuable since your methods are different to those used in existing studies, which might initially cause concern among your markers if they doubt the relevance of the technique you have chosen.

It is worth spending some time considering your research design carefully before you fix on the methods to use and launch into data collection since these aspects are related and need to tie in with your research objectives. If the design is not thought through, you could waste time obtaining the wrong data or selecting an approach that will not allow you to test what you had wanted to.

In more detail, your research design will involve several interlinked aspects. It incorporates the research questions or hypotheses; the sources, types and extent of the data; the methods you will use to gather and analyse the data; the ordering and timescale over which each aspect of the investigative work in your project will take place. Before beginning their investigative work, some students find it useful to sketch out in writing all of these components of their research design, as doing so helps them identify any potential inconsistencies or other issues before they waste a significant amount of time going up a blind alley.

8.2.2   How to choose the methods

A risk-return trade-off applies with the choice of methods. If you stick with the same approach that has been widely used in the established literature, the risks are low, but the work is less likely to be ground-breaking. On the other hand, attempting to apply an entirely different technique (such as using surveys to address a particular research question when every existing study has used market data from Bloomberg) could lead to exciting new findings that are vastly different from anything already out there. But there is also much more scope for the study to be criticised or for the method not to work as anticipated. Hence, most students take the safe route for their chosen topic and use the established methods used previously in the literature.

The challenge of working in an area that is new to you and using methods that you are not familiar with will develop your skills and knowledge. But do you want to be challenged in this way, and do you have the time and energy to devote to the additional reading and learning required?

Note that this does not mean it is wrong to try different methods than those used in existing studies. In fact, quite the reverse – using an alternative approach is an excellent way to provide new and exciting evidence on the topic. But it is riskier since you would be breaking new ground rather than treading a well-worn path with an established framework to follow. Consequently, you need to provide additional confirmation that you have reflected on the appropriateness of the alternative methods and that you are aware of the difficulties that you might encounter. Your supervisor will also help you ensure that you have the requisite skills and possibly recommend specialist training or additional resources if these are needed. Moving out of your comfort zone is risky – you are more likely to face problems along the way and possibly even make mistakes – but if you overcome these issues, your learning development will be significantly enhanced.

Alongside the choice of topic, thinking about your strengths and weaknesses and what you enjoy doing will help you select a methodological approach that could be applied. You will learn new skills if you move slightly out of your comfort zone and try something somewhat different from what you have done before. But there are evident dangers if you try to move too far and stray deep into an approach that you have never been taught and have limited time to learn before the deadline. For instance, it ought to be well within most students' capabilities to learn how to implement a new econometric model if they have already attended a module on econometrics as part of their programme. On the other hand, using a qualitative approach such as interviews or detailed case study analysis would be highly challenging if your programme has taught only quantitative techniques, and you had also not covered qualitative methods previously.

The following checklist might help you to think about the kinds of approaches you could use. Do you know how to do the following, and do you enjoy using such techniques? Each technique is presented alongside some examples of the types of projects to which they would be suited.

1. Deriving formulae using algebra – an economic theory-type project or sophisticated empirical approach would suit this
2. Analysing data using statistical models – an empirical approach would suit this
3. Writing code in languages such as Python or C++; again, an empirical project but where new models are being constructed would suit this; similarly the conducting textual analysis or pricing derivatives contracts will require the use of a programming language rather than an econometrics package
4. Understanding and writing arguments for or against a particular viewpoint – this might suggest the use of a case-study or archival approach or perhaps using interviews or surveys to seek people's opinions
5. Working with conceptual or theoretical models – this would be done where the purpose is to develop a framework to understand a particular phenomenon (although probably without testing it)
6. Talking with people and understanding how they make decisions – the use of interviews or surveys would fit this type of interest best

7. Setting up and running computer-based experiments in a lab – this requires some prior background in psychology or other experimental settings since there is unlikely to be sufficient time available to learn the technical skills needed to conduct them validly
8. Working with historical documents in archives – this would be appropriate if using case studies or gathering historical data for analysis
9. Understanding practical problems faced by firms or individuals and identifying resolutions – again, the use of surveys or interviews would work well here

Each of the research methods in the above list will imbue the user with various competencies and knowledge, but among these, data handling, statistical and programming skills are particularly valued nowadays by potential employers. You may wish to bear in mind the possible positive impact on your CV of having experience with particular methods as one factor to consider when selecting a topic and the methods you will employ to study it.

Another suggestion to help you determine and implement your methods is that if there are any research seminars pertinent to your topic being given by staff or PhD students in your department, ask the seminar organiser permission to attend (which will almost always be granted). Watching the seminar will be a unique opportunity to access first-hand the latest research on the topic. It might be presented in a more informal and accessible format than a journal article, it will be easier to understand, and the methods and data handling are likely to be covered in considerable detail. At the end, you should have the opportunity to chat with the speaker about their work and, more importantly, about yours. That person (provided it is not your supervisor, with whom you will already be working) could be a useful point of contact at a later stage if you have already made an introduction and built a rapport with them.

8.2.3   The methods available for a project in accounting or finance

Accounting and finance are often considered both as sciences and as social sciences, and the methods used to tackle research problems reflect this variety of possible techniques. Case studies, surveys, interviews, conceptual models, and the empirical analysis of existing data are all used in various ways. Each of these techniques will now be discussed, but first, it is helpful to categorise each approach as being either quantitative or qualitative in nature.

Qualitative versus quantitative research – what's best?

Qualitative research is scarce in finance and less frequently used in accounting than other social sciences such as politics, philosophy or sociology, where the approach originated. In many ways, that it is so little used is a considerable loss to scholarship in our subject since it can generate richer insights and answer numerous important questions that could not be addressed with a quantitative study.

In general, qualitative studies can be preferable where the researcher wishes to investigate why particular outcomes occurred related to people's behaviour, opinions or feelings. Such an approach is also useful where the study focuses on the interactions between people (e.g., are there leaders and followers on a trading floor, and what factors determine the group to which each person belongs?) Qualitative research can also be expedient to see how a process works in action (as opposed to how it should work in principle), particularly in a stressed environment. For instance, how does a firm react when it discovers an accounting fraud by its Chief Financial Officer?

All of the above situations have in common that the data and information needed to draw conclusions about the issues cannot be observed or recorded without explicitly asking the people involved what they think or observing them in the situation. Qualitative research also has the added benefit of flexibility as its relatively unstructured nature is amenable to modification on the go as the findings begin to emerge.

Objectivity is crucial to build into such investigations but challenging to achieve because of the researcher's perspective and preconceptions, and the scope that they have to design the methodological framework, establish the sample and set the questions in many different ways with little or no capacity for later replication.

Since it can be more time-consuming to gather the data for qualitative studies, which must usually be done manually, sample sizes tend to be small. Consequently, in some ways, the choice of qualitative versus quantitative research is one of depth versus breadth, i.e., between looking in detail at a small number of subjects versus examining a larger number but much less closely.

Perusing a cross-section of the research in contemporary accounting or finance, it is clear that most studies adopt a quantitative design involving either the empirical analysis of data or the construction of artificial data (simulation). In accounting research, there is more balance, but still, quantitative work dominates. Even if this will also be your chosen method, it is useful to be aware of the numerous other types of research available under the qualitative umbrella, such as case studies and interviews.

Both quantitative and qualitative methods each have their advantages and disadvantages, and these will now be discussed in turn, which should support readers in making an informed choice about the approach that is most appropriate for them to employ given their background, interests, and research objectives.

The disadvantages of quantitative research

Qualitative research is sometimes chosen over more technical approaches because the researcher is concerned about the limitations of the statistical analysis of data, which include:

- Quantitative research can confuse correlation and causality – just because two variables change together does not mean that one causes the other since, in reality, it could be that a third variable causes changes in both. This is a hard issue to address
- Quantitative research neglects the context in which data are measured and assumes that all measurements of a given variable are equal

- Empirical work is usually conducted in the context of real data, and thus, the investigator will have little control over the quantity or quality of information available or the scope of the variables
- Some concepts are very hard to measure objectively at arm's length (such as expectations, beliefs, or emotions). Yet these variables are crucial in underpinning many theories in accounting and finance
- Long lists of assumptions may be required – either implicit or explicit – and these could be pivotal. The assumptions are essential to conduct the analysis but slight changes in them may lead to big variations in the results
- Quantitative research is not genuinely value-free as is sometimes claimed because the research is conducted by investigators who will have their own preconceptions and biases that will influence their research design, methods, data and interpretations of the results
- The quantitative approach encourages researchers to focus on the details at the expense of a bigger picture, meaning that it may give precise answers to trivial questions but maybe unable to provide solutions to the most fundamental problems
- The research design is rather fixed, and this can diminish the opportunities for a bigger intellectual contribution and a fundamental shift in the way people think about a particular phenomenon. It is too easy for quantitative researchers to switch into autopilot mode and follow down a well trodden path to produce incremental research that makes at best a small contribution

The advantages of quantitative research

Quantitative research usually involves developing an empirical model that links a dependent or explained variable with one or more independent or explanatory variables. This approach embodies several advantages compared with qualitative research:

- The data can be analysed formally with statistics, and the results are usually more generalisable since they are not context-specific
- Related to the previous point, the findings can be compared more readily across countries or over time
- It is possible to produce precise, numerical descriptions of the relationships between variables and also accurate forecasts about plausible future values of a variable
- It should be relatively straightforward for other researchers to replicate what a given study has done, thus validating the results
- The findings are less likely to be affected by the views or approach of the investigator than qualitative studies, and thus there is less scope for biases to creep in

If you are using a quantitative method, it is probably just a question of pushing your knowledge boundaries further in implementing a model or technique that you have not used before. It is then a matter of understanding how the model works at a conceptual level, how to implement the model using software, and how to interpret and check the output's validity.

The range of possible quantitative techniques is vast, but fortunately, there are many resources available, including numerous excellent textbooks. Still, as you would expect, I recommend my own, Introductory Econometrics for Finance (IEfF), Brooks (2019), available from the publisher and in e-book format from Amazon and Apple.[1] I also co-authored software guides to accompany the textbook for Python, R, Stata and EViews – these can be downloaded in pdf format from my page at SSRN,[2] or in Mobi or Epub formats from Amazon and Apple Books, respectively – the software guides can be downloaded free of charge on all platforms.

Although IEfF was written primarily with finance students in mind, most of the material presented is also relevant for the statistical analysis of accounting-related data. In addition to the software guides, a substantial volume of other free resources is available to accompany IEfF from the publisher's website, including answers to end of chapter questions, an electronic glossary, a self-study multiple choice question bank and video lectures.

Quantitative work is usually associated with 'the scientific method' for conceptualising and understanding a problem. It involves establishing a theory or a set of testable hypotheses that are then transformed into an empirical model that can be estimated using statistical software. Next, a relevant dataset is collected and analysed using quantitative models, and the hypotheses are either supported or refuted by the data and appropriate conclusions drawn. The process operates according to the flowchart in Figure 8.1, taken from Brooks (2019).

8.2.4 The role of hypotheses in research

A hypothesis is a statement that is specified and then test using data. In essence, it is simply a well-informed guess (based on theory or prior knowledge) about what will happen in a particular situation and why. Note that the part in parentheses is essential – the hypothesis has to be grounded within the knowledge base and not just a randomly generated suggestion.

More formally, a hypothesis could be defined as a proposition that arises from your theoretical or conceptual model, but it may or may not be correct. By definition, if you knew that the hypothesis was correct before you tested it, there would be no point in proceeding, and it would instead be a law or generally accepted principle, not a hypothesis. Hence a hypothesis should not be so broad or obviously correct (or incorrect) that it is not interesting to test, and knowing the result of the hypothesis test should be relevant and useful to other people for it to be worthwhile.

Like good research questions, effective hypotheses should be sufficiently involved that they cannot be answered by looking at figures that could be obtained

---

[1] https://www.cambridge.org/gb/academic/subjects/economics/finance/introductory-econometrics-finance-4th-edition?format=PB

[2] https://papers.ssrn.com/sol3/cf_dev/AbsByAuth.cfm?per_id=14685

Figure 8.1: Steps in the quantitative approach to research

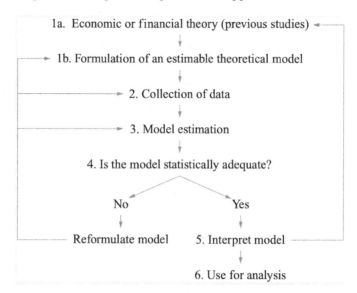

from the internet, which is why incorporating causality into hypotheses based on specific, pre-defined variables can be worthwhile. For instance, the hypothesis:

'H1: people in the public sector save more for their pensions than those in the private sector'

would not be very interesting because a quick use of a search engine would reveal the answer. But if this was specified with some possible reasoning as:

'H2: people in the public sector save more for their pensions because their schemes are more generous, they can take the benefits sooner, and they are on average older than those in the private sector'

then it would be more exciting. This would probably be best split into three separate sub-hypotheses, none of which has an immediately obvious answer. You probably couldn't tackle this without conducting a survey or interviews as the information would not already be available, and the data you would obtain could be examined using several different techniques, including, if you wished, a formal statistical analysis.

Falsifying hypotheses

The Austrian philosopher Karl Popper (1959) argued that hypotheses should also be falsifiable. In other words, if the hypothesis is wrong, the testing method should be designed to be able to reject it. If a researcher is unable to refute the hypothesis, then it is supported by the data. Even if a scientific statement passes every attempt to refute it, it can still never be proved correct or definitively accepted as true. But only one piece of evidence against a hypothesis or theory is sufficient for it to be rejected. Popper gave the example of the hypothesis, 'all swans are white': even if there are vast numbers of only white swans on a particular lake, this does not prove the hypothesis correct. But a sighting of only one black swan is required to prove it false. Consequently, hypotheses are either rejected or not rejected by the data, and just as in classical statistics, they are never accepted. If a hypothesis or theory is falsified (i.e., proved to be wrong), it could be modified and retested or rejected entirely.

However, we also need to remember that, unfortunately, because no testing framework is entirely accurate, is it even possible to reject a correct theory, which is analogous to a Type I error in statistics. Therefore, just because we find evidence against a theory, it could still be right, and if we find evidence in favour of a theory, it could still be wrong! While researchers always try to set up the testing framework to minimise the chances of both types of error as much as possible, there is a trade-off: making the rule for rejecting a hypothesis more strict means that the probability of incorrectly rejecting a correct null is reduced but the probability of incorrectly not rejecting a wrong null is increased. The way to reduce the probabilities of both types of error is to improve the size and quality of the sample. This is why repeated investigations of a given research problem using different techniques and in various settings are so valuable.

Popper argued that it is the possibility that an assertion can be falsified that sets science apart from non-science, and any hypothesis or theory that is not open to being refuted is not scientific. A hypothesis must be sufficiently explicit (i.e., not vague) that it is testable – i.e., it needs to be set up in such a fashion that it can be demonstrated to be wrong if it is so. In other words, hypotheses should be as tightly defined as possible, which makes them more testable.

In this vein, we could perhaps argue, for instance, that the efficient markets hypothesis is a scientific theory since it is possible to test and refute it (which it has been in a vast number of studies), but many concepts in behavioural finance are not. To illustrate, if we find that investors update their beliefs too quickly in the light of new information, we might argue that they suffer from recency bias; if they are too slow to update their beliefs, then they suffer from anchoring bias. Hence, either way, we could argue that they suffer from behavioural biases when they form their beliefs about future price movements with no way to demonstrate that they do not. Therefore, when considered in this way, the behavioural finance explanation is not falsifiable unless the hypothesis is set up to specify precisely which bias is being tested.

How to establish meaningful hypotheses

Hypotheses need to be precisely written to be testable, and they need to convey something beyond what is already known. For example, consider the hypothesis:

'H1: Men and women have different degrees of risk tolerance'.

This hypothesis would not be useful since it is too vague. In particular, it does not state whether men's or women's tolerances are expected to be higher, and it does not specify the domain (finances, driving, job choices, sports, etc.) or the cause.Replacing the hypothesis above with:

'H2: Men are more financially risk-tolerant than women'

would resolve some of the issues, but it would still not be a strong statement since this issue has been investigated very many times before, and so the findings are already widely available in the literature. A hypothesis:

'H3: Men are more financially risk-tolerant because they are more confident than women'

would tick all the boxes. This hypothesis is not only written in a precise and testable language, but also the added clause would relate to a new and exciting question where there is some existing work, but it is still an open area where research has yet to reach a firm conclusion.

Hypotheses, research aims and research questions

Returning to the point made above about different means to express the research problem, it is worth noting that H3 could alternatively be written in other ways. The general research problem could be written as:

'it has been observed in numerous studies that men tend to be more financially risk- tolerant than women. A range of explanations for this phenomenon has been proposed, with one idea focusing on differences in their average levels of confidence.'

This statement then leads to two alternative ways to write this problem as an aim or as a question:

- As a research aim – e.g., 'I aim to investigate whether men are more financially risk-tolerant because they are more confident than women;'
- Or as a research question – e.g., 'Are men more financially risk-tolerant because they are more confident than women?'

These three approaches (research hypotheses, research aims, and research questions) are equivalent, but some researchers prefer not to state hypotheses explicitly, and the style varies somewhat from one field to another. Most fields within management seem to like the use of hypotheses, but in accounting and finance, the convention is mostly to write research problems in the form of aims or questions. This style is more useful if your research is somewhat exploratory, and it is not possible to express your ideas as formally as a hypothesis, although the advantage of hypotheses is that they limit the scope for excessively vague ideas to be included. Questions including 'why' can be too vague to be testable, but conveniently they cannot usually be formulated into a hypothesis. Returning to the previous example to illustrate this, we might have asked:

'why are women less risk-tolerant than men?'

This would take us back to H2, which was deemed not to be sufficiently precise.

The hypothesis, stated aim or research question needs to cover all contexts rather than being specific to the sample you are investigating. For instance, it might be that you are exploring the final hypothesis, H3, listed above using a selection of undergraduate students at your university. But even though your data are limited to that group, your hypothesis would relate to all men and women, not just students. However, you might need to justify why you believe that the results are generalisable from your specific sample.

Notice a distinction in style between the hypotheses as they are constructed here compared with those specified in statistics and econometrics. In the latter cases, there is a formal approach where there are null and alternative hypotheses, specified using an equality and an inequality, respectively. In accounting and finance research studies and other branches of business and management, these statements would generally be set up somewhat less formally as individual hypotheses rather than pairs, with no null or alternative, but instead, a single statement expressed in words.

8.3   The role of theory in dissertations

The word 'theory' is used in various contexts and to capture something at different levels of abstraction. As a basic working definition, we could think of a theory as a statement or set of statements that embody several ideas about how something operates or what causes a particular phenomenon. Theories are usually ideas that link concepts together, embodying one or more hypotheses. For positivists, theory is the key to explaining causal relationships and making predictions. On the other hand, for interpretivists, theories are not tested using data; rather, they are constructed after fieldwork.

In finance, the term theory is used confusingly on many different levels, so it is crucial to explain precisely which theories you are referring to. The word is employed both loosely to talk about a general set of ideas before empirical implementation and formally to define precise notions of why specific groups of individuals behave in a certain way in a given situation. For instance, signalling theory (where one party in a transaction or negotiation has better information than the other, and so provides a signal to convey that information) is one aspect of capital structure theory (which refers to the way that firms select combinations of equity, bonds and loans in their project financing mix).

Theories can also be classified as being either positive or normative: positive theories dispassionately relate to the facts of what is happening without passing judgement, whereas normative theories embody a set of values or moral judgements about what is right or wrong (in other words, how things should be).

Unlike a 'law', which is a statement that scholars generally accept to be true, 'theories', 'models', and 'hypotheses' may or may not be true, which is why they must be subject to testing and then tentatively rejected or supported by the data. If the data refute the theory, it needs to be modified or replaced and then subjected to further testing, although this sort of iterative process does not strictly follow the positivist tradition that the theory must come first. In practice, however, many (perhaps the majority of) researchers engage in what might be termed 'post hoc rationalisations of their empirical findings' where they estimate an empirical model, see what the data are telling them, and then try to identify an 'off-the-shelf' theory that is consistent with what they observe from that data. But when they write up the theory and methods, they do so as if they had proposed the theory first, which then miraculously works when they test it empirically.

Perhaps an advantage of the grounded theory approach discussed in chapter 1 is that it explicitly acknowledges that theory can be developed after observing the data. A further problem with the scientific method is that rigid, pre-conceived ideas from an existing theory about the relationship between variables can narrow the research agenda's scope from the outset.

Why theory is needed

It is, of course, possible to conduct research without having a theory, but arguably such research is purely exploratory, it would lack a framework or structure, and some scholars might argue that any findings emerging from such research are not rigorous and could be statistical flukes that are specific to that sample and context. In essence, they might state, the conclusions are the result of data mining.

While the empirical analysis of secondary data is by far the most common type of method employed in our field, good research is rarely purely empirical. The empirical model should arise from an accounting, economic or financial theory, and this theory should be presented and discussed before the investigative work begins. Theory shows what features in the data and what relationships would be expected based on some underlying principles. Theory can give order to empirical results and ensure that the findings are not the result of a data-mining exercise.

Although theory strengthens and adds depth to empirical work, it is important to note that theory should only be used when it is useful and relevant. If an inappropriate theory is 'bolted on' to investigative work, the theory would detract from it. The theory and empirics need to complement each other, else it will cause confusion since the theory should allow the investigator to step back and put the empirical findings into a wider context. If theory is not a useful tool, it should not be included.

Characteristics of a good theory

Ideally, good theories should embody the following characteristics:
- Theories are usually deliberately broad and high-level, abstracting from most of the specific details, and hence they are often called 'theoretical frameworks' or 'underpinning theory'
- Following from the previous point, a theory should not attempt to explain everything and should be capable of being specified in at most a few short statements. In other words, it should embody the concept of parsimony, explaining as much as possible while remaining compact
- A useful theory will be generalisable and predictive, so it should enable the researcher to determine what is likely to happen in a given set of circumstances. It should also be capable of being used in different contexts to the one where it was developed

- Following from the previous point, a theory needs to be abstract enough to generalise the research findings, but not so abstract that it has no practical applicability

Theory relates to what a researcher expects to find *ex ante*, rather than what they actually do find *ex post*, and theories should be independent of the data they are designed to model, not developed after looking at the outcomes (except for grounded theories – see chapter 1). The theory should lead naturally to the methods and data selection, and it has no value if it does not link with the empirical aspects of the work.

Some researchers have argued that theory is not useful since it is implausible that people making decisions will be aware of it, let alone understand it. Therefore, such a perspective would argue, how could decision-makers follow theory? However, the economist Milton Friedman (1953) argued that it does not matter whether agents are aware of the relevant theory, the only relevant question is whether they behave as if they followed the model, and if they do, then the theory is worthwhile. Friedman provided the analogy of billiards players who perform as if they have employed mathematical models to work out the correct trajectory and force to apply for a shot even though they might have had no training in physics. Consequently, so long as people end up behaving in the same way as a theory describes, then it is useful even if they get to that behaviour through a different path. Moreover, according to Friedman, 'descriptively inaccurate' theories are perfectly adequate so long as they are 'analytically relevant' (i.e., they still work in predicting outcomes).

8.3.1 Where do theories come from?

Researchers usually develop theories from first principles based on a consideration of why and how relevant individuals (sometimes known as 'agents' in this context) make choices, given the information and knowledge that those decision-makers have and what they aim to achieve. Theories can also arise from the expected outcomes from interactions between groups of agents – for example, different groups of stakeholders within a firm (shareholders, customers, employees, the government or regulators, etc.).

Often, to operationalise a theory and to predict or mathematically model the outcome will require a set of assumptions to be made since, without them, the model is intractable and therefore of no use. In other words, the model could not be solved, either mathematically or in a more informal sense, so that it would not be possible to determine the expected outcome. Many such models in accounting and finance are based on economic principles. Therefore, the assumptions usually revolve around matters such as rational agents (always preferring more to less, and only taking risks if there is sufficient reward) or markets being frictionless (no taxes, freedom to buy and sell in any quantity, and so on).

It is also clear that theories will often incorporate concepts from psychology or sociology since people rather than machines ultimately make the decisions. Hence, the role of personality, emotions, biased expectations or inaccurate forecasts of risks or payoffs for individuals are built into theories of how people behave. Also relevant are the interactions between people when they operate in groups (such as the effects of herding or information cascades), which affect their decisions and, therefore, the outcomes.

Numerous studies in finance, in particular, develop their theoretical frameworks into a set of mathematical equations that are then solved to determine the outcome. So we can think of a model being that aspect of a theory that is expressed mathematically. The model's solution can be obtained either by algebraic substitution and rearrangement of the equations (a so-called 'analytical solution') or, if the problem is too complex to disentangle algebraically, by simulating the model with artificially generated data to determine the expected outcome conditional on the assumptions made.

However, theoretical models don't need to be set up formally as equations, and they can remain at a more intangible level, with the outcomes determined using logical arguments in words rather than numbers. This approach is more likely to be used in accounting and most other branches of management – for example, in marketing or strategy. In such cases, authors sometimes refer to their collection of interlinked ideas as a 'conceptual model' or 'conceptual framework'. The concepts can be based on variables that can be observed or measured (such as risk aversion, wealth, auditor independence, etc.) or they can be abstract notions such as utility.

The difference between a concept and a theory

Although the terms theory and concept are related, they are often used as if they are interchangeable, but in reality, there is a subtle distinction between them. A concept is more of an abstract idea and is not necessarily testable, whereas a theory is usually thought of as more formal, testable and scientific. Theories are built up from concepts, but both should only be employed if they are useful, and they are tentative, so they might be incorrect.

A conceptual framework arises when several concepts are brought together and linked in some way. For example, there could be a causal relationship between several variables (e.g., 'if X1 and X2 both happen, it will cause Y to occur'). The causality could be in one direction, or there could be feedback so that changes in Y then lead subsequently to shifts in X1 or X2. A theoretical framework will be more formal than a conceptual framework and based on a model of how and why specific variables interact arising from first principles of decision-making. Both conceptual and theoretical models abstract from reality with the aim to simplify rather than explain everything.

As should be clear from the discussion above, the term theory can mean very diverse things to different groups of researchers. Here are two examples of recent research that I co-authored, and that used very different kinds of theories from sociology and psychology to underpin empirical studies in finance.

1. The paper by Brooks *et al.* (2019) mentioned in chapter 4 sought to explain

why academic finance had grown and remained so strong despite being so little used to influence policy or practice in the financial services sector. A conceptual framework due to the French sociologist Pierre Bourdieu was employed to argue that scholars of finance obtain their sense of worth and the capital that they possess from metrics generated within universities including the recognition of their peers through publication in top journals. Therefore, conducting research with practical value is, in most cases, not something that matters to them.

2. In an entirely different recent study, Hillenbrand *et al.* (2021), we were interested in examining the impact of retail investor characteristics, their emotional states and their attitudes towards finance on the kind of investment products they were most attracted to. Specifically, we aimed to determine the factors that affected whether they were more likely to select short- or long-term investments and those that focused on protecting the value of the capital versus a type having more growth potential.

To develop the hypotheses in Hillenbrand et al. (*op. cit.*), we relied upon the theory of construal level from psychology, which explains how investors will determine their inter-temporal discount rates when they compare an object to be received soon with the same one to be obtained further into the future. We also used regulatory focus theory, which relates to how people make decisions to attain their goals. Applying these two sets of established theoretical frameworks and their interaction allowed us to develop our hypotheses.

We found that adverts for short-term products with growth potential attracted sensation-seeking investors who were highly risk-tolerant, and people with positive emotions towards finance were drawn to products that were focused on the preservation of capital rather than growth, while those with negative emotions were more prone to short-termism.

Developing a new theory involves an in-depth examination of a particular phenomenon, market, type of firm, or behaviour with a view to establishing a causal framework that could explain how or why specific outcomes occurred. The theoretical model developed could be testable or untestable. A testable model would be one where the necessary information can be observed or collected, and a statistical framework used to show whether the theoretical model is supported or refuted by the data. The development of a solid, well-reasoned theoretical framework is a substantial undertaking, especially if it is highly novel, and so it would probably not be necessary to empirically test the model in the same research project, although it would add strength if the work did both.

A model might be untestable because its concepts are too high-level and so are not observable. However, this sort of model might still help researchers organise their thoughts into a framework and conduct a counterfactual analysis ('if X were to happen, what would be the impact on Y'?)

Although most dissertations will not propose or develop new theories since to do so would require specialist skills that generally take many years to hone, they will use theory to underpin any empirical work and make sense of the findings. The careful use of theory will considerably strengthen a research project and should be utilised to underpin the research hypotheses or questions. When the data are analysed, you can then return to the theory and explain whether it is supported by your findings or refuted. Could the theory be modified to make it fit your data better, and if so, how?

If you have a conceptual or theoretical framework, it makes the process of data collection and analysis more straightforward because the framework will inform which variables you need to measure, how, and why. Theory is the backbone of empirical investigations, and its absence can leave a study looking weak. It allows the researcher to make predictions about what the relationships between variables will or will not be. If there is no theory, a researcher can simply experiment with large numbers of candidate variables until several statistically significant coefficient estimates are found. Any relationships found this way without recourse to theory could be entirely spurious and the result of data mining, which is sometimes termed a 'fishing exercise' where you would dip your finishing rod into the river with no idea what kind of fish you might pull out.

8.3.2   Examples of relevant theories

Many established theoretical frameworks underpinning recent empirical investigations have been around for a long time. Each field (including finance, accounting, sociology, psychology, and economics) has its own theories, with differences in how they are specified and tested. But there is also a considerable degree of cross-fertilisation, with some fields borrowing theories from others. In particular, since accounting and finance are social sciences where decisions are ultimately made by people, theories that originated in psychology and sociology are widely adopted to account for how individuals make choices either individually (psychology) or within the context of group interactions and dynamics incorporating the influences of others (sociology).

The lists below provide a few examples of some fundamental theories that have been developed and widely implemented in each field (accounting, economics, finance, management, psychology, sociology and politics), alongside brief definitions or explanations in each case. However, merely a handful of illustrations are presented to give some ideas and the lists are by no means exhaustive since for all of these fields there are very many other examples that could have been provided. These are, in some cases, the 'highest level' grand theories that cover many situations and aspects of behaviour and hence are harder to isolate and test than narrower theories. The theories presented from the fields of psychology, sociology and politics focus on the ideas of most relevance to accounting and finance.

It is worth noting that which field's researchers developed a particular theory might be contested – for instance, when psychologists lay claim to having developed an idea that is also employed (perhaps under a different name) by sociologists.

Accounting, in particular, is short on theories developed within the field and has adopted many from other disciplines. Researchers sometimes appeal to more than one theory, or they combine theories to explain a particular phenomenon.

I have not provided any references or suggested further reading in this section as there are simply too many for that to be useful, and each researcher needs to select a relevant theory given the nature of the problem they are investigating.

Accounting
- Residual theory of dividends – argues that firms should continue to invest in any projects with positive net present value and only distribute funds as dividends once such project possibilities have been exhausted.
- Behavioural accounting theory – considers the impact of psychological factors, including personality and emotions, on the interpretation of accounting information and accounting decisions.
- Positive accounting theory – a very high level, all-embracing set of principles that has been variously interpreted as corresponding to the use of positivist, scientific principles to study accounting issues by some authors and interpreted by other writers as relating to how corporate accountants determine their firm's accounting policies and how they respond to changes in externally imposed standards.
- Structuration theory – originated in sociology but is now widely applied in management accounting to analyse accounting frameworks, recognising the importance of social systems and social structures, also considering the impact that accounting systems can have on organisational development.
- Legitimacy theory – relates to the notion that a firm has a 'social contract' with its stakeholders, is expected to act in certain ways that conform with ethical norms and principles, and that fulfilling this wider role provides the company with the credibility to conduct its core business.

Economics
- Expected utility theory – where people make the choices that will maximise the expected utility of the decision (where they weight the outcomes by the probabilities that each will occur).
- Theory of optimal taxation – the notion that taxes should be set (in terms of their level and coverage) to maximise societal welfare, causing the least possible distortion in economic activity.
- Theory of information asymmetry – this relates to how people behave when one party in a transaction has much more information about the situation than the other. For example, in the 'market for lemons', George Akerlof explained how markets could fail in the context where a car seller has much more information about its condition than the buyer so that only poor-quality cars ('lemons') will have a market.
- Theory of comparative advantage – countries specialise in producing goods

and services where their production costs (measured in terms of opportunity cost) are lower.
- New growth theory – argues that by the process of consumption and investment to fulfil their wants and needs, individual actions will lead to economic growth over time. It emphasises the importance of knowledge and information in driving rises in gross domestic product.
- The classical theory of central bank lending – central banks should act as lender of the last resort and always provide liquidity to the banking system in times of stress but at high rates of interest where appropriate, and insolvent banks ought to be left to fail rather than bailed out.

Finance
- Greater fool theory – linked with speculative bubbles, this idea explains why people buy assets even when they know the prices are too high (i.e., the securities are over-valued) because they believe that a 'greater fool' will purchase the asset from them at an even higher price in the future.
- The theory of capital structure irrelevance – the idea that corporate financing (i.e., how firms finance expansion via retained cash, bond or stock issue) and dividend decisions do not affect firm value since investors could generate the same impacts themselves through the combinations of assets they buy and sell.
- Efficient market theory – that securities' prices will fully and immediately encompass the effects of all available and relevant information.
- Short interest theory – the counter-intuitive notion that the prices of stocks having a large volume of short sales are expected to rise since, at some point, these short positions will have to be covered by purchasing the shares, which will cause net buying pressure.

Management
- Stakeholder theory – a perspective on how firms will operate based on the notion that they will make decisions that benefit all the agents whom the firm interacts with, including customers, workers, and the government, rather than just maximising profits for shareholders.
- Agency theory – describes the interactions between the principal in a firm (i.e., its owners or shareholders) and the agents (managers), who will act in a self-interested way that can lead to conflicts of interest and may not maximise value for owners.
- Stewardship theory – the idea that corporate managers will primarily aim to serve the best interests of the organisation for which they work rather than acting for their own personal gain since they feel a sense of responsibility and professional pride. The predictions from this theory go against those from agency theory.
- Resource dependency theory – suggests that a firm will have dependencies on others due to its requirement for raw materials and further inputs, and equally,

there may also exist firms that depend on it. Therefore, having control over its resources gives a firm power.

Psychology

- Cognitive theory – argues that decisions are based on the way people process information and form their beliefs, which is in turn related to memory, attention and perceptions.
- Prospect theory – when making financial decisions, people do not maximise expected utility but instead exhibit loss aversion due to asymmetries in their utility functions. These arise because people feel the pain of a given monetary loss more than they feel the pleasure from an equal amount of gain.
- The ripple effect theory – moods are contagious within groups, so spending a great deal of time among people in a negative mind state will encourage an individual to develop such negative feelings.
- The theory of offsetting behaviour – embodies people's tendency to take greater risks when in a safer environment. For instance, drivers tend to be more aggressive when wearing a seatbelt, and children take more risks when playing near a river if they can swim. Hence their modified behaviour offsets the risk reductions in other aspects of their environments.
- The theory of multiple intelligences – the notion that people have several different 'intelligences' so individuals are good at particular tasks depending on which intelligence they are stronger in, including linguistic, musical, spatial, and mathematical.
- The theory of planned behaviour – suggests that a person's behaviour depends on three aspects: their attitude to this action, the view of others regarding it, and the extent to which the individual believes they can control it. According to the first of these, the person is more likely to go ahead and do something if they view it positively, i.e., they believe it will benefit them. Second, the person is more likely to take this action if the people in their social circle view it positively. Third, if the person believes they have the skills and ability to do something, they are more likely to do it.

Sociology and politics

- Symbolic interaction theory – people use labels (i.e., language) to make sense of the social world, which exists only through those individuals' actions and perceptions. The experiences that people have with particular entities (both people and objects) will modify what the words attached to the entities mean to them.
- Conflict theory – argues that the world is permanently in a state of conflict because resources are limited. Those with wealth develop the means to hold onto it through the exercise of domination and power over others.
- Labelling theory – people act according to the way that they have been labelled. For instance, if someone is branded a criminal, they are more likely to behave

in that way. Deviance from social norms occurs not as a result of an individual's behaviour but rather as a result of the label that is attached to their behaviour by others defining it as a deviant action.

- Social learning theory – people learn via observing others in action, identifying their behaviour and imitating it, and seeing whether these behaviours yield good or bad consequences and are either reinforced or frowned upon by others.
- Public choice theory – covers many ideas relating to how those in the public sector make decisions on behalf of the general population, often in a self-interested manner that focuses on the former's utility rather than the latter's.

Further reading

- Many books have been written on research methods in general, and one of the most relevant is by Creswell and Creswell (2018)
- There are also two good books explicitly aimed at research methods in accounting or finance: Paterson *et al.* (2016) and Smith (2020)
- There was not sufficient space in this book to cover either qualitative or quantitative methods at great length, and therefore readers might wish to consult more detailed treatments. For books that cover a range of qualitative techniques, I suggest Hinnink *et al.* (2020) or Ritchie *et al.* (2013). My own textbook, Brooks (2019), covers a wide range of quantitative techniques
- Each of the major categories of research methods also has several specialist texts that are worth considering once you have selected the approach you will use, including Yin (2018) on case study methods, Fink (2016) or Fowler (2013) on surveys, and Cassell (2015) on interviews

Chapter takeaways – top tips for success

- ⊛ Be aware of the wide range of research methods available to you, noting their strengths and weaknesses, and in particular how much time each would take to implement
- ⊛ Your dissertation should state clear research aims, hypotheses or questions and you should address each of them in your analysis
- ⊛ The research methods must match your aims and objectives
- ⊛ If you opt to use an approach that is unfamiliar to you, seek appropriate training through courses or self-study
- ⊛ Ensure that your dissertation integrates a conceptual framework or an appropriate theory to underpin your investigative research. The theory could come from economics, psychology or sociology as well as from accounting or finance themselves

9. DATA COLLECTION & ANALYSIS

Learning outcomes: this chapter covers

- ✓ The differences between primary and secondary data
- ✓ What a sample is and different sampling techniques
- ✓ How to choose the software for quantitative data analysis
- ✓ How to run a survey
- ✓ How to conduct an interview
- ✓ How to validate your data

9.1 Approaches to investigative work

An array of methods is available to students when conducting the investigative parts of their projects in accounting and finance in order to collect and analyse the data. This section will discuss these various methods below, including an empirical analysis of downloaded data, conducting a survey or interviews, or developing case studies.

Whatever method you choose, it is essential to clearly explain the methods you are using to inspire confidence in readers that the techniques are appropriate and that you know what you are doing - if not, the results could be considered worthless. In particular, since the vast majority of student research projects are empirical, involving gathering and analysing data, you will probably need to think about the following questions if you have not already had to do so when you wrote the proposal:

- What data will you collect?
- From where will the data be obtained?
- Why is this the relevant data to address your research aims?
- How will you analyse the data, and what do you expect the analysis to show?

Wherever your data arise from – surveys, archives, or databases, and even if your aims involve estimating complex econometric models, ensure that you begin with rudimentary analysis. Always plot the data (where feasible) and present summary statistics and simple correlations between the variables. This will help you build the more complex models effectively and allow a sense check of the data's quality. It will also enable you to sharpen your research questions or hypotheses and gently lead the reader into the more in-depth analysis that follows. Qualitative studies, however, will usually have few tables or charts, if any, which will be limited to basic summary measures and hence the presentation of the findings will be all about the narrative.

A large amount of useful information can always be gleaned from simple means, variances, plots over time, and so on. However, while including summary information is vital, try to avoid swamping the reader with endless tables, and unless the sample is tiny, do not paste the raw data into the dissertation, even in an appendix. It will take a vast amount of space, yet it is unlikely that anyone will look at it.

9.2   Primary versus secondary data sources

9.2.1   The difference between primary and secondary data

It is surprisingly tricky to define primary and secondary data precisely, but we can think of the former as applying anywhere that new information is created for the first time – for example, through interviews or surveys, while the latter occurs when existing information is reused or re-interpreted.

Collecting primary data is an essential component of conducting a research project in some disciplines such as many of the sciences and some social sciences, including psychology. Still, in accounting and finance, it is usually optional and rare given the widespread availability of extensive off-the-shelf databases and the speed with which they can be put to use. Therefore, rather than using surveys, interviews or experiments using the techniques discussed above, most students will download their data from an established source.

Advantages of primary over secondary data

Primary data collection has several advantages:

- A range of techniques is available, including web-based surveys, which could allow you to gather a sample of comparable size to secondary sources but on a more diverse range of topics
- It allows you complete flexibility over what you study since you are in control and creating the data rather than relying on the choices that someone else has previously made

- Secondary data sources will not have been set up with your research aims in mind, and so it might be the case that you cannot obtain the information you need unless you create your own data
- Secondary databases can be used freely if your school subscribes to them, but if not, the access fee could be prohibitively expensive.

Disadvantages of primary over secondary data

There are, of course, also downsides to using primary, rather than secondary, data:

- Market-type finance and accounting questions can realistically only be addressed using an established secondary database. For example, anything to do with the prices, yields, volumes or volatilities of assets, unless you wanted to conduct a study in the context of an experimental or simulated market
- Collecting and organising primary data is likely to be much more time-consuming than using an off-the-shelf solution. Many students conclude that they simply don't have the scope to obtain primary data within the time available, and if they do, there is a danger that collection will take the time that should have been used in analysing the data
- Opting for primary data use runs more risk that something will go wrong, and the sample will be inadequate in some way; on the other hand, there is less scope for problems with secondary data
- Collecting primary data is usually only feasible in your own country, where you have contacts and expertise. Therefore, if you intend to study another country (either on its own or as part of an international sample), there is probably no chance to use primary data

9.3 Data Collection and sampling

Data collection will be a core activity in almost all dissertations. Collecting an appropriate volume of relevant data is vital for the successful completion of the project. If you have too much data (in terms of its breadth or when it requires considerable cleaning or pre-processing), it will be challenging to perform an in-depth analysis of it, with the danger that your investigation will be superficial and only skim over the surface. In this case, it might also be the case that the task of collecting and examining the information becomes overwhelming or impossible to do systematically.

On the other hand, if your data are insufficient, either in volume or scope, there is a risk that you will be unable to answer the research questions you have posed. In econometrics, we would say that the tests will lack power if the sample is insufficient, leading to the likelihood that no statistical tests result in significant parameters. This lack of power means that you will not be able to confirm any meaningful relationships between variables. As a consequence of these trade-offs, determining your precise data needs is crucial before diving in and collecting it.

9.3.1   Sampling from the population

A question that project students who are collecting data often ask is how large their sample should be. Before getting to that question, it is worth discussing what a sample is and the properties of a good sample. Brooks (2019, p.48) defines a population as 'the total collection of all objects to be studied. For example, in the context of determining the relationship between risk and return for UK stocks, the population of interest would be all time-series observations on all stocks traded on the London Stock Exchange,'

Similarly, if you were interested in gauging management accountants' opinions in UK manufacturing firms about whether offshoring to China is likely to continue, the population would be the set of all accountants working at all such manufacturing firms.

On the other hand, a sample is 'a selection of just some items from the population' (Brooks, *op. cit.*). Usually in statistics it is assumed that the sample is randomly selected so that each item from within the population has an equal chance of being drawn.

The reason for sampling is that it is usually infeasible to obtain the entire population of data because the data collection and analysis tasks would be too great. Instead, researchers obtain a sample and then use this to infer the likely characteristics of the whole population. There are various approaches to sampling available, as discussed below. But in almost all cases, the sample should be as large as possible because each sample observation represents a valuable piece of information that will allow the inferences to the true population values to be as reliable as possible. In statistics, this reliability is measured through standard errors, and everything else equal, the larger the sample, the smaller will be the standard errors, so the more likely it is that parameter estimates will be statistically significant.

There is never a minimum acceptable sample size, but instead, the results' reliability will gradually increase along with the sample size. The size required to achieve a given level of reliability will depend on the complexity of the relationships that the researcher is attempting to measure and the extent of variation in the sample. If all entities within the sample behave in roughly the same way, the required sample size will be smaller.

For example, suppose you were interested in measuring the average fee that a financial advisor would charge their client to advise on the age at which the latter could comfortably retire. If you took a sample of 15 advisors and they all charged fees within a narrow range, you would have a high level of confidence that the average you computed was fairly representative of all advisors.

But if your sample showed huge variations in the fees charged, your confidence level would be low, and you might need a much larger sample before you had faith in the average that you computed. Also, suppose that instead of just calculating the average fee, you wanted to build a model of the determinants of advisor fee levels as a function of the client's characteristics, the latter's wealth level and educational attainment, and the age and experience of the advisor. Then the additional parameters needing estimation would again imply that a much larger sample would be necessary for reliable results.

9.3.2 Choosing your sample

Whether you are engaged in primary or secondary data collection, it is worth defining your population at the outset and reflecting on the size and coverage of the sample you hope to obtain. Some discussion of these issues relating to surveys is given below, but they are still relevant if you download data from existing records through a provider such as Bloomberg.

Once you have identified the population, you need to establish the sampling frame, which defines how you will select the entities from within the population. If the data are secondary, the first choice, which should be made based on data availability and the requirements to answer your research questions, will be between time-series, cross-sectional or panel datasets. The secondary choice then concerns the coverage (geographical coverage, spanning which assets or markets, or time period, etc.)

Although, as stated above, the larger the sample, the better, there will no doubt be constraints that might either be in terms of the scope of the information covered in the database or the volume of data that you could process during the time you have available to complete the project. While it makes sense to download time-series going back as far as they are present on the system, you may not want to conduct the same analysis repeatedly for many countries as it would be repetitive unless that is an integral part of your research design.

Types of sampling

Random sampling is usually considered the best approach since, provided that the number of data points is sufficiently large, its properties will converge upon those of the underlying population, and hence the former can be used to make valid inferences about the latter. Sampling in a non-random fashion could lead to biases favouring one sub-group rather than another, thus breaking the link with the population characteristics. Random sampling is sometimes known as probability sampling because each entity within the population has an equal probability of being selected. To illustrate, suppose that we wanted to examine the impact of news wire announcements for a random sample of ten FTSE100 companies. It might not be possible to examine all 100 companies due to time constraints, but the ten selected would imply that each company has a 10% chance of being chosen.

A related possibility would be to use a stratified sampling technique, where the population would be separated into strata (layers) and random sampling takes place within each stratum. For instance, we could split the FTSE100 firms by size (say, small and large) and by sector (into five broad sectors), which would yield $2 \times 5 = 10$ categories, with one firm chosen from each. This would ensure that, despite the small sample, it would be more representative of the population of interest and would include an appropriate spread along the size and industrial classification dimensions.

However, in some instances, the bias from non-random sampling may be desirable and even necessary, in which case non-random or non-probability sampling would be implemented. Here, the sample would be selected to achieve a higher proportion of (or contain exclusively) individuals with particular features. For example, we might be interested in investigating whether people who get into extreme difficulties with their debts are more likely to have particular personality types compared to the rest of the population. But the proportion of the overall population that has got into severe debt management problems might be so low that a modest random sample would pick up just a tiny number of them or possibly none at all, in which case it would not be possible to conduct any valid quantitative analysis. In that case, we might prefer to systematically over-sample from that specific group.

In the case of qualitative research, there is often no interest in generalising the findings, but rather the purpose is simply to demonstrate how one particular instance works. Returning to a previous example, a researcher might be interested in writing a case study of a trader they know who was convicted of having illegally manipulated market prices for personal gain. In this instance, the focus could be on the individual's motivations, how they felt at the time, whether they feared being caught or losing money, how they hid their activities, and so on. There would probably be no attempt to suggest that the insights gained would apply to others engaged in market price distortion, let alone other types of traders. Therefore, the concepts of sampling, inference and populations usually have little relevance for qualitative research.

9.4   The empirical analysis of secondary data

This is by far the most common method used in accounting or finance research projects and allows the student to adopt a formulaic approach and write up the investigative work in the manner of a standard scientific paper. A dataset is downloaded from a third-party website, then the data are cleaned and organised, and some statistical models are estimated. The results are then presented in tables and graphs and discussed with appropriate conclusions drawn. This kind of project is arguably the lowest risk technique and allows the researcher to make quick progress with less scope for things to go badly wrong, which partly explains its popularity.

Data selection requires some careful thought. Sometimes, the precise nature of the data you need will be defined by your research questions, but often, you will have considerable flexibility to vary the context in which you study the phenomenon of interest. For example, if you were conducting a study of whether director share dealings had any predictive power for subsequent earnings announcements, this could be achieved using data from any one of a large number of countries. So which country will you select for analysis? If the database you have access to only covers one country, then the decision is made for you, but many electronic databases have at least some global coverage, leaving a wide array of options. One possibility would be to select a country (or other setting or market) that has not been covered before in the existing literature as a source of novelty for the project. Since most of the world's largest financial markets are in the US, this tends to be the first country where new models are applied. Alternatively, you could also select your home country, which could provide a competitive advantage if you have some location-specific knowledge that would not be widely available to researchers from other places.

9.4.1   Sources of secondary data

It is worth planning your analysis and carefully considering what you will do with your data before beginning the collection process. Sometimes your data will need to be downloaded from a system where you have restricted access (e.g., you have to book a slot in advance). If that is the case, make sure that you take everything that you might need when using the system as your opportunities for another dip later may be limited.

You will hopefully have access to a range of commercial databases through your university department (such as Reuters/Eikon/Datastream, Bloomberg, FAME, CRSP and Compustat, OptionMetrics, etc.), and if so, these will provide a rich resource amenable to a wide range of topics and approaches. These databases are so vast, each with a distinct user-interface, that it might require formal training or at least some time getting used to the interface before you can download the information you want. No further details are presented of these sources since, if your institution subscribes to them, full information will be available from there, and possibly free training on how to use the databases.

Many internet-based sources offer free data without registration, which might be your only option if your university does not subscribe to (often eye-wateringly expensive) commercial databases. Some useful links to free data on the internet include:

Financial Data
- Yahoo! Finance – an incredible range of free financial data, information, research and commentary[1]
- Ken French's data library – this contains the Fama-French factor data, mainly US-focused but also international factors[2]
- Robert Shiller's stock market confidence and cyclically adjusted price-earnings ratio data[3]
- An archive of US stock data from 2009-2017[4] and daily data on the VIX volatility index from 2004-2018[5]
- US and German annual company accounting data (income statements,

---

[1] https://finance.yahoo.com
[2] http://mba.tuck.dartmouth.edu/pages/faculty/ken.french/data_library.html
[3] http://www.econ.yale.edu/ shiller/data.htm
[4] https://github.com/eliangcs/pystock-data
[5] https://github.com/datasets/finance-vix/blob/master/data/vix-daily.csv

cashflow, share prices, etc.)[6]

<u>US-based data sources (mainly macroeconomics)</u>

- Federal Reserve Bank of Chicago – including interest data and useful links[7]
- Federal Reserve Bank of Dallas – including macroeconomic, interest rate, monetary and bank data[8]
- US Bureau of Labor Statistics – US macroeconomic series[9]
- US Federal Reserve Board – US macroeconomic series, exchange rates, interest rates, household finance series[10]
- FRED, the St. Louis Fed – a vast array of (three-quarters of a million) US and international macroeconomic series, even including cryptocurrency prices, available daily, weekly or monthly[11]
- All US Treasury – a wide range of US interest rate series[12]

<u>UK and other European macroeconomic data</u>

- The UK Treasury – a range of UK macroeconomic and other series[13]
- The Bank of England has several series, including exchange rates and yield curves[14]
- European macroeconomic data are available from the EU Open Data portal[15]
- UK house price series[16]

<u>Global macroeconomic data</u>

- The IMF[17]
- The World Bank[18]
- The Bank for International Settlements, which provides a range of macro-financial series sourced from the world's central banks, including data on exchange rates, debt securities, property prices, liquidity, and payment systems.[19]

---

[6]https://simfin.com

[7]https://www.chicagofed.org/research/data/index

[8]https://www.dallasfed.org/research.aspx

[9]https://www.bls.gov

[10]https://www.federalreserve.gov/econres.htm

[11]https://fred.stlouisfed.org

[12]https://www.treasury.gov/resource-center/data-chart-center/interest-rates/Pages/TextView.aspx?data=longtermrate

[13]https://www.gov.uk/search/research-and-statistics

[14]https://www.bankofengland.co.uk/statistics

[15]https://data.europa.eu/euodp/en/data/dataset?sort=views_total+desc&vocab_theme=http%3A%2F%2Fpublications.europa.eu%2Fresource%2Fauthority%2Fdata-theme%2FECON

[16]https://www.gov.uk/government/collections/uk-house-price-index-reports

[17]https://www.imf.org/en/

[18]https://data.worldbank.org

[19]https://www.bis.org/statistics/index.htm

If you have no choice but to use these, the range of topics you will be able to tackle will be severely constrained compared to the commercial databases, but nonetheless, it is possible to use them for good quality research, and they are sufficiently credible that the reliability of your findings will not be called into question. There are other, more dubious internet-based sources where, for example, illegal copies of commercial data have been uploaded, or the source of the information is unclear. But for precisely these reasons (illegality, and a lack of credibility and reliability), these are best avoided.

Many of the URLs listed above include extensive databases, and furthermore, many markets and exchanges have their own web pages detailing data availability. However, one needs to be slightly careful to ensure the accuracy of freely available data; 'free' data also sometimes turn out not to be.

Do not be afraid to send established researchers an e-mail if they have used specialist data or they have written some code that would be of value to your project. If the information has a commercial origin (e.g., the researcher's university has purchased it), then it is unlikely that the terms of their licence would enable the data to be sent to you. Academics are also keen to hold on for some time to information that they have collected if they intend to continue to publish from it, to avoid other researchers being able to free-ride from their initial efforts to get research on the same topic out quicker. But aside from these situations, scholars are often happy to share their data and code for others to use, especially research students and early career researchers – after all, that is an important aspect of why they chose a university career.

9.4.2 Choosing the software for quantitative analysis

If you are conducting quantitative analysis using secondary data, you will need to use a package to do the computations. Selecting the appropriate software to analyse the data is a significant decision since it will affect how you are able to conduct the investigation and how long it will take. If you intend to conduct only straightforward analyses of your data, such as constructing summary statistics (means, standard deviations), cross-tabulations, correlations, etc., or standard linear regressions, you may find it easier just to use a spreadsheet such as Microsoft Excel.

However, for more sophisticated analysis, including specialist econometric models, it will be preferable to use a statistical software package. Although a wide range of such packages exists, the quickest way to make progress will be to stick with the package you have been taught as part of the quantitative methods module(s) on your degree programme. If you have not received any such training before, identify the packages that are available to you free of charge as a result of your university's site licences. If you have to purchase a commercial package licence, it will likely cost several hundred pounds (although some suppliers offer student versions at a substantial discount).

Clearly, the choice of computer software will depend on the tasks at hand.

Projects that seek to offer opinions, synthesise the literature, and provide a review may not require any specialist software. However, even for those conducting highly technical research, project students rarely have the time to learn an entirely new programming language from scratch while conducting the research. Therefore, it is usually advisable, if possible, to use a standard software package. It is also worth stating that marks will hardly ever be awarded for students who 'reinvent the wheel'. Therefore, learning to program a multivariate extreme value model estimation routine in C++ may be a valuable exercise for career development for those who wish to be quantitative researchers but is unlikely to attract high marks as part of a research project unless there is some other value added. The best approach is usually to conduct the estimation as quickly and accurately as possible to leave time free for other parts of the work. Table 9.1 provides details of some of the packages on offer and their advantages and disadvantages.

It is unlikely that you will need a relational database package such as Microsoft Access given the dissertation's scale and scope unless the data originate in Access format when you receive them. Access is valuable when the dataset is vast and multidimensional, but it cannot be used for statistical analysis, except for elementary functions, and is much less useful than a spreadsheet package in most cases.

9.5 Surveys

A survey, usually conducted using a questionnaire, provides a poll of the views, experiences, or behaviour of a representative sample from within a specific population of possible respondents obtained by asking a series of questions. A vital attribute of a survey is that every participant is asked the same questions so that the responses can be aggregated and analysed quantitatively. Questionnaires are an ideal method for gathering data when you want to know about opinions or choices and how these are formed, specifically among individuals or particular classes of individuals within organisations. This sort of data will not exist in any secondary database, and hence research that aims to deal with opinions or decision-making will have no choice but to collect the information from scratch.

Conducting surveys and interviews is more involved than it might first appear, and adopting an appropriate design is essential for the results from the investigation to be considered valid – in other words, for readers to have confidence that the claims you write are genuine and apply in reality.

Nowadays, surveys are typically conducted on-line, with the responses being automatically dropped into a data file at the end. This saves a significant amount of time compared with previously when surveys were completed on paper, and then the responses had to be coded and manually entered into a spreadsheet. It is not worth using a paper-based questionnaire unless the only way to meet your target respondents is face-to-face, where they will not have access to a device. Not only do paper surveys look old-fashioned, but you would also then be required to key in all of the information, which would take hours, if not days, of tedious work.

Table 9.1: Software choices for quantitative analysis

Package	Commercial or Freeware	Advantages	Disadvantages
Microsoft Excel	Commercial	Straightforward to use, you almost certainly already know how to use it, and your data will probably already be in the correct format. Very easy to configure the output to an attractive layout to drop straight into a document.	Only very basic analyses are possible without a lot of function writing. It is also inefficient if you have a large amount of data or need to run the same models repeatedly. Since the data, models or functions and results are kept together, it is easier than other packages to damage the raw data or make errors without realising it.
EViews	Commercial	Straightforward to use and quite powerful with numerous built-in models and a programming language available within the software as well as a menu-driven system.	The programming language is less intuitive than others, and some built-in functions have limited options.
Gretl	Freeware	Menu-driven but freely available. Most of the main classes of models are available. Fairly straightforward to use.	Only available on the Windows platform and not for Mac. Limited range of built-in functions, although since it is open-source, a programmer could extend the available routines.
R	Freeware	The extensive and rapidly growing range of functions is available make it very powerful, and it is becoming the standard package for sophisticated analysis.	Requires some programming skills and will take longer to get up to speed than some other packages.
Stata	Commercial	Wide range of built-in functions and guides on how to use it. More straightforward to use than programming languages.	Requires some limited programming skills. Expensive to purchase if your institution does not have a site licence.
Python	Freeware	Particularly useful for textual analysis, extraordinarily flexible and increasingly in demand in the corporate world.	It is a programming language, not a statistical package and takes much longer to get up to speed than the latter. The toolboxes for econometrics are currently less well developed than the specialist packages.
RATS	Commercial	Straightforward to use and powerful with numerous built-in models and a programming language available but with most routines accessible through simple one-line commands.	Less widely used than some other packages, and so your institution is less likely to hold a licence.
SPSS	Commercial	Very straightforward to use with an Excel-like interface and sometimes considered the standard tool for student project data analysis. There is also a similar-looking cutdown freeware package available, PSPP.	Considerably less flexible and less powerful than some other packages, particularly for econometrics, including time-series analysis.

Surveys provide an important means by which new data can be created since there are many potential topics for which secondary data do not exist. If you run a survey, you can ask (within certain boundaries) whatever you wish, creating the possibility to conduct a much more comprehensive range of investigations.

Several software packages are available to construct and run surveys efficiently on-line, including Google Docs, Qualtrics and SurveyMonkey. All of these are free to set up and to run if you source your own respondents, only charging a fee if they collect the responses for you. Qualtrics has a limit of 100 respondents for the free version, but this will be unlimited if your university has a licence for the system, which many institutions do. All three systems are straightforward to use, and once your questionnaire is set up, you can send potential respondents a link to complete the survey remotely, with the results being collated in a tabular format for exporting to a spreadsheet or statistical software.

Surveys have widespread applicability over various situations and can be adapted to address a range of different types of research objectives. The information obtained from a survey can incorporate quantitative (responses to pre-defined questions on a scale) or qualitative (free-flow text input) data, or both.

Most dissertation surveys are cross-sectional in design, meaning that they try to gauge participants' opinions or knowledge at a particular point in time. It is also possible to conduct a longitudinal survey, where the sample data are collected at different points in time to try to gauge how attitudes or experiences have changed. These can be particularly useful in examining the impact of major events – for instance, it would be fascinating to compare people's views of the effectiveness of the corporate audit process in normal market circumstances with perspectives in the immediate aftermath of an accounting scandal on the scale of the Enron fiasco. Ideally, the same participants would be used in each wave of the survey, but if not, any random differences in the characteristics of the participants across samples can be controlled for.

Longitudinal surveys are defined as those covering the same questions over a period of time, although the respondents might be the same or different for each wave of the questionnaire. Such surveys are seldom used in student projects for the obvious reason that there is barely sufficient time to conduct one survey, let alone two.

Getting survey respondents

A particular difficulty with conducting surveys is persuading a sufficient number of people to complete them that you have a large enough response sample to analyse. Unfortunately, the move from postal or hand-distributed surveys to on-line questionnaires has made the non-response problem even worse as it is harder to engage with potential participants. They might think of a questionnaire sent through the post to them personally as worthwhile completing whereas they would simply delete an e-mail request that arrives with tens of other junk messages in their spam folder.

One way to increase participation would be to recruit participants by paying them a fee (e.g., £5) for completion, although this is usually prohibitively expensive for unsponsored students. It is common to use entry into a prize draw as an incentive to complete the survey, but if you offer this, you must follow through, selecting one of the participants at random and presenting them with the prize. This reward could, for example, be a £50 voucher for an on-line retailer.

As an alternative to trying to identify and persuade people to complete your survey, is to get a company to do that for you. Organisations such as Qualtrics, Prolific and M-Turk will collect responses from databases that they hold of people willing to complete surveys. But these individuals are paid (usually minimal sums of money) by the company, and the organisations would pass this cost onto you by charging you a fee (probably ranging from £200-£2000 or more) for the service, depending on how long your survey would take for a respondent to complete and how many such participants you want to obtain.

Third-party survey distributors, although expensive, can often procure large numbers of responses (more than sufficient to ensure statistical validity) of good quality within a few days. In such cases, the researcher can also specify a sampling frame to control participants' characteristics tightly (e.g., gender balance in the sample, 50% high-income individuals, 25% above retirement age, etc.). This would be known as a stratified or quota sample and can be extremely useful in ensuring that the selection is representative across several dimensions of the population that you intend to target.

However, for students who are advertising and managing participation themselves, it might be a struggle to get sufficient numbers of people who are willing to engage with the survey, and the percentage of completions is likely to be low. In that case, obtaining a representative sample would be a distant dream, and the best you could hope for would be a response rate that is not so low that it diminishes the validity of the study. What is acceptable here will also depend on the sample size, but in general, it is often suggested that a response rate of 25% is probably the minimum that is okay. However, some real consumer surveys have rates as low as 1%. In all cases, the higher, the better. Some useful information on how to calculate the numbers of participants and response rates that are needed for a valid survey is on Genroe.com.[20]

Social media platforms such as Twitter and Facebook can be used to advertise your questionnaire, but the number of people willing to complete it is likely to be low as there is little incentive for them to do so. If you simply circulate the survey to random members of the general public – assuming that you could seek out a list of their contact details from somewhere – the response rate is likely to be extremely low. The sample would then be too small, and the results unrepresentative of the population from which you were trying to appraise and therefore unreliable. As a very rough guide, depending on the homogeneity of the sample, at least 50 responses

---

[20]https://www.genroe.com/blog/acceptable-survey-response-rate-2/11504

are required as an absolute minimum to conduct any meaningful analysis, especially if you wish to perform some hypothesis tests. A sample smaller than this will be very unlikely to generate any significant and robust findings; 100-200 responses would be much better but probably still not sufficient for a study to be publishable.

Low response rates are a problem for they may render the sample too small for a detailed analysis but this issue is related to a more serious difficulty known as non-response bias. This occurs if the choice of a potential participant not to respond to the survey is correlated with what the researcher is trying to measure. Returning to the debt example discussed above, suppose the objective of the exercise is to examine the role of personality factors in determining how well people deal with problems servicing their debts. It might be that people of certain personality dispositions are both more likely to deal badly with financial difficulties and less likely to fill in on-line surveys, in which case the sample of respondents will be biased and the results from analysing them potentially misleading. Non-response bias can therefore be a serious issue that warrants careful consideration for all surveys.

If you are conducting a survey or interviews, it might be the case that you have to rely on your friends, relatives and classmates to be the subjects of the investigation. Known as a convenience sample, although they don't constitute a representative or random sample, this might be the best you can do given the time and resources available. While not ideal, there is a long history of doing this in experimental research. It is common for scholars to use their students as subjects, for which the latter receive course credits, thus providing an incentive to participate. Much of the evidence base on human behaviour is derived from experiments conducted using 18-22-year olds studying in psychology departments. If this is the best you can do, then so be it: provided that you have gone through all of the steps appropriately, you would be unlikely to lose many marks for using a convenience sample.

Surveys can be an excellent way to collect both numerical and textual information that is unique. But setting up survey questionnaires, running a pilot study and collating the responses is usually a time-consuming activity that is likely to be spread over several weeks. The lengthy nature of the data-gathering process leaves many students to conclude that doing so is infeasible within the time allocated to their dissertations, which is why they instead choose to rely on secondary data sources.

Another disadvantage of surveys is that the background around which it is being completed and the reasoning behind the selection of particular responses rather than others cannot be identified due to the process's anonymity. In other words, you cannot ask a respondent why they chose one specific answer rather than another unless you had already built that question into the survey. These difficulties could be overcome with interviews, although they are even more time-consuming to conduct than surveys.

A further issue arises when respondents complete the survey but fail to treat it seriously or give ill-thought-out and rushed responses. This can be the case in particular for those who receive payments to complete surveys as the compensation rates are usually meagre, and hence the only way to earn anything like a reasonable hourly rate is to proceed through them extremely quickly.

Does a survey constitute quantitative or qualitative research?

This is a pertinent question that is the cause of considerable confusion among both students and research methods textbook authors. One response, although probably not a very helpful one, would be to say neither since a survey or questionnaire is a method of obtaining data and not a type of research as such.

A different answer would be to say that it can be either depending on the nature of the questions that are asked and the way that the responses are analysed. A survey could ask purely open-ended questions to a relatively small number of individuals in a specific grouping with the answers written into a narrative and quoted in some cases. This would be a qualitative study, almost like a structured interview (subsection 9.6.2).

At the other end of the spectrum, a survey can be constructed to include only questions coded into numerical values (for instance, Yes and No become 1 and 0 and responses to strongly disagree through to strongly agree are mapped onto a scale coded as 1-5). This information would be purely quantitative and analysed using numerical analysis – either with simple summary statistics or more sophisticated econometrics – which would make it a quantitative study.

A final possibility would be that a survey includes both fixed-response and open-ended, free-flow questions, and so the answers could be analysed statistically or by discussing the textual inputs (or better, by both methods). In this case, the research would have the characteristics of both a quantitative and a qualitative study.

Possible types of survey questions

A range of question types are possible in a survey, including the following:

- Free-flow text entry. Here, respondents are presented with a box and can enter their own choice of text, usually subject to an upper character limit.
- Selecting from a list. Here, respondents can either select one item from a list or are asked to tick all that apply.
- Ranking a list. Here, respondents examine a set of items and then rate them according to some criterion. For example, the question might be to 'Rank the following in terms of how much you would trust them to provide valuable suggestions on how to save for your pension', and the items to rank might be 'bank', 'building society', 'financial advisor', 'academic', 'government representative', 'money website'.
- A yes or no question, for example, 'do you invest in the stock market?'
- A question requiring a response on a scale, such as a Likert scale, which usually has five or seven points, such as: 'To what extent do you agree or disagree with the statement "Auditors are not sufficiently independent from the companies whose accounts they are inspecting,"' with possible responses on a 5-point scale from Strongly disagree through Disagree, Uncertain, and

Agree to Strongly agree.
• Related to questions on a Likert scale are those known as semantic differentials, where there might still be a five-point scale from one term to its polar opposite. The question might be, for example, 'I would consider a career in auditing to be' with responses from Very Boring through Dull, Indifferent, and Quite Interesting to Exciting.

9.5.1 Survey design

There are many aspects of survey design that require careful thought if the completion rate is going to be the best possible and for the results to be valid and useful. This section discusses several practical tips to enhance the quality of the survey.

When setting up a survey, try to limit the questions to those that are necessary and avoid repetition. People are much more likely to respond if you can honestly tell them that they will be able to complete it in less than five minutes. Equally, don't exclude any questions that you consider would be useful since you will not be able to go back and ask the same people additional questions later.

Also, don't forget to ask demographic or background questions where these will be useful in the data analysis. This information will also help you ensure that your sample covers the part of the population you intended to and is not biased (for example, if 90% of your respondents were men but you had wanted a gender-balanced sample). Here are some practical tips for setting up an effective survey:
• Check that your survey is nicely formatted, with no questions or responses spilling over from one screen to the next.
• Ensure that there are no spelling or grammatical errors.
• Nowadays, people tend to respond to surveys on their phones (even if you expressly ask them not to), so check that your questionnaire will scale well to a tiny screen and consider shortening the questions and responses if necessary.
• Try to avoid vaguely worded questions or responses where it is difficult for respondents to understand unambiguously what you mean and be aware that varying the language will lead to different answers. For instance, suppose that you are trying to measure how people feel about building up debts and how such a debt accumulation could arise. If you ask: 'I sometimes don't pay my bills on time' with the possible responses 'Yes' and 'No'. Most people would choose 'Yes', but that would not indicate how often respondents got behind in paying their bills or whether it was a serious problem for them. This ambiguity arises because of the vague word 'sometimes' combined with only the possibility of a binary response. This wording could be modified to: 'How often do you pay your bills on time?' with the response scale, 'Never', 'Occasionally', 'Sometimes', 'Frequently' and 'Always'. This wording combination for the question and response items clarifies what is intended for both the participant and you, the investigator, when analysing the data.

- When designing questions, avoid double (or triple) negatives, which will tie participants up in knots so that their responses don't mean what they intended them to. For instance, the question above could have been written as 'I never fail to pay my bills on time' with possible responses on a strongly disagree to strongly agree scale. This new version would be more confusing than the one above that was written in a positive way.

- Avoid using compound questions where, in effect, you are asking two things at the same time that ought to be separated. For example, if you ask, 'Do you have a bank account or a stocks and shares ISA?', virtually every adult will have a bank account. But although the proportion with a stocks and shares ISA will be much lower, it will be impossible to detect that given the way the two types of product have been combined in the question.

- Even if you opt for only closed questions, you should still have at least one free-text 'Comments' box at the end so that participants can communicate with you about anything they did not understand or with which they are not happy.

- When considering the ordering of questions in the survey, it is usually preferable to begin with more straightforward and closed-end questions, proceeding later to more challenging questions and those inviting a free text input. The reason is that respondents often take a while to focus on the task and get in the right frame of mind, so starting with a few easy questions provides an excellent warm-up. If the initial questions require a great deal of thought, there is a danger that either you will get ill-considered responses or that the participant will believe that all the subsequent questions are going to constitute equally hard work, discouraging them from continuing so that they give up.

- Electronic survey platforms can usually be set up to randomise the ordering of questions (and possibly also randomise the order of the responses), which can mitigate against any impacts of question ordering on the results.

- There is a sizeable literature on the impact of question order on the answers that survey respondents provide, so it is often preferable to begin with uncontroversial items such as demographic information and leave more tricky issues until closer to the end.

- Also, try to ask non-controversial questions first in your survey – items that respondents will find evidently relevant but which would not upset or bore them. For the latter reason, it can be preferable to leave basic demographic information until last. The tricky questions where the participant has to think carefully or confront something that they might feel uncomfortable with (e.g., admitting to having a fiery temper or being lazy) are best asked in the middle when they have built some momentum with filling in the questionnaire and are least likely to abandon it or provide false answers. Keep all questions succinct, ensure that they are clear, and use as little technical terminology as possible. Where specialist language must be used (such as where the survey is about attitudes to investing in stocks and shares, in which case discussing risks and returns is unavoidable), try to define any words you use that are not widely known among non-specialists. For example, you could refer to 'price movements up and down' rather than 'volatility', refer to 'stocks and shares' rather than 'equities', and refer to 'UK government bonds' rather than 'consols'.

One of the most challenging issues with questionnaire design is ensuring that the participants have sufficient knowledge and understanding of the subject matter to provide valid answers to the questions that they are being asked, rather than merely picking a random response. Remember, the participants have probably not studied your subject area, let alone your topic. Indeed, if you are surveying the general public, many of them will not have studied anything at all for decades, so don't assume too much.

People are often reluctant to select 'Unsure/Don't know', even if that applies to them as they feel embarrassed. So, where possible, try to phrase the question so that choosing this answer would not be a mark of shame. Or the response could be written differently, such as 'I have insufficient information to answer this question', which would give the impression that the question was the problem, not the respondent. This would allow the person to feel better about themselves and so be more inclined to select that answer if it applied rather than one of the others, which could damage the validity of the question.

Relatedly, participants might feel uncomfortable about selecting other responses that cast them in an unfavourable light. A low proportion of people might be willing to agree with the following statements, even if they apply, e.g. 'I tend to be lazy at times'; 'I am bad at managing my finances'.

Points on a scale

If you ask respondents to select a response on a scale, ensure that this has an appropriate number of points. For instance, 'To what extent do you agree with the statement: I am willing to take risks with my money if I might receive higher returns?' Seven- and five-point scales are most common, but I prefer the latter, due to its simplicity in being represented as 1 = 'strongly disagree'; 2 = 'disagree'; 3 = 'neither agree nor disagree'; 4 = 'agree'; 5 = 'strongly agree'.

Some researchers prefer a 4-point scale that omits the central point so that a 'neutral' response is not possible. They do this because respondents frequently select the central one of five points merely as a default if they are not really engaging with the survey, and with a four-point scale, every choice must be an active one to at agree or disagree. However, the disadvantage with this approach is that forcing people to jump in one direction or another would not allow those who have considered the question carefully but genuinely have no particular opinion to express that.

If you have too much granularity in the scale (such as 10 or 12 points), differences between one point and the next are likely to be spurious as most people will not be able to enumerate their feelings or opinions to that level of precision (e.g., some people would choose three and others four when they felt the same).

9.5.2 Validating survey data

Once you have obtained the raw responses from the survey, they might need to be coded (although his might be done automatically if you use a package such as Qualtrics to distribute the survey questions), which means turning qualitative information into quantitative information. For instance, you might ask respondents their gender and code men as 0 and women as 1. Once this has been completed and entered into a spreadsheet, all of the data need to be checked along various dimensions:

1. Is there evidence of apparent errors or inconsistencies in responses? For instance, a respondent ticks that they are over 90 years old for one question but that they are employed in the hospitality sector in another. Or a respondent who is 18-21 years old but holding a doctorate. Of course, either of these could be the case, but they are highly doubtful.

2. Is the sample you have collected sufficiently broad and representative of the population you wanted to measure? For instance, if your primary means of finding respondents was through a university rugby team (of which you are a member) and their friends, did you end up with the vast majority of male participants?

3. Did respondents answer all questions? If particular respondents failed to answer several items, consider dropping those people entirely from the sample if you have a sufficient number remaining.

4. Is there evidence of any 'straight-lining' where participants have put the same answer for many questions in a row, or similar questions elicit totally different responses from the same person? If so, consider dropping those people entirely from the sample if you have a sufficient number remaining.

5. Is there evidence that particular questions did not resonate with your audience so that middle 'neither agree nor disagree' responses were selected an overwhelming proportion of the time? This indifference would indicate a weak question; ideally, it would again be removed from the analysis, although you may have just to note the lack of engagement and use it regardless.

6. Calculate the mean and standard deviation of the scores across all participants for each question. If the standard deviation is very low, that would indicate that the particular question is a poor discriminator between participants and will likely not be very useful in the analysis, and you might consider dropping it.

7. Are the responses to any open-ended questions sufficiently detailed and insightful to be worthwhile analysing?

There are also more sophisticated ways to check the reliability of survey data, although they require a specific setup of the questionnaire:

- *the split-half coefficient*, where the survey is split into two parts and all respondents answer both parts and then the responses to the two parts are compared. This method will only be useful if the two parts of the survey cover the same instrument (i.e., they are asking questions on the same topic).

- *the test-retest coefficient* – here, the same test is completed by the same respondents with an interval in between. A reliable test should have very highly correlated responses between the first and second sittings of the questionnaire.

- *Cronbach's alpha* – this involves calculating a coefficient that measures how closely the items in a survey work together. Again, it can only be used for a set of questions on the same topic (e.g., a survey with several question items to measure someone's current mood). Like the R^2 in a regression, the alpha will be between zero and one, with a higher alpha indicating that the questions are reliable. A value of at least 0.8 is usually considered appropriate, although it should be noted that alpha is always increasing in the number of question items. Also, if the value is excessive (e.g., 0.95), this would be indicative of too much overlap between the items and that in essence almost the same question is being asked repeatedly. Such a high value might be taken to suggest that there is redundancy in the questionnaire so that one or more items could be deleted without losing much.

Data checking and validation is an essential step before the analysis of survey responses. Low data quality can profoundly impact the statistical results and diminish the value of your study. Since it is far more likely that genuine patterns in the data will be destroyed than artificial patterns created by noise in the responses, insufficient checking and failure to dispose of unreliable data points could reduce the chances of finding statistically significant results that would have supported what you had hoped to find.

9.6 Interviews

Alongside surveys, in-depth interviews provide an important means by which researchers can generate new and exciting findings. Interviews can be particularly valuable when they embody the opportunity to ask key decision-makers why they made their choices, how they felt, and what their thought processes were. This sort of insight provides an opportunity to conduct a thorough analysis of a particular situation that could not be obtained from an arm's length survey or secondary data. The emphasis here is on quality rather than quantity, with the objective usually to conduct a small number of detailed discussions with highly relevant individuals.

Interviews may appear more straightforward than either surveys or experiments, and in many ways, they are. As with surveys, however, the setup costs involved in conducting compelling interviews are substantial and should not be underestimated. An ill-thought-out chat with specific people, even if they hold senior roles that are highly pertinent to the research questions, will not generate useful findings. Conducting compelling interviews is a specialist skill that requires considerable training and planning. As for surveys, ensuring sufficient 'buy-in' from potential participants is crucial. They need to be willing to provide their precious time when there is little incentive but many risks for them, which is always challenging to achieve.

Running successful interviews also involves a degree of charisma and charm that is not needed for other, more anonymous data collection methods. You need to draw up a list of questions in advance and order them to flow naturally as a conversation. Also, be prepared to deviate from the script if the responses to previous questions lead to relevant digressions that will help address your research aims.

Interviews can be categorised according to whether they are structured (sometimes known as pre-coded), semi-structured or unstructured (sometimes termed open). Each of these types of interviews is now defined.

Structured interviews

A structured interview is one where the questions are fully prepared prior to it taking place, and the interviewer simply reads them out in order and circles or notes the responses. There will be little, if any, variation from the schedule, so in essence, structured interviews can be considered one-to-one oral surveys or researcher-administered surveys. The latter have the additional benefit over surveys completed on-line that the researcher is able to follow up on any misunderstandings, and the respondent is likely to be more focused with a higher chance of completing the survey if being watched.

Although researcher-administered surveys have some advantages over their self-administered equivalents, the former are considerably more time-consuming for the investigator to implement and limit the sample to those whom the latter is able to make direct contact with, either in person or over a phone or video call. Compared with free-flow interviews, any opportunity for worthwhile digressions, follow-up questions or open-ended responses is usually lost with structured interviews, thus arguably defeating their core purpose, and thus many scholars prefer a less structured approach.

Unstructured interviews

On the other hand, unstructured interviews are more like a steered chat between the two parties, where the agenda is much more freestyle. The interviewer poses a question that is like an opening gambit for a discussion around the topic that the interviewee can respond to in whatever way and at whatever length they want. The interviewer will probably draft a list of topics beforehand but will not specify the questions fully.

Semi-structured interviews

Semi-structured interviews are, as the name suggests, somewhere between the two extremes where there will be an initial set of questions drafted beforehand but with the flexibility to change the order or deviate from the list as the interview progresses and the researcher gets a feel for how it is going.

The primary advantage of unstructured and semi-structured interviews is that they are open-ended and so can be adapted as they progress to 'go with the flow' in whatever direction the interviewer wants to take the conversation following the interviewee's previous response. This flexibility can provide unexpected insights that would not have been possible with a more anonymous and formulaic information gathering technique such as a questionnaire.

Although clarity and precision in the questioning are still crucial, it is easier during interviews to determine whether a respondent understands a line of inquiry from their facial expressions and to change tack or provide examples if the current approach is not working. This feedback is a benefit of a structured interview over an on-line survey, although the former is much more time-consuming to implement. The interviewer can look out for any emotional cues, and if the interviewee is clearly feeling uncomfortable, they can ease off with the intense questioning until later in the session and move to an aspect the interviewee will find less controversial.

Preparing for your interview(s)

You are likely to have only one opportunity to interview each individual, so think very carefully in advance about precisely what questions you will ask and how you will keep the communication going if the interviewee is not very talkative and provides a series of one-line answers. Also, consider how you will respond if the interviewee refuses to answer or becomes angry at one of your questions. Great care is needed to ensure that the questions are not loaded in any way since the interviewee will probably feel much more comfortable agreeing with the interviewer than disagreeing, leading to the potential for biased responses.

Surveys are anonymous by their nature, whereas interviews require a considerable amount of interaction, whether they are completed in-person, by on-line video conferencing, or by telephone. This interaction means that conducting compelling interviews requires a different skillset. Someone who is a strong communicator, engaging, and gives the impression of being an interested listener, will conduct useful interviews. You need to inspire confidence, demonstrate that you understand the issues that the interviewee is referring to, and act as if their responses are highly valued even if they merely state the obvious or ramble. All these characteristics will encourage them to give further, honest detail in subsequent answers.

If you have never conducted formal interviews before, it is worth conducting a trial run with fellow students to test out your approach and the questions you intend to ask. A dummy run will also allow you to time the proceedings to ensure that the tempo is about right and you do not run over schedule, which could imply that you are unable to cover some of your most crucial questions.

Running effective interviews

Interview questions need careful thought so that they are designed to elicit the kind of responses the researcher wants and can be used in their project. It is essential for the researcher to get to know all they can about the interviewee and the organisation they work for before the interview. This knowledge will stop the interviewer from appearing ill-informed and unprepared, and it will prevent time from being wasted going over questions when the answers are on the organisation's website.

If you opt to use interviews as your primary method for data-gathering, there are several steps you can take to ensure that you get the most out of them:

1. At the beginning of the interview, you will need to introduce yourself, explain who you are, what you are doing, and what you intend to get out of the process. Choose your opening words carefully – if you speak for too long, it will eat away at the time that you have with the interviewee; if you don't explain sufficiently carefully what kinds of responses would be most valuable to you, the replies might not be on-topic or of the right depth.

2. You will need to reassure participants that their views will remain anonymous (unless you have a prior agreement that the interview will be 'on the record', with everything the respondent says being attributed to them) and explain the ethics approval procedure that your research design has gone through.

3. Avoid questions that encourage a one-word answer; make plenty of use of 'why'- and 'how'-type questions.

4. Also, avoid the temptation to suggest an answer to the interviewee as it is likely they will agree with it even if it is not quite right, e.g., 'how frequently do you check the value of your pension fund? Maybe just once a year?'

5. Many of the points about good survey question design also apply to interview questions. For example, avoiding asking leading or loaded questions and avoiding questions that mix several different ideas into one or asking two or more questions simultaneously. In such cases, the interviewee will struggle to remember all parts of the compound question and may skip over some vital aspects.

6. Allow the interviewee plenty of time to gather their thoughts and fully answer one question before moving onto the next.

7. At the end of the session, ask the interviewee if they have any further comments they wish to make or whether they can think of any relevant aspects that you have not covered. Also, ask them whether they want to receive a copy of the transcript or the completed study.

9.6.1   Gaining access to interview participants

If your research involves obtaining information from organisations, or interviewing specific personnel, making the right first contact is crucial. Usually, people at the middle management level who are in the division or department relevant to your research are the best people to approach: very senior people are hard to reach, while juniors may have insufficient authority to grant access.

Avoid sending the same e-mail to multiple individuals from within a given organisation simultaneously. If one person cannot help you, they will likely forward your note to a colleague, and if the latter has already been contacted and then receives the same message several times, they will be irritated and less keen to assist. It is acceptable, of course, to send a follow-up e-mail to that individual or others in the organisation if you do not receive any response to the first communication within a reasonable time (e.g., a week). When there has been no response via e-mail, try telephoning instead, which makes it much harder for you to be fobbed off.

If your supervisor has some specific contacts that they are willing to employ on your behalf, that will considerably improve the likelihood of success. Some organisations are incredibly bureaucratic, however, and will routinely decline all requests for information or help. If that happens, you will need to look elsewhere for the information you need, and there is little point in pushing harder on a permanently closed door.

Handling the interviewee

You need to find a way to get the conversation flowing so that the participant feels at ease and talks freely. Start by asking an uncontroversial but demonstrably relevant question on a topic that the interviewee will be happy talking about.

You might need to change tack as the interview progresses if it is not going as planned. If some aspects of a participant's responses are particularly insightful, fascinating or unexpected, you may wish to divert from your intended schedule to investigate these issues more deeply with follow-up questions to expand on precisely those points. If the respondent provides excessively brief answers with insufficient detail, try reframing your questions to make it clear that you expect more comprehensive replies or ask them whether they 'can say a bit more on ...'

Dealing with excessively talkative participants is even more challenging since you don't want to appear impolite and uninterested by cutting them off abruptly. Try to identify brief gaps in their talk to move on to the next question or remind them at the earliest opportunity that their time is pressing. Ultimately, if none of these discrete approaches work and the time available cannot be extended, you might have to limit your question set to only the most pertinent issues or, although not ideal, try asking compound questions where you combine related points together. Hopefully, this step might reduce the amount of detail offered on each aspect to allow you to get through your question list.

You also need to think about whether you will make audio or video recordings of the interviews. Doing so will make the subsequent analysis of the information much more straightforward than if you are forced to rely on hand-scribbled notes made while you are trying to listen and ask questions. You will also be able to retain all of the evidence in case some of the responses are surprising or controversial. But making recordings will require the interviewee's permission, and they are likely to be more guarded in what they say, so the really 'juicy' pieces of off-the-record information that you might otherwise have received will not be forthcoming.

9.6.2 Analysing interview notes and transcripts

By their nature, the relatively unstructured nature of interviews makes the analysis of the information arising from them much more challenging than for purely quantitative datasets. Analysing qualitative data is problematic because the researcher is usually presented with a vast mass of information, often with no obvious way to organise or classify it.

In order to properly analyse the output from interviews, it is usually best to have a formal electronic transcription of the conversations. Software exists that can do this automatically, but there are likely to be significant errors to contend with and identifying and correcting them will require going through manually. It is common to produce verbatim transcriptions of interviews – in other words, to include everything, even hesitations and misspoken phrases where the interviewee later corrects themself. You could also note down facial expressions that link with particularly obvious emotions, which can then be analysed alongside the transcript of what was said.

Even if the researcher imposes some form onto the proceedings by having a pre-defined set of questions, the small sample of interviewees and variation in the kinds of answers they will provide makes it near impossible to conduct any conventional quantitative analysis. Quoting directly from the responses can bring a dissertation to life and amplify the arguments you are making. But it may lead to accusations of anecdotalism and that you had 'cherry-picked' certain parts of the conversation to suit the argument that you wanted to make, and this needs to be combined with a more comprehensive analysis.

There are many different techniques to analysing interview transcripts that can be adopted. If the interviewer has also produced the transcript, they will already know it well, but if this has been done by a third party or automated from audio files, the researcher will need to undergo a process of familiarity with the data. This is essential so that the researcher has a map in their mind of precisely what was said at what stage in the process and in response to which question.

The next stage is usually to code the transcript, which refers to a process of organising, labelling and categorising the information, aiming to identify patterns that tie in with the research questions and identifying them with a tag amongst a vast mass of material that will ultimately not be used. The list of codes to be applied can either be decided based on theory or existing knowledge before the interviews are conducted (*a priori* coding) or after conducting the interviews and reviewing the output (*a posteriori* coding). Altogether, this can be an extremely time-consuming process, and there is no template-driven approach that can be adopted as for the quantitative analysis of data.

Then it is possible to conduct a thematic analysis, where you try to identify and investigate the distinct themes (around 5-12 is considered a sensible number of them), which are recurring concepts or patterns that arise within the coded transcript. Codes can directly map onto themes, but in other cases, a theme will comprise a group of codes, while some might be dropped altogether if in the final analysis they appear not to occur sufficiently often or are not useful. Since you will be presenting and examining the themes in your dissertation, these need to be adequately descriptive of what they are trying to explain that they will make sense to readers who had not read the transcript.

A final stage would be to analyse the themes, seeing how frequently they appear, whether they link together, and interpreting them. The emerging themes might require several iterations of specification and combination with the codes when some of the former are found to have insufficient support, some have contradictory codes, and some are found to overlap too much and would be merged. A final set of themes will be specified and the discussion in your results section can be organised around them and their implications.

Examples of the use of interviews

An interesting use of interviews to investigate how accountants are dealing with climate change issues and the impact that the profession is having on the debate is given in Lovell and MacKenzie (2011). The paper is available for download free at the University of Edinburgh repository.[21]

Another fascinating illustration of the use of interviews in accounting research is by Tucker and Parker (2014). They use both a survey and interviews with high-ranking management accountants to determine whether, and to what extent, scholarly research in that sub-field influences accounting practice. Tucker and Parker encourage their respondents to reflect on the relevance of accounting research and whether it is even feasible, let alone desirable, for academic research and the industry to be better linked.

Their methods begin with an e-mailed survey of 125 senior academic accountants from 55 universities in 14 countries, of whom roughly half (64) produce usable responses. The survey was based on seven sections:

1. Demographic information
2. Perceptions of how well-connected academic accounting is with practitioners The following three sections were designed to tease out views on the perceived barriers to greater integration.
3. Discovery – how can practitioners find out about academic research?
4. Translation – whether practitioners can comprehend academic research in accounting
5. Dissemination – how hard is it for practitioners to access the academic research that is relevant for them?
6. Change – to what extent does academic research have relevance and value for practitioners to solve real-world problems, and can they implement it?
7. Open questions on any 'specific initiatives' respondents could think of to bridge the gap between the academic and practitioner worlds

---

[21] https://www.pure.ed.ac.uk/ws/files/11098137/PDFAntipode2011AccountingforCarbon2.pdf

The researchers then conducted follow-up interviews, primarily via voice and video calls, with respondents. These were semi-structured and were the chosen method to obtain the respondents' detailed opinions and judgments, which could not be obtained through a less personal means.

Through a thematic analysis, Tucker and Parker are able to identify two separate, quite pervasive viewpoints. One set of senior researchers argues that academic research in management accounting is not engaging sufficiently with the industry and that there is an increasing divergence between the two worlds. The other group suggests that a separation between the agendas of scholars and practitioners is desirable and appropriate. This set of respondents emphasised the importance of theorising, which is of limited interest to the industry, and generating new knowledge rather than acting as consultants.

A similar set of questions regarding the relevance of research for practice was considered in the context of finance by Brooks *et al.* (2019) in a paper available from the University of Reading repository.[22] Brooks *et al.* start with the premise that scholarly finance is 'punching below its weight' in influencing policy and practice, and their study is largely focused on trying to explain why this is the case from both theoretical and empirical perspectives. The theoretical underpinning is based on work by the French philosopher Pierre Bourdieu. His concepts of 'habitus' and various forms of 'capital' are used to argue that scholarly and practitioner finance have different incentive structures, objectives and outcomes, in the academic and financial market contexts. They were both able to grow and thrive through the past two decades, to a large extent independently of one another.

Brooks *et al.* adopt a very different set of methods and data collection compared with Tucker and Parker, instead using a large database of secondary data on publication patterns and analysis of journal publication patterns and choices of methods and data by the researchers who had written articles in the 'leading' finance journals.

This divergence in methods between the two sets of authors illustrates that there are often numerous different approaches that can be used to tackle the same broad research aims, and the variety of techniques that can be used in accounting and finance leads to a rich array of evidence.

Content analysis and text mining

Contemporary text mining software can make the process of analysing interview results more rigorous, with programs available to explore and scrutinise the transcribed files. Sometimes such software is referred to by the acronym CAQDAS (Computer-assisted qualitative data analysis software). For example, using textual analysis to count the number of times that specific phrases are used across several interviews in a process known as discourse analysis. The packages can allow users to visualise the information better, enabling them to spot patterns using heatmaps

---

[22]http://centaur.reading.ac.uk/76975/

or clusters. NVivo is a package widely used in universities, and you might have free access to it through a site licence agreement, although Amazon, Google and Microsoft also have their own versions. Several freeware packages are also available – see this list at listoffreeware.com.[23]

It should also be noted that the quantification of interview transcripts and other qualitative information has been subject to criticism. In particular, it is argued that such a step defeats the purpose of conducting interviews as much of the richness and subtlety in what is said and how by the interviewee will be lost in the process of coding and thematic analysis. The research agenda can narrow, and many of the criticisms of quantitative analysis presented above could apply. This critical perspective would claim that if the interview transcript is distilled into a set of numbers and lists, it was hardly worth conducting, and the researcher might as well have used a survey with closed questions that would have been easier to analyse. In addition, learning how to use software packages such as NVivo effectively will take considerable time and effort.

More conventional documents (books, articles, company reports or announcements) and interview transcripts can also be subjected to content analysis, which aims to extract the original source's essence through a systematic analysis of the words used. It is related to textual analysis, an exciting subject area that has proliferated in accounting and finance in recent years. Content analysis can involve trying to determine the tone or sentiment of a particular document (such as an accounting narratives, disclosure statements, news item content, or Twitter postings).

Traditionally, content analysis would have been conducted manually by coding words or whole sentences and comparing them with a pre-defined list, which would have been a laborious task that would severely constrain the scope of analysis that could be conducted. Nowadays, however, content analysis would typically be conducted using an automated approach (i.e., using a computer language), which has the enormous advantage that a large amount of material can be assessed very quickly, accurately and consistently. This kind of analysis can be used to determine not only the nature of a document (for example, if an announcement relates to new products, increasing competition, director turnover, etc.) but also its 'tone'.

One approach treats the text being analysed as a 'bag of words' so that the technique involves simple counts of the numbers of words that fall into a particular category. For instance, we could define them by classifying words as either positive (optimistic) or negative (pessimistic) and then subtracting the percentage of one type from that of the other to generate a net tonal measure. A more sophisticated method, sometimes known as 'latent content analysis' aims to go further than the bag of words approach by identifying a sense of the meaning of the text.

Textual analysis can be conducted using freely available code – for example, searching using a phrase such as 'textual analysis in Python' leads to several relevant

---

[23]https://listoffreeware.com/best-free-text-analysis-software-windows/

articles and sources (although there are many other relevant sites):
- A useful article as a starting point with several links[24]
- Python code segments for content analysis onGeeksforGeeks[25]
- Python code segments for content analysis ontutorialspoint[26]
- Some sample code and links to a package to perform sentiment analysis on PythonCode[27]

There is also a much simpler to use commercial package:
- DICTION[28]

A textual analysis example

A recent study using text mining that I was involved in is the paper by Tao *et al.* (2020), where we use textual analysis of news announcements to explain the 'MAX effect', whereby stocks that experienced the highest maximum daily returns over the past month tend to experience negative returns in the following month. It has been argued that such stocks act like lottery tickets, and investors push their prices up excessively so that they fall subsequently. One possible line of intuition behind this phenomenon is that where stocks have been subject to news announcements over the previous month when the MAX is observed, their higher valuations have more justification and are therefore less likely to be reversed.

Tao *et al.* construct a news dataset for US equities for the period 1979-2016 based on stories published either on *Dow Jones Intra News* or in the *Wall Street Journal*. A sentiment measure for each news article is determined by summing the number of positive words and subtracting the total number of negative words.

The authors find that the size of the MAX anomaly, defined as the return spread between the highest MAX and the lowest MAX decile, is −1.74% per month on average for stocks with no news that month, whereas it is +1.34% for stocks that did have news. Naturally, there are very many other empirical results in the paper, which can be downloaded freely from SSRN.

The downsides of text mining

Automated text-mining is an exciting, relatively new development with a vast range of potential applications in accounting and finance, but there are nevertheless limitations to bear in mind:

1. Determining which words appear on the list and classifying them correctly is crucial. Often, to save time, scholars continue to use lists developed previously by other researchers (often from linguistics rather than being accounting or finance specialists). But there are inherent dangers that any systematic misclassifications will go unnoticed and infect all research on the topic

---

[24]https://towardsdatascience.com/getting-started-with-text-analysis-in-python-ca13590eb4f7

[25]https://www.geeksforgeeks.org/text-analysis-in-python-3/

[26]https://www.tutorialspoint.com/text-analysis-in-python3

[27]https://www.thepythoncode.com/article/vaderSentiment-tool-to-extract-sentimental-values-in-texts-using-python

[28]https://dictionsoftware.com

2. Reducing the rich, qualitative information in a statement to a word count can hide the essence of the message that the writer had intended to get across, leading to inappropriate conclusions

9.6.3   Disadvantages of the interview approach

While the use of unstructured or semi-structured interviews can allow the researcher to address otherwise unanswerable questions and provide rich insights, as a technique they are subject to several important limitations:

- As discussed above, interview findings can lack the generalisability that is achievable with larger-scale quantitative techniques
- Related to the previous point, any human errors on the part of the interviewee (for instance, if they have incomplete memories or misunderstandings of a key issue of relevance to the study) can have a significant effect upon the findings due to the very small number of participants (and possibly only one)
- Conducting effective interviews and analysing the data methodically and in detail can be enormously time-consuming
- The amount of information contained in interview transcripts can be vast, the bulk of which is not valuable. Separating the wheat from the chaff is challenging and laborious
- The way that the researcher structures the questions and asks them can have a profound influence on the outcome, possibly leading to biases in the findings. It is impossible to eliminate the effects of this entirely; the best that the interviewer can do is to ensure that they are aware of this, taking a reflexive approach. This can relate both to biases from the interviewer side that damage the neutrality of the investigative process, and also to changes in the behaviour of the interviewee as a result of being in an interview situation. The interviewee might, for example, be embarrassed about the truth and lie about their views or actions to please the interviewer. With a more anonymous form of questioning (such as an on-line survey), they might have been fully honest

9.6.4   Pilot surveys and interviews

Once you begin a full survey or set of interviews, you will generally only get one shot at them with no opportunity to come back and add or replace items at a later stage. Therefore, all of the questions you include must be 'road tested' so that they are written in good English, make sense to the reader, and ask what you want to ask. The best way to achieve that is to run a pilot, which is a small-scale initial version with the specific purpose of identifying issues. For instance, it is common to use a soft launch of a survey released to a few people for feedback and to ensure that their responses are as expected.

Similarly, a pilot interview will enable you to determine whether your questions elicit the kind of responses you want, or perhaps some are in danger of misinterpretation or one-word responses indicating that those questions did not resonate with the interviewee or covered a topic they did not like to discuss. Pay attention to the interviewee's facial expressions for signs of their emotional reaction throughout the process – are your questions making them feel alert, excited, angry, bored, or concerned, for example?

It is much better to check everything at this stage than to identify problems further down the line when it is too late to remedy them, and running a pilot will support the rigour of the research. Once any bugs in the initial version have been removed, the full launch can be made to the entire survey sample or interview list. If you made no alterations or merely minor changes between the pilot and the full launch, you could include the responses to the pilot as part of the dataset, but you cannot question the same people a second time.

9.7 Focus groups

A focus group can be thought of as a multi-person unstructured interview with much the same objective. Amongst many other uses, focus groups have been (infamously) used by politicians to obtain insight into the general public's views before implementing potentially unpopular new policies. In some ways, they are a little like interviews, but several people are asked the questions simultaneously, with each participant responding whenever they wish.

These are extremely rare in accounting and finance, but in my view, as a data collection technique they are under-utilised. A focus group involves establishing a set of thematically linked people specifically chosen for their relevance to the research. Typically, they will have 6-10 participants plus a moderator or facilitator who runs the sessions, which will normally last an hour or so. This number of people is ideal: fewer than that can lead to insufficient ideas and energy being generated, while more might cause some of those involved to feel intimated, refusing to become actively involved or difficulties in handling the group and retaining control of the room. The number of separate groups that are run will depend on the resources available (in particular, how much time the researcher has) and whether the research aims require a range of different types of participants that cannot be combined into a smaller number of groups.

Focus groups are an ideal way to gain insight into how people think about particular topics and why they behave the way they do. Usually, three or four separate focus groups would be more than sufficient. Each group could have a particular kind of participant, where you might choose to keep them separate because combining could cause awkwardness and a lack of willingness to participate or offer honest opinions. For instance, it might be unwise to combine people at different levels of seniority within an organisation or profession, as the likely outcome would be that the more experienced individuals would end up leading the discussion with those lower in the hierarchy feeling intimidated and simply nodding and agreeing with everything their seniors said.

The sessions tend to work better when all participants have undergone some of the same experiences and can discuss and share them without feeling intimidated, although equally, there needs to be some variation within the group otherwise the findings will lack interest if there is complete consensus.

Focus groups are fascinating because the responses that arise in a group setting might be more enlivened than would be the case when speaking to individuals since members will gain ideas from the others in the room. Once one particularly outgoing individual in the group has admitted a particular view or feeling, others might feel emboldened in a way that they would not have done in an individual interview setting. Provided that the discussion is managed delicately, particular viewpoints can be explored and questioned by others in the group.

As a result of the above points, focus groups are more fun to run and be a participant of than interviews and can allow you to obtain a large volume of material in a relatively short space of time. If group participants are made to feel at ease, divergences of experience or opinion and the reasons for them can be teased out in a way that would be impossible with individual interviews.

The person running the focus group is sometimes known as a facilitator, or moderator and to do this effectively requires some particular skills and can benefit from specialist training. The person needs sufficient charisma that they can supply the enthusiasm that the group needs to get going, but they may also need to firmly steer the conversation if it is veering away from addressing the research aims or causing discomfort to one or more of the participants.

The facilitator might also have to deal sensitively with participants who are either speaking too much (excessively dominating the discussion and imposing their views on the group) or not enough (for example, not engaged in the discussion or feeling shy) without causing offence but at the same time ensuring that all can contribute. Other issues that might need to be dealt with are when the whole group is lacking confidence and so it is hard to get a good conversation going, or when sub-groups are having their own discussions, which could easily veer off track or not be properly captured.

The facilitator might or might not also be the person conducting the research; if not, it would nonetheless make sense for the latter to be on-hand both to answer any questions and to ensure that the session is as useful as possible for its intended purpose.

To gain the most valuable insights from focus group requires extensive thought and planning prior to the activity taking place with regard to how to recruit the participants, how to run the sessions and what questions to ask the group(s). Although the participants within a group might be thematically linked in some way, the selection of individuals to be in a given group requires careful consideration to ensure balance and that the sample is not biased in a particular direction that will influence the findings in an unexpected or undesired way. The selection could be to ensure a balance among various lines: gender, age, incomes, educational level, subject or department specialism in an organisation, etc.

Given that the number of participants is fairly small, it is feasible and indeed desirable to approach them individually to maximise the chance that the most useful people are selected and agree to be involved. However, identifying, rather than approaching, relevant participants is likely to be the most challenging aspect.

As with interviews, it is essential to begin with a set of clearly identified research objectives. Many of the issues to consider when conducting interviews also apply to focus groups, such as where to hold the sessions, whether they should be recorded (either audio only or video too) with a device or notes taken by hand in the traditional way.

There is also a need to begin the session slowly by creating an atmosphere that ensures all participants feel at ease and happy to contribute. For example, they could be invited, in turn, to introduce and say a few lines about themselves, starting with the facilitator. The latter should also explain the purpose of the session and lay down a few rules regarding what is and is not appropriate to discuss, explaining that every viewpoint is welcome and equally valid. A few fairly straightforward questions could be discussed initially to warm up the participants before proceeding to the core business that aims to address, perhaps, between four and six themes or groups of questions. Finally, the facilitator might wish to return to any particularly controversial or unclear aspects before asking participants whether they have any final remarks prior to closing the session.

As for interviews, the discussion output needs to be transcribed, coded, and organised thematically before it an be analysed. The analysis can be even more challenging for focus groups due to the sheer volume of discussion that can be created by 6–10 people and the likely divergence of opinions making it hard to gauge whether and to what extent there was consensus.

There are some useful on-line resources that could be pursued:
- MasterClass[29]
- UserInterviews[30]
- YouTube Playlist[31]

One area of application of focus groups that I was involved with was a project to develop a new attitude to risk questionnaire (ATRQ) to be utilised by independent financial advisors when meeting with their clients. After we had invented the new questionnaire, we then ran two sets of focus groups: one with financial advisors and a separate one with members of the investing public. In both cases, we wanted to explore what the participants thought of the ATRQ, whether they understood the questions, and whether they had suggestions for improvements or different items.

We felt that we could obtain a more in-depth understanding from a focus group than we could with an anonymous survey, and it was more efficient and livelier than conducting a large number of one- to-one interviews. It would often be the case that

[29]https://www.masterclass.com/articles/how-to-run-a-successful-focus-group#quiz-1

[30]https://www.userinterviews.com/ux-research-field-guide-chapter/focus-groups

[31]https://www.youtube.com/watch?v=gjQtu6yeC1E&list=PLkODyp8qUsBjt05Zp_XZb1lmLpTs7bNWt

the session would be audio recorded, although we chose not to and instead made hand-written notes so that participants felt as relaxed as possible to provide honest responses. We did not need a recording to transcribe as ours was not a scholarly study as such with the requirements that might come from peer-reviewed journals.

9.8 Experiments

The use of experiments is ubiquitous in the natural and physical sciences, but they are also occasionally used in the social sciences, including finance and accounting. For clarity here, when we discuss experiments in a 'lab', these will be based around individuals in a computer room rather than a laboratory with chemicals and a fume cupboard.

Experiments are valuable when it is of interest to establish a group of highly controlled conditions and to examine, for example, how people behave in certain fixed circumstances or how they react to particular types of information. For this reason, experiments are used in behavioural finance and economics to examine how a range of factors affects decision-making. For instance, one class of experiments aims to prime respondents to have a specific emotional state (e.g., instilling fear by asking them to recall and write about previous events in their lives that they felt fearful about) and then getting them to choose between safe and risky assets in various scenarios. Another group of respondents then performs the same task but without the priming.

This technique provides a method for answering otherwise imponderable questions due to the precisely controlled nature of the lab conditions, and they also allow the researcher to infer causality (i.e., the result can be attributed directly to the treatment given after allowing for random differences in covariate characteristics between the treatment and control sets). Attempts are made in the experimental design to ensure that these covariates or extraneous factors have no effect on the outcomes. This will happen naturally to some extent due to the randomisation but also through collecting all relevant information about participants and using that as additional explanatory variables in any regression models used to analyse the results.

Experiments can be enormously valuable in allowing the researcher to examine various aspects of a decision under controlled conditions. This level of control allows the investigator to home in on particular explanations for particular phenomena and to isolate the impact of all the others, which should result in a high degree of internal validity. Thus, experimental data are highly amenable to causal analysis using regression-type frameworks.

Experiments comprise establishing a tightly controlled set of conditions, typically using a treatment group and a control group, with participants randomly assigned to one group or the other. The former will be given some additional details (e.g., they are given additional information) not shown to the latter, or they will be subject to an additional stimulus or manipulation not applied to the control set. Randomisation of participants between the treatment and control groups is used to ensure that the distribution of treatments is unrelated to any participant characteristics.

However, in situations where the sample is expected to be unbalanced along certain dimensions, then it might be that participants are assigned to the treatment and control groups in order to match the sample as far as possible for that dimension. For example, if it is expected that overseas students would approach the task differently to home students, but there are far fewer of the former in the cohort, it might be that the sampling frame is set up to split the overseas students equally between the treatment and control sets. Unfortunately, matching the samples in this way would mean that it would be impossible to assess the impact of a student's origin on their performance of the task. But if this was not the primary aim of the experiment, it would be better than leaving open the possibility that almost all of the overseas students ended up concentrated in one of the groups by chance.

Disadvantages of experiments as a research method

To conduct solid experiments requires specialist skills and equipment that will not be available to the majority of bachelor's or master's students in business schools. Hence their use among this group of students is rare. Setting up experiments also requires a substantial infrastructure (such as a lab with computers and a set of willing participants who fit the screening criteria) to produce valid findings. The use of theory is still important in an experimental setting to guide the design, facilitate the interpretation of the results, support the external validity and to put the findings into context.

There may be additional difficulties in getting the experimental conditions to match those of real life, and not achieving this can diminish the value of the results. Returning to the previous example, if the context is financial decision-making, and you ask participants to select between risky and risk-free choices, the outcome of the decision they make during an experiment will have no impact on those making it whether they make a good or bad choice. The situation is akin to 'playing poker for match sticks', where the player's strategy is likely to be very different from the one that they would use if real money were involved. This problem is sometimes known as hypothetical bias, where it is difficult to artificially get participants into the frame of mind that they would be if they were really making an important choice.

Indeed, some scholars would argue that in order for an experiment to be worthwhile, only practitioners of accounting or finance should be used as subjects since they alone have the relevant skills and information to make realistic decisions. For that reason, some journals are reluctant to consider studies for publication if the participants were students. Other scholars have argued that provided the experimental setup and incentive structure are realistic, valid results can be obtained from student subjects.

Natural experiments

Numerous studies in accounting and finance make use of 'natural experiments', which occur when there is a significant exogenous (externally driven) change in an important aspect of how something works, such as regulations or market structure. For instance, in the UK from April 2015, the government changed the law to allow people much greater freedom in how they could access their private pension funds, in effect enabling retired savers to withdraw the entire pot in cash (whilst paying tax on the income) if they wished.

A possible implication of these new freedoms is that they could encourage greater savings among younger workers who will be aware that they would be able to access their pensions in a way that was previously not possible upon retirement. This situation would be a natural experiment since a researcher could conduct a comparative study of savings rates into pensions and retirement fund access choices before and after the legislative change.

Natural experiments provide a powerful setting for researchers in accounting and finance since they enable us to examine what has happened under a specific set of conditions in a way that would normally not be possible since it is infeasible to change legislation on a whim just to see how people react. We could, of course, aim to replicate the effects of legislative changes using a lab-based experiment and study how participants react, but this would arguably be much less realistic, again suffering from hypothetical bias. The natural experiment, on the other hand, relates to a real event rather than an artificially constructed one. If you are able to identify such a natural experiment and can make use of it in your research design, you would have an exciting and worthwhile project.

9.9   Case studies

9.9.1   A single case study

Case studies can be single or comparative. A single case study involves examining a specific event or phenomenon through a forensic, highly detailed analysis within its own environment of what happened and all of the circumstances around it. The phrase *within its own environment* is key here since the purpose of much scientific research is precisely to decontextualise studies (i.e., to remove them from their original context) to make the findings more generalisable and to allow focus on the phenomenon under study rather than the background. In case study research, however, the entity under study and its environment are examined as one. This entity under study could, for instance, be a person, a firm, a market or a government.

The case study approach is particularly useful where something of interest occurred only once or twice, and so a quantitative, data-heavy approach is not feasible, or when a phenomenon is new or complex and cannot be separated from its environment. Thus it is the uniqueness of the individual or situation which is of most value. In such cases, generalising the findings would not be relevant or useful anyway and therefore nothing is lost by focusing on this one instance *in situ*.

Case studies can either focus on historical events or on a currently occurring phenomenon. Those based on historical information will primarily aim to answer 'how' questions, such as investigating how procedures within an organisation function, how individuals or groups interact, or how decisions are made. For example, single case studies have been undertaken on accounts of the activities and downfall of 'rogue traders', such as the fascinating account by Greener (2006) of Nick Lesson, who famously caused Barings Bank's collapse. Case studies can also examine current phenomena using, for example, interviews which will also enable them to answer 'why' questions.

Research focusing on a single case study provides the chance to grasp the intricacies of a situation, including the relationships between all of the agents involved and how these interplay to generate the observed outcomes. It is usually straightforward to expand or contract the study's scope to fit the time allocated and modify the nature and content of the investigation as it progresses.

In some ways, case studies are not even formal methods, but instead, they merely attempt to provide a historically accurate account of an event or occurrence, sometimes explicitly written to put forward a particular perspective. Often, case studies will involve either a detailed examination of the relevant secondary documents (e.g., from other academic studies, newspapers and archives) or interviews with individuals most closely linked with the event under investigation.

Case studies can be tackled using a range of approaches to data collection, including interviews, printed media (both scholarly and popular), archives, and participant or non-participant observation, which provides considerable flexibility. The use of varied data sources allows each to provide a cross-check of the others and supports the validity of the analysis despite the fact that only one or a small number of entities is being examined. Case studies have particular value in situations where there is a lack of formal theory or the number of available observations is small, although they could be a precursor to a wider analysis using a larger sample.

Case studies tend to be descriptive in nature, although conceptual models could be developed based on what is observed using an inductive approach. Causality might also be discussed, with arguments presented as to why relationships should arise in particular directions, but there can, by definition, be no formal tests of causation with a case study, and so the reader must simply accept the writer's argument (or not accept it). Having an in-depth knowledge of the circumstances surrounding the issues presented in the case study is crucial, and the writing style must be engaging and authoritative for it to be convincing. A single case study can be adopted as a precursor to conducting a wider analysis – for instance, where a researcher wishes to examine the feasibility of a particular line of enquiry before committing the time and resources to extensive interviews.

There is no standard template for structuring a case study or what to include, so if you plan to use this approach, it is best to examine a range of existing such studies and identify the approach that seems to work best. It should, of course, incorporate evidence to back up any claims you make, which can include tables, charts, flow diagrams, or quotations from relevant individuals. Strong case studies will incorporate both quantitative and qualitative evidence, and while the time will not be spent on detailed statistical analysis, the narrative needs to be very polished. By their nature, case studies are immersive and focused, but must still nonetheless be positioned within a relevant academic literature.

It would be best to begin by sketching out the case study's outline, listing the key elements in order. While the unstructured nature of case studies is a major strength, it also embodies some dangers due to the potential for investigators to misrepresent the situation or bias the findings due to their own preconceptions, thus diminishing the reliability of the study. It is common for case study authors to write up their research as a story without going into great detail about how they reached their conclusions from the data, or how they selected the particular items of information used rather than others that they could have employed. Many authors also fail to consider or discuss possible alternative explanations of their findings or pinpoint aspects where the meaning of the data is ambiguous.

Therefore, it is essential to establish the research design at an early stage as would be done for a survey or quantitative analysis of secondary data. Specify the research questions in advance, at least in outline form, and reflect on what you want to obtain from the case study before you begin. You also need to consider carefully your data needs before approaching any organisations since they are likely to want to know how much of their time and what access to their facilities you will require. You also need to build in contingencies in case anything does not go to plan – for instance, if you do not get access to all the sources you anticipated, or you do not uncover the new controversies you had hoped for.

A case study of a case study

Although case studies are extremely rarely used as a research tool in finance and are also not particularly common in accounting, there is a handful around. An excellent example of the latter is the study by Larrinaga-Gonzales and Bebbington (2001). They use a single case study in the context of a Spanish electricity generating company conducted over a two-year interval from 1992 to 1994. When environmental reporting becomes more onerous, organisations can adjust in one of two ways: either the organisation adapts and modifies its operations or twists the environmental agenda but ostensibly continues to function largely as before, which the authors term 'institutional appropriation'.

The case study approach was ideal in this situation because:
* The electricity industry, in which the firm that is the subject of the case study operates, is a substantial emitter of greenhouse gasses and thus must be central to any national objectives to reduce emissions
* Many of the issues around sustainability that affect numerous firms in this and other industries are present here
* One of the authors was heavily involved with the organisation as an external consultant and therefore had detailed specialist knowledge
* The case study draws on a range of different types of sources, including

company papers, interviews with stakeholders, observations and attendance at
meetings

The authors begin by describing the country context and industry background,
charting its development from the 1970s until the time of writing the article. They
also describe the regulatory environment for electricity generation in Spain at that
time, which incorporated a National Energy Plan. The Plan was ambiguous in terms
of its objectives, but Larrinaga-Gonzales and Bebbington argue that it is unlikely to
have incentivised greenhouse gas emission reduction as greater electricity generation
was rewarded financially.

The authors also conduct a thorough review of the literature on research in
accounting relevant to the link between organisational structure and corporate
environmental policy change. They explain how 'appropriation' can take place
and at what levels in the organisation.

Despite conservation of the environment being a considered objective and the
establishment of a Director of Environmental Affairs role within the company
(p.276), Larrinaga-Gonzales and Bebbington highlight variations in the extent
to which senior stakeholders within the organisation believed that environmental
considerations should be at the heart of the firm's strategy. They find that
the organisation's ecological agenda was narrow, focusing on those aspects of
environmental performance that are most regulated, and satisfactory performance
was equated with compliance. The authors state that 'attempts to intervene in
organisational life using accounting did not work... the accountants in the case
study appeared to find environmental issues irrelevant to their work, despite these
issues being converted into accounting mechanisms' (p.285). They conclude that
the incentive structures at the industry level discouraged firms from getting to grips
with environmental considerations. In such a situation, despite the appropriate
management structures being present, accounting did not embody the power to cause
changes in the company.

9.9.2   A comparative case study

Single case studies are particularly valuable when the desire is to focus on one
particular individual or organisation because they are in a unique, self-contained
situation or where a phenomenon occurs that is extremely uncommon.

Precisely as the name would suggest, a comparative case study adopts the same
approach as a single case study but involves the joint examination of two or more
events or phenomena using an identical method for comparison. In this way, one
case can provide a context or benchmark and a contrast for the other to bring out
the similarities and differences between them. The comparator in such a case study
could be either the same entity but at a different point in time or a distinct entity but
linked somehow to that under study. For instance, a case study could be undertaken
on the introduction of a new financial derivatives market in a developing country
with a comparison to what happened previously during the inception of the same

type of market in a developed country.

Comparative cases can consider anything from two entities up to, perhaps even ten, although the use of more than four or five is rare and would be unwieldy and possibly repetitive. The analysis usually begins by examining each case individually before moving onto a comparison between them.

A further class of comparative case studies is where an entity is contrasted with itself at a different point in time. This would be a longitudinal study that could examine how and why changes in a particular organisation or situation occurred.

Comparative case studies can add both depth and rigour compared with single case studies, since the number of entities examined will be larger. They can also help to spread the risk that one of the foci of examination for some reason works out less well than anticipated.

Case studies – of either the single or multiple varieties – are relatively common in accounting research, but extremely rare in finance, where the preference remains to use large secondary databases for addressing any research questions. They would usually constitute exploratory or descriptive research, although they may also aim to be explanatory.

A case study of four case studies

Holland *et al.* (2012) employ a multi-case study to engage in exploratory research on how four Japanese financial organisations (three fund managers and a venture capital firm) develop and use intangible intellectual capital in their investment decisions. They employ an underpinning theory of knowledge-creating firms, with the data being drawn from archives and semi-structured interviews with relevant personnel at the companies. The study by Holland *et al.* (2012) is available in the Glasgow University repository.[32]

9.9.3 Disadvantages of case studies

Case studies, by their nature, involve looking at one, or at most a small number, of exemplars of a phenomenon and so they are sometimes regarded as merely anecdotal and it would be meaningless to discuss whether they are rigorous or not. They could have been chosen precisely because they represent extreme rather than typical illustrations, and, as already mentioned, there is no attempt to generalise the findings. Therefore, the results need to be accepted purely for what they are in the situation they are embedded within.

Case studies are only feasible if you have access to all of the relevant sources, and they are made even stronger if your contacts are unique to you so that you are able to do something that other researchers could not. For instance, this might be because you are related to someone working at senior level in an organisation that will permit you to view their archives and historical records, or grant interviews that would be refused to other researchers.

---

[32]http://eprints.gla.ac.uk/71970/

However, a further issue with case studies may arise due to their focus on a single entity – which might be a single individual or a single company. This could lead to problems where that person or organisation feels that they have been over-utilised and so is unwilling to provide further access and the gates close before the data collection has been completed. Critics argue that they are anecdotal and purely illustrative, lacking in analysis and rigour. While case studies might have a high entertainment value if well written, they can struggle to offer additional insights beyond those already available in the existing sources that the researcher consulted to obtain the information.

9.10   Archival data

Archives, including company records offices, The National Archives in the UK and local records offices, provide a rich source of information for historically focused dissertations in accounting and finance. However, using such archives systematically and validly requires specialist training and skills that is probably beyond the time available in a student project for those without a history background. Therefore, archival research is not covered here, although readers are referred to the book chapter by Ventresca and Mohr (2017) and the citations therein for detailed information; Eilifsen and Messier (2000) provide an illustration of a particular use of archival research in the context of financial statement analysis available from Research Gate.[33]

9.11   Mixed methods

The use of 'mixed methods' for data collection and analysis, sometimes known as methodological pluralism or multi-strategy research, has become fashionable. It involves the simultaneous use of more than one approach to cover the weaknesses inherent in individual techniques and obtain a more comprehensive viewpoint.

There are several ways to set up a mixed methods design. A first possibility is conducting a so-called two-phase study where one technique is employed first, with the results then informing how the other is used. For example, an investigation of secondary data can be supplemented by a small number of interviews with key decision-makers to get further insight into those specific cases. Alternatively, an interview could be used to gain insights into a phenomenon from a typical individual's perspective before conducting a more comprehensive survey using a large sample of respondents.

A second technique is to conduct the two phases in parallel, with neither the quantitative nor the qualitative aspects informing the other. This approach would

[33] https://www.researchgate.net/profile/Aasmund-Eilifsen/publication/260273218_
The_Incidence_and_Detection_of_Misstatements_A_Review_and_Integration_of_Archival_
Research/links/02e7e530715e120256000000/The-Incidence-and-Detection-of-Misstatements-A-
Review-and-Integration-of-Archival-Research.pdf

save some time and might be preferable in the situation where it is a large study with separate academics conducting each part.

A final option would be where the focus is predominantly on one side of the study, with the other playing a limited role – for example, conducting a broad-based survey with a practitioner expert commenting on the results and offering their perceptions of what the results mean.

While this combined approach can lead to deeper engagement with the research questions, it is probably infeasible for most undergraduate or taught postgraduate degree dissertations given the time constraints. It would also require a strong familiarity with both quantitative and qualitative approaches, which very few scholars possess. When mixed methods are used in academic studies, it would typically be by a team of authors with different backgrounds who can pool their skills.

From a philosophical perspective, it might also be difficult to combine methods that require the researcher to see the world from very different viewpoints. For instance, those conducting large-scale quantitative studies typically consider that phenomena can be objectively measured, whereas qualitative researchers usually believe that all knowledge is subjective. For this reason, it is also more challenging to write up mixed method studies since qualitative and quantitative studies tend to have somewhat different narrative styles and structures. Given the additional challenges from implementing more than one research approach in a single study, the number of examples is relatively small but a good illustration is the paper by Tucker and Parker (2014) discussed in more detail in subsection 9.6.2.

9.12   Validating the data and results

9.12.1   Checking quantitative data

In terms of assessing your finding's robustness, two concepts used in a specific way in psychology research are useful: reliability and validity. In the context of accounting and finance, we can think of reliability as referring to whether your results are secure and are likely to be repeated if tested again with slightly different data or in a different context. Validity is a more general notion embodying two aspects:

1. One aspect is known as content validity (sometimes also known as face validity or measurement validity), which refers to whether your model actually measures what it aims to.

2. Measurement validity may be impossible to assess fully, so a second aspect of validity is often used, known as construct validity. This is taken to mean that all details of the methodological approach adopted are credible and consistent with best practice, leading the reader to have confidence in your conclusions.

It is sometimes argued that without validity, reliability is not worth measuring. Although there is no scope in this book to cover quantitative methods for data analysis in any significant detail, a point to emphasise is how vital it is to sense check all of your data and results. Sense checking means not going into autopilot and taking everything at face value but instead looking carefully for outliers, data entry errors, or issues relating to inconsistent data transformation in both the raw inputs and the findings. Even one observation in the dataset that is a long way from the others could render the results utterly invalid. For example, in a survey, it might be that someone is typing their age as '38' but presses the key too hard, so it registers as '388'. It would be easy to include that data point alongside all the others and not notice that it makes no sense; any subsequent analysis you conduct using an 'age' variable would be worthless.

It is also vital to conduct a similar check of the results tables and figures. If something doesn't look right, go back and identify where that number came from and see whether you can explain why it has that value, particularly if you did have to type in the results manually. Common mistakes are forgetting negative signs, putting the decimal point in the wrong place, or typing the wrong number of zeros.

9.12.2   Checking qualitative data

Validating qualitative data such as that from unstructured interviews is even more important than for most quantitative data but much more challenging. The former's sample size will be minimal – perhaps only a handful of different records and certainly not more than ten for a student project. Thus, the statistical arguments available for quantitative data cannot be applied, and concepts such as random, representative sampling will also not be applicable.

Moreover, since interview data tend to be employed in studies adopting an inductive approach, the lack of prior theory can lead to accusations that the results are coincidental and anecdotal so that another researcher could have started with the same research objectives and arrived at a very different answer. However, there are several steps that can be taken to inspire confidence among readers that a qualitative dataset has validity. These primarily involve taking steps to minimise researcher and respondent biases:

- Ensuring that the questions asked are detailed, well-informed by the existing literature, and focused squarely on the study's research objectives.
- Ensuring that the data fully justify every statement you make, and if there are ambiguities or inconsistencies across participants, that must be the conclusion on this particular issue rather than trying to claim that there is consistency where there is not. In other words, are your analyses and conclusions credible given the evidence that you have presented?
- Using as many different instruments or data sources as possible to corroborate each other in a process known as triangulation.
- 'Completing the loop' by getting participants to confirm that they did indeed state what you have written about the interview and that they have not been misquoted or misrepresented will help to ensure the credibility of your conclusions.
- Being willing to include findings that go against what you are aiming to show, but you would then intend to argue that the contrary perspective is

somehow considerably weaker or less prevalent than your central argument and providing evidence that this is the case.

- Related to the previous point, focusing particularly on negative cases that do not follow the behaviour of other participants and trying to identify why this might have occurred.

- Allowing the reader to judge how likely it is that your perspective and prior experiences have biased your interpretation of the data by stating these and explaining in detail how you mitigated any such distortions. Use appendices where necessary to include as much information as possible on your research methods to allow them to be scrutinised.

- Peer de-briefing, which means discussing your research methods and emerging findings with staff and other student researchers at every available opportunity to gain different perspectives and interpretations of your work.

Chapter takeaways – top tips for success

- ⊛ Check data availability at the earliest possible stage
- ⊛ Think about your data sample and whether it is sufficiently large and representative of the underlying population
- ⊛ If you are using a survey or interviews, determine how you will obtain respondents and how you would deal with a failure to get sufficient numbers or buy-in
- ⊛ If you are using a survey or interviews, ensure that you check it thoroughly and run a pilot before launching the full investigation
- ⊛ Your data analysis should be accurate and comprehensive. Ensure that all tables and figures are explicitly mentioned in the text and discussed at an appropriate level of detail
- ⊛ Confirm the validity of your data, whether it is of a quantitative or qualitative form

Writing and polishing

10. WRITING UP THE PROJECT

Learning outcomes: this chapter covers

✓ The academic style of writing
✓ How to structure your dissertation
✓ What to include in each chapter
✓ How to write in an entertaining way

This is the big moment when it all starts to come together, and your dissertation begins to take shape. It's an exciting stage, but one that many students dread. How will you organise all that material, and how will it fit together? This chapter will cover all aspects of the process of writing up the project document from the cover page to the appendices and aims to make the task as painless and effective as possible.

It is advisable always to start writing at the earliest possible stage and to continue progressively with it rather than leaving all the writing until the final stage because:

- Writing can help to pin ideas down and make them more concrete
- It can help you identify problems with the research design and improve the quality of the investigative work before you waste a lot of time
- Intermingling the writing, data collection and analysis may reduce the boredom related to spending all your current research time on one type of activity
- Writing is something you can always continue to ensure that time is not wasted when you hit blocks with the investigative work – for example, waiting for e-mail replies about data or waiting for surveys to be completed or trying to fix bugs in non-functioning code

- You might be able to get early feedback on sample chapters or sections from classmates or your supervisor that can be taken on board to improve the style of the final draft

10.1   Preparing to write and laying the foundations

Writing is hard work and draining yet requires creativity, so it is hard to do it well if you are tired, stressed or distracted; always try to schedule your best time for writing. It is also evident that different people need varying environments to motivate them to get the job done. Some need deadlines to discipline them, but others find it hard to work under pressure. Set yourself realistic targets (or agree on these with your supervisor) and try to stick to them even if they are artificial and not formal submission points. Some researchers need to 'crank up', which means that they start slowly but build up momentum, writing very little initially but then progressing much faster once they get into it. If you are such a person, don't be concerned if you find you are making slow progress with your drafting initially.

The most important aspect is to set aside regular quality time for writing – indeed, it is worth noting that almost all professional writers treat it as they would a job, working consistent hours each day rather than in fits and starts. Frequent, short blocks of one to two hours will probably be best, alongside realistic targets of how many words or which sub-sections to write in each sitting.

Many people find writing difficult, and they sit for hours and write very little. One reason they are slow is that in their own mind, they have convinced themselves that it should be possible to write something brilliant, and so they agonise over every word and end up writing almost nothing. Their own self-criticism prevents them from making any progress. Others insist on having a detailed structure for the draft worked out and penned before they can begin write a single word of the actual piece. However, this is not necessary since, often, the project or section will assume both structure and shape at the same time because the process of thinking about what to write clarifies the appropriate ordering and flow of the material.

For those who prefer to have a structure to work towards, a good way to start can be to develop a roadmap for the chapter, which explains to the reader what will be covered there. This will satisfy two objectives: it will be a valuable guide for the reader in the final version but more importantly it will satisfy the writer's desire to work from a pre-existing outline.

Writing something reasonably good is better than aiming to write an outstanding piece and not getting past the first sentence. Remind yourself that you are starting, not finishing, and the redraft will be easier than the first draft. There is a saying that 'you cannot edit a blank page'. Writing the first draft is by far the hardest aspect, while improving what you have already written is relatively straightforward. Once you begin constructing the chapters, the 'writer's block' will quickly clear, and the words will start to flow more easily.

Most researchers for whom writing does not come naturally find it harder to get started than to continue or finish. Such individuals are best just to write something relevant to get 'in the zone', and in that case, it is likely to be more effective to write the most straightforward part first, then do the hard parts and fill in the gaps later.

Related to this, you should not feel obliged to write a piece in the correct order. In reality, almost no academics or professional writers do that. A common approach would be to write an initial draft of the literature review first, followed by the methodology, data and results next, and then finally create a story around them that builds into a coherent picture. This strategy implies that you would probably write most of the introduction, conclusion and abstract last.

Some researchers, albeit a declining number, also find that hand-writing early drafts helps them, especially for those who can write more quickly than they can type. They might also note down a skeleton plan or structure first before writing the actual piece, which helps them organise their thoughts. But you should use the approach that seems the most natural and works best for you. Hand-writing initial drafts will of course take longer overall than moving straight to a word-processor but is worthwhile if it helps you to be more creative.

10.1.1   At what are you aiming?

It is worth reading carefully through the rules at an early stage to know precisely what you are aiming at and to avoid wasting much time doing unnecessary work while skimping on essential aspects. If you can, try to get hold of a finished project document from a previous cohort. Even if you have already taken a look through these at the ideas and proposal-writing stage, it is worth doing so again since now you will be focusing on different aspects of the work. Specifically, you will be examining the presentation – the structure, length, chapter headings, layout, font and margin sizes, and so on. Completed project documents will provide a useful guide as to what you are aiming to produce. You can also assess the strengths and weaknesses of the sample project so that yours is even better.

Before you dig deep into the writing phase, it is worth stepping back and considering the structure – what will be the main sections in the project, how long will they be, and in what order? Thinking about this at an early stage will be worthwhile because it will allow you to write according to a formula to some extent – if the skeleton outline is already there, it is just a matter of filling in the gaps. You will then also have a reasonable idea if you have perhaps written too much on some aspects and not enough on others.

A typical project in accounting, finance or management is likely to be somewhere between 25 and 50 pages long, including everything - front matter, main body, tables, figures and references, although the actual length may vary significantly depending upon the subject matter. Both the layout and the overall length will probably be roughly similar to those of a published paper in the project's subject area. Note, though, that published articles often look much shorter than they are because the small font and tight spacing turns a 50-page working paper into a 20-page published

Table 10.1: Suggested lengths for each chapter in a research project

Chapter	Expected length	Expected number of words	Expected percentage of entire document
Introduction	4 pages	1,600 words	16%
Literature review	6 pages	2,400 words	24%
Methods and data	6 pages	2,400 words	24%
Results (including tables)	5 pages	2,000 words	20%
Conclusions	4 pages	1,600 words	16%
Overall length	25 pages	10,000 words	100%

paper.

Although every project will be different and there is not just one format that will work, in general, there needs to be a sensible balance between the amount of space devoted to each of the major parts of the document. As a very rough guide, I propose the following for an example of a project where the main body is 25 pages of 400 words each (total, 10,000 words), with the front matter, references, and any appendices considered separately, as suggested in Table 10.1.

Note that the suggestion in the table is a rough suggestion rather than a fixed rule, but there should be a sensible balance between the project's main components to avoid giving the reader the impression that some parts are overwhelming the others. For instance, as discussed in chapter 5, it is common for research proposals to be review-heavy, and the same is true of dissertations, which is undesirable since it is primarily your ideas and new work that the reader is interested in. On the other hand, a project where half of the pages are taken up with detailed tables of results would also be unbalanced.

The suggested proportions for each component indicate that the description and discussion of your investigative work will be at the heart of the project, constituting about half of the overall space available. Note that counting the number of words or pages accurately is surprisingly tricky and probably a fruitless endeavour as there are several plausible ways to do so that could lead to quite different numbers. For instance, do tables count towards the word total? How about footnotes? If you reduce the margins or reduce the font size, have you reduced the word count? (of course not, but it can make the document length look substantially different).

Each chapter in the document should flow seamlessly from the previous one so that they fit together like a book. Consequently, the chapters do not have to be self-contained, and you can assume that readers will go through it in page order from the front to the back cover and will therefore be familiar with any material that you had discussed previously (although reminding them of the meaning of unfamiliar acronyms or esoteric words might still be helpful).

10.1.2 Some Tips for Successful Writing

The importance of clear, persuasive drafting should never be underestimated. As a leading academic economist, John Cochrane, argues, 'Many economists falsely think of themselves as scientists who just "write up" research. We are not; we are primarily writers. Economics and finance papers are essays. Most good economists spend at least 50% of the time they put into any project on writing.' The same principle applies equally in accounting and finance as economics.

Even if your core idea was not very good or the results didn't go in your favour, you can make up for a lot of that and improve your mark substantially with a good layout and precise, polished writing. Learning to write with clarity, reasonable structure, accurate grammar and in an engaging way is also a useful life skill that many employers value. You can save time by thinking in advance about what you want to write, thus avoiding the need for endless redrafting.

Your writing needs to be succinct – i.e., using as few words as possible to get the point across. Your supervisor and other markers are likely to have several (one year, some time ago, I had 20) projects to read, and so writing that is too wordy and doesn't get to the point will frustrate them. Their minds will drift, they will begin to skim read, and your mark will suffer.

Whenever you write, whether it is for the dissertation or anything else, it is essential to consider your audience:

1. For whom are you writing?
2. What do they want to read?
3. What is their prior level of knowledge and understanding, both about the general subject area and also about your topic more specifically?

Your supervisor and markers (other faculty members) are your primary audience here, and you can think of them as being knowledgeable about accounting or finance in general, but they may or may not be experts on your precise subject. You need to bear that in mind, in particular, when drafting the literature review and methods chapters. Write for intelligent people familiar with the area, broadly described, so you do not need to cover elementary material ('accounting and finance 101').

Try to be clear, succinct and use language that is neither stilted (i.e., old fashioned, e.g., never write, 'one needs to write formally') nor too informal (like a text message that you might send to friends). Writing is like many other crafts, with some people being naturally talented and being able to express themselves quickly and effortlessly, and turning out polished, final drafts in just one hit; others will never be powerful writers, but everyone can improve with practice.

Writing is probably best thought of as an art rather than a science – in other words, there are numerous different ways to get the same message across to your readers, so there is no magic formula and no single right answer. Writing is an exercise in explaining yourself clearly, trying to place yourself in the position of the reader who has probably read less of the literature than you (or at least, read it a while ago and now remembers less of it) and thinking carefully about ways to make them understand it better. The ordering of the material is important, so make sure that you introduce new concepts first and then discuss and make use of them; it is very easy to get this the wrong way around, especially when you write the project out of page order.

10.1.3 The 'scholarly style' of writing

Although each academic writes differently, with some being more successful than others at communicating their message, a certain literary style pervades academic work. Focusing predominantly on accounting and finance as disciplines, we could characterise it in the following way:

* Academics tend to write at length and with depth, and so most studies written by scholars tend to be longer and more exhaustive than pieces written on the same topic by non-academics.
* The presentation should be clear and straightforward, visually appealing but not glitzy, focusing on the writing quality and the underpinning investigative work
* The style is formal. For example, even though I have used contractions in this book because I think the informality makes it easier to read given its length, I would not use 'don't', 'can't', etc., in an academic paper. Similarly, loose, overly friendly, informal, and slang language should be avoided. For instance, don't use words such as 'gutted', 'ballpark', or 'dodgy'
* Try to avoid writing sentences that are too long or contain too many clauses as it makes the draft dense and hard to follow. In general, if a sentence is more than a couple of lines long, see if it can be broken into two sentences.
* The project structure can be varied slightly, but the key ingredients and order are almost always the same. This is what is expected in an academic piece, and to depart substantially in the dissertation from the usual formula would be highly risky and could generate a low mark
* Technical terminology is frequently used, but the specialist language is always carefully defined the first time that it is used in a document with an appropriate level of knowledge assumed of the reader
* The arguments are always somewhat understated. There is no boasting, and there should be no exaggerating the strength of the findings. Precision and accuracy in descriptions are expected. It is common to see wording such as 'the results are suggestive of...' or 'the parameter estimates point to...' rather than 'the results prove ...'. Remember, your results are tentative, not definitive, so avoid giving the impression that you believe them to be indisputable. Perhaps another researcher with slightly different data or models would have come up with dissimilar findings
* Related to the previous point, your arguments' tone should be balanced and not in any way emotional, whether you were particularly impressed or unimpressed by a study. It is fine to say that one author's approach is more robust than

another or that the findings are more plausible, but don't suggest that one paper is excellent while another is weak

- There is an emphasis on ensuring the robustness of results, and so it is common to repeatedly vary the methods and data slightly to determine whether the main results remain unaltered. The proliferation of similar results tables and discussion can be somewhat dull for the reader, so a careful balance is required to avoid excessive repetition. A common approach is to put the robustness checks in a clearly named, separate section so that they can be skimmed over unless the reader wants to focus specifically on these additional details
- As discussed in chapter 7, critique is an essential part of academic writing, but it is always subtle and polite
- Viewpoints should be balanced, and even if you end up following one line of reasoning, the alternatives should always be presented and discussed, with explanations as to why these approaches are not appropriate or optimal
- The writing is heavily referenced with citations to existing studies. This is a key difference compared with formal non-academic writing, such as reports written by management consultants or regulatory bodies, which might share many of the other characteristics described in this list
- The number of citations per page of text needs to be just right, which is a delicate balance to achieve. Too few citations implies an under-referenced document that is not sufficiently well embedded in the existing literature while too many will disrupt the flow of text and make the work appear excessively derivative of prior studies so that the present piece seems to be adding little that is new
- Even more important than adopting a good style is to adopt a consistent one, so ensure that all your chapters are written in the same fashion and to the same standard
- Always substantiate any claims you make with evidence – this can be drawn from your own research findings or from the previous literature, where you would then include a citation in parentheses to the existing study which identified it. In general, unsubstantiated opinions are best avoided, except perhaps in the concluding chapter of your dissertation, which could, for instance, be somewhat speculative about future research or the implications of your findings. But if you are making a value judgement, you should state that rather than giving the impression that the statement being presented is a fact

While slang should be avoided entirely, it is acceptable to write in the first person ('I evaluated X and then I also examined Y') or use the passive voice ('X was evaluated and then Y was also examined...'). Whether the active or passive style should be used is the subject of much disagreement between authors. Automated grammar checkers usually frown upon the use of the passive voice and recommend that it is changed to an active style. But the passive approach is the standard way that scientific studies are described to give an impression of independence between the research and the researcher. Not having personal pronouns (I or we) allows the focus to be on the research rather than the researcher(s). On this point, we might conclude that academic writing is different from that for other purposes, and thus both active and passive styles are suitable.

10.1.4   Are you an informer or an entertainer?

When you write, your primary task is to explain what you are doing, how and why, with as much clarity as possible. After all, writing is first and foremost an exercise in communication: you know what you think about your research topic and what you have done, and now the task is to get that across as effectively as possible to your supervisor, and other readers of your dissertation document.

But your secondary role is as an entertainer. Just as some individuals give lectures that send the listener to sleep, so too do some writers bore the reader. Make your writing as lively as possible so that the reader is keen to keep turning the page rather than finding it a chore with their mind wandering to putting the dishwasher on or what to feed the cat. Entertaining doesn't mean filling the pages with jokes or funny pictures; it means writing in a lively and engaging way. There are many webpages on improving academic writing but be careful with these, as many are simply a front to advertise an essay mill. I found the Oxford-royale site to have some useful tips.[1] Here are some further suggestions to make your writing more entertaining:

- Your writing needs to be reasonably formal, and so this makes it challenging to introduce humour or use the style you might see in a blog piece. For example, although it is acceptable to include funny images in a slideshow presentation to illustrate a point, it would seem out of place to do so in a dissertation. But you can make the material pleasant to read by being clear, not repeating yourself, and varying both the phraseology and the presentation. This means not using the same phrases repeatedly – try to think of different ways to explain things
- Use some bullet points or numbered lists rather than just long paragraphs – this helps to make the material more digestible and breaks up the sections of text
- Spend plenty of time on your abstract and introduction – these are the first parts the reader sees, and they set the scene for the rest of the project. These are also the aspects where you can use some imagination in what and how you write. By contrast, the methods, data and results are much more factual and harder to draft appealingly (although they should still be clear and succinct)
- Including pictures, tables, or quotes (where relevant) helps break up the sections and make them visually more interesting. Anecdotes, examples, or short case studies help bring a narrative to life even if the project's core focus is a quantitative big data study
- It is common for working paper versions of academic studies to gather all of the tables and figures at the end of the document after the references. But

---

[1] https://www.oxford-royale.com/articles/make-writing-interesting/

when the document is typeset into its published form once accepted by a journal, the tables are shifted into the relevant places within the text where they are first mentioned. I think the latter is also a much better style for a dissertation than putting them all at the end where they probably won't even be seen. Intermingling the tables and figures with the writing makes the project more fun to read

10.2 Getting the document structure right

The more 'scientific' fields tend to favour a larger quantity of numbered sub-headings. In contrast, more discursive work (such as that in historical accounting, behavioural finance, or critical accounting) makes less use of them, typically using only main headings, with sub-headings limited in frequency of use and unnumbered.

Write the project around the contributions that you are making. Your investigative work should be the star of the show, with everything before building up to it and everything after explaining what you have done, what it means, and why it is important and for whom.

Try to avoid repetition since this will waste valuable words and take the place of more original content you could have included. Having said that, you will still need to summarise the key findings three times: in the abstract, introduction and conclusions, as well as explaining them in detail in the results section. Hence a valuable skill is learning to write ostensibly the same thing using different language. Never just copy and paste the same blocks of phrases from one part of the document to another – the reader will probably spot this, it makes the work tiresome to read, and you will appear lazy.

If you look carefully at the best-written journal papers, you will notice a subtle change in style through the article. The introductory section, while being more general in terms of the subject matter covered, also tends to be written in a somewhat less formal style, perhaps referring to articles in the popular press or blogs as motivational tools. This slightly journalistic style might also apply in the final paragraphs of the conclusions, where the author aims to make some long-lasting impressions about the relevance and gravity of the findings. The parts in the middle, though – the data, methods, and results sections – will probably be written formally in a style as dry as unbuttered toast.

Try to avoid using too many footnotes – they disrupt the flow of the document so that the reader has to keep moving between the body text and the bottom of each page unless they entirely ignore the footnotes, which would defeat the object of including them. Endnotes, where the notes are gathered together in a single list at the end of the document rather than in the footers of each page, are even worse from this perspective. If the footnoted (or 'endnoted') material is essential, include it in the main body instead; if it is not vital, drop it altogether.

Also, aim to link each section or sub-section together so that the narrative flows seamlessly through the document. This can be achieved in various ways, including linking sentences at the end of a section or the beginning of the following one. For example, 'the previous sub-section described how accounting standards developed in the UK over the past half-century. This section now proceeds to discuss the Financial Reporting Council's contemporary role in setting standards since 2004 and how it is funded and governed.'

10.3 How to structure the project

Different projects will, of course, require somewhat varying structures, but it is worth outlining the form that a good project or dissertation will take. As stated previously, unless there are good reasons for doing otherwise (for example, because of the nature of the subject), it is advisable to follow the format and structure of a full-length article in a scholarly journal. Many journal articles are, at approximately 8,000-12,000 words long, roughly the same length as a student research project. A suggested outline for an empirical research project in accounting or finance is presented below, with each component then examined in turn.

A basic structure for a typical dissertation or project

Title page
    Abstract or executive summary
    Acknowledgements
    Table of contents
    Chapter 1: Introduction
    Chapter 2: Literature review
    Chapter 3: Data
    Chapter 4: Methodology
    Chapter 5: Results
    Chapter 6: Conclusions
    References
    Appendices

10.3.1 The title page

The title page is usually not numbered and will contain only the title of the project, your name, student number, the date, and the name of the department, faculty, or centre in which the research is being undertaken. Try to make the cover page neat and tidy with appropriate font size and spacing. The dissertation may be marked anonymously, in which case your name should be omitted, so check the submission rules in your department.

The title should be succinct but contain sufficient detail to explain what the work is about rather than trying to be too smart with only a pun or idiom. 'Back to the Future' would be a bad choice of title as it essentially gives the reader almost no idea of what the project will be about. But 'Back to the Future: Revisiting Out of Favour Models for Forecasting Earnings Revisions' would be much better. The first part of the title could generate interest, linking with a series of films from the 1980s, while the second part explains clearly what the project is actually about.

Similarly, a recent paper that I co-authored was entitled: 'Tomorrow's fish and chip paper? Slowly incorporated news and the cross-section of stock returns.' The first part links with an idiom or old saying that 'today's news is tomorrow's fish and chip paper,' referring to the traditional practice that fish and chip takeaways were wrapped in old newspapers. The saying suggests that news is only relevant for a single day, and then it no longer has any information value. In both cases, of course, dropping the first part altogether would also be acceptable but be less striking and with less entertainment value.

For another illustration of the sorts of titles that work and that don't, look at the following suggested titles for the same project. Which do you think is most appropriate?

1. Asset Pricing Tests
2. Tests of the CAPM
3. Empirical Tests of the Four-moment CAPM
4. Empirical Tests of the Four-moment CAPM in Frontier Markets
5. Empirical Tests of the CAPM in Frontier Markets using Daily Data from 3 January 2007 - 31 October 2020

Clearly, the first title is far too broad and gives the reader little idea of what the dissertation might be about as there are so many tests that could be conducted in many different ways. The second title is an improvement since it narrows down the scope to a single model, but it could still be more explicit, and there will undoubtedly be vast numbers of existing projects and academic studies with precisely this title.

Title 3 is again an improvement as the number of applications of the four-moment CAPM is smaller still compared with those of the CAPM more broadly defined. Within this list, however, title 4 probably nails it: the addition of the clause stating the markets that the model will be tested on makes the title quite unique, and it clearly explains what the project will be about while remaining succinct. The final title pushes in the wrong direction compared with title 4 by adding excessive and unnecessary detail; the reader doesn't need to know the sample data period and frequency at this stage, so it works less well.

It is also possible and sometimes effective to generate intrigue within the reader by phrasing the title as a question, encouraging them to delve inside the document's covers to see the answer. Continuing the theme of the examples given above, a title containing a question might be, 'The Four-moment CAPM: Do Empirical Tests in Frontier Markets Show More Promise than those in Developed Countries?'

If you are stuck as to what title to select for your project, one way to decide is to write down a set of keywords that describes your research:

• What is the topic?
• What main investigative method are you using?
• What data, covering which markets or countries, and over what period?

Remember that this part should not contain too much specific detail

Once you have listed perhaps six keywords or short phrases that describe the project, try to write a sentence that includes them all. Then delete any non-essential or recurring parts, and you should have a working title.

The title needs some careful thought because that, and the abstract, are by far the most important parts of the whole project because these are always the aspects that will be read first. The title, abstract and the first couple of paragraphs of the introductory chapter represent your opportunity to draw the reader into your dissertation, so you need your writing to entice and excite them. If these pique the reader's interest and generate a good impression of the likely quality of the work as a whole, it will mean the mark that is beginning to form in your supervisor's mind will be a good one. On the other hand, if the title is vague and the abstract is noticeably rushed, the supervisor/marker will have the idea that the work is not of high quality, and the rest of the document would have to be truly impressive to win them back over.

10.3.2   The other front matter

Your dissertation definitely needs a table of contents but also adding lists of tables and figures will give the document a professional feel; you do not need an index, however. As suggested above, you might consider incorporating in the front matter a glossary of technical terms used if your topic is esoteric and includes a lot of acronyms or specialist terminology.

10.3.3   The abstract

The abstract is a short summary of the problem being addressed and of the research's main results and conclusions. The maximum permissible length of the abstract will vary, but as a general guide, it should not be more than 300 words in total, and the maximum can even be as few as 100 words for some journals. Perhaps 150-200 words is an ideal number to aim for in a research project. A conventional (and usually good) style is for the entire abstract to be contained in a single paragraph or two.

Unlike the introductory chapter, the abstract will simply state what is done in the project without referring to specific parts of the document. For instance, it is not considered necessary to incorporate phrases as follows, 'This dissertation presents and compares several approaches to measuring financial literacy. I review the literature in chapter 2; then, using a large survey of UK-based investors of varying ages, in chapter 3, I demonstrate...' There is no need to mention the literature review in the abstract as it can be taken for granted in this part that you conducted one. There is also no need to refer to 'chapter 3' and so on here either, so that phrase should be dropped as this sort of material belongs in the introduction where there is more space.

The abstract should usually not contain any quotations, and it should not be unduly technical even if the subject matter of the project is. It should not include any references – these should be left for the main body of the project and the abstract written in general terms without citing any specific studies. It should summarise the research problem and main aims of the work, the broad methodology used, and the main findings and conclusions. In other words, the abstract needs to summarise the entire dissertation, not just the results. Academic papers are not like murder-mysteries, where you don't find out 'whodunit' right until the end. You should put the punchline right at the front in the abstract and the introduction – this will cement the importance of the work in the reader's mind from the outset.

An abstract is always the most crucial aspect of a research paper. It will be the first thing that is read, and if it is dull or hard to follow, the most likely outcome is that the reader will stop going through the whole paper. The abstract is often used as a sort of advertising blurb for the full article, where it is included on websites and is searchable and viewable without restriction or payment in a way that the whole paper is not. Abstracts are frequently listed on websites without the rest of the article, and so they should always stand-alone – in other words, they need to make sense if, together with the title, that is all the reader sees. This is the primary reason why they should not refer to other sections in the dissertation and should use as little technical terminology as possible given the subject matter.

Likewise, in a student research project, the abstract is arguably the single most important aspect of the entire document. Once you had gone through a few journal articles, no doubt that you started using the abstract as a filter: if what was written in it did not grab your attention, you probably put the paper on the 'read later if time permits' pile. Your supervisor won't have the luxury of discarding your project if the abstract is uninspiring, but it will set their expectations for the remainder of the work at a low level. Consequently, this aspect must be as strong as possible, yet unfortunately, it is often rushed and significantly less well written than the rest of the document. A further common pitfall is to write the abstract as if it were the opening paragraph of the introductory chapter - in other words, it is all or mostly background information and allocates insufficient space to discussing the work in the dissertation.

It is often best to write the abstract at the very last stage since then it can most accurately reflect the contents of the whole project document as it stands at the end, rather than representing what you initially thought you would be writing about. But every word in the abstract should be carefully considered for the first impressions reason outlined above.

It is surprising how many times the abstract does not hit the target and is not as strong as it could be. Indeed, sometimes the abstract is the very worst part of a project because a student writes it last but by then has run out of time or enthusiasm and so just rushes it through. I have also seen situations where the main body of a dissertation is relatively well written because the author paid a proof-reader to go through the grammar, but they did not do so for the abstract, which they wrote after the proof-reader had already finished. Yet since it is arguably the most crucial part of the whole dissertation, it should be the best; it's only a couple of hundred words, so put in the effort.

10.3.4 Acknowledgements

The acknowledgements section is a brief list of people whose help you would like to note. For example, it is courteous to begin by thanking your instructor or project supervisor (even if they were useless and didn't help at all). Remember, this person is also likely to be the first marker so put them in a good mood by flattering their ego. Thank any agency that gave you the data, PhD students who helped to debug your code, a librarian who showed you how to use a database, anyone you interviewed, friends who read and checked or commented upon the work, and so on.

It is traditional 'academic etiquette' to put a disclaimer after the acknowledgements in research papers, worded something like 'Responsibility for any remaining errors lies with the author(s) alone.' In some ways, this also seems appropriate for a dissertation, for it symbolises that the student is entirely responsible for the topic chosen and for the contents and the structure of the project. It is your project, so you cannot blame anyone else, either deliberately or inadvertently, for anything wrong with it. The disclaimer also reminds project authors that it is not valid to take others' work and pass it off as their own. Any ideas taken from other papers should be adequately referenced as such, and any sentences lifted directly from other research should be placed in quotations and attributed to their original author(s) as discussed in chapter 4. You will probably have seen this quoted line written in many papers, although its use is declining as it is increasingly seen as somewhat old-fashioned, and therefore it is up to you whether you include such a statement.

10.3.5 The table of contents

The table of contents should list the chapters and sections (and possibly also the sub-sections) contained in the report. The chapter and section headings should reflect accurately and concisely the subject matter that is contained within them. It should also list the number of each chapter's first page or section, including the references and any appendices.

The abstract, acknowledgements and table of contents pages are usually numbered with lower case Roman numerals (e.g., i, ii, iii, iv, etc.), and the introduction then starts on page 1 (reverting to Arabic numbers), with page numbering being consecutive thereafter for the whole document, including references and any appendices.

You should never number the title page, and it will appear sloppy if the first page of the introduction is numbered 5, for example. Also, do not let the page numbering restart from 1 on a differently formatted page (e.g., when moving from portrait to landscape layout), which Microsoft Word has a habit of doing by default.

10.3.6 The introduction

The introduction should give some very general background information on the problem considered and why it is a vital area for research. An excellent introductory section will also describe what is original in the study – in other words, how does this study help to advance the literature on this topic, or how does it address a new problem or an old problem in a new way? What are the aims and objectives of the research? If these can be clearly and concisely expressed, it usually demonstrates that the project is well defined. The introduction should be sufficiently non-technical that the intelligent non-specialist can understand what the study is about, even if the investigative work is narrow or arcane.

Setting the context in the introductory chapter is vital. This part explains to readers where the current state of thinking is and how it got there. Hence, this aspect needs to include some of the historical background (but not too much), laying the foundations for you to explain precisely what you are working on. Without this context, it is difficult for readers to see where your material fits.

The first paragraph is the most crucial to get right since the evidence suggests that markers will make up their minds about the quality of a piece of work quickly after reading just a few sentences. It is, of course, possible to win the reader back over and to recover after a poor-quality introduction followed by much better investigative work, but it will then be an unnecessary uphill struggle.

The introduction also needs to present the 'motivation' for the study. This aspect explains why the research you are doing is useful in the context of what is already known and what is not known. This part of the introductory section is your chance to sell your ideas and approach to the reader, hooking them in with statements about why the work is important and for whom.

Some authors choose to begin the introductory section with their contribution, and then they broaden it back out, using a similar writing approach as a journalist writing in a newspaper. Other researchers give a gentle build-up first, trying to motivate why the general area is important – in essence, they are identifying a knowledge gap (the whole world's knowledge gap, not just theirs) which the research conducted through the dissertation can then fill. I prefer the latter ordering, but it is really just a matter of style.

An example of the gentle build-up style is presented below from a paper by Rendall, Brooks and Hillenbrand (2021). The alternative approach of jumping in with the contribution after providing some preliminary definitions before moving back to discuss the wider literature is given in Brooks, Chen and Zeng (2018):

> 'Previous studies suggest that institutional ownership keeps growing in US stock markets and has an important role in both corporate strategy and equity pricing [references removed from here]. Institutional investors manage portfolios that are not only much greater in financial terms than those of most retail investors but also contain much larger numbers of stocks. Compared to retail investors, there is a much higher probability

that institutional investors will become owners of the stocks on both sides
of a proposed merger deal — i.e., they hold shares in both the acquirer
and the target. In the context of mergers and acquisitions (M&As), this is
termed an "institutional cross-holding."

In this paper, we investigate the externality of institutional cross-
holdings for corporate strategies through an important corporate event:
M&As. Unlike non-cross-owners, who only hold the stock on one side
of a merger deal, cross-holders tend to make decisions from a broader
perspective that nets off any potential losses from one side (usually the
acquirer) with gains made on the other (usually the target) and will
consider how the newly formed joint entity would sit within their portfolios
compared with the two existing separate stocks.'

(Brooks *et al.*, 2018, p.187).

While it is good to put the problem that you are investigating into a wider context
and to initially avoid being esoteric or using highly technical jargon, equally, try to
avoid starting with a well-used philosophical cliché such as, 'financial economists
have long been fascinated by the question of whether markets are efficient...' It is
often useful to include some simple summary statistics or a quote from the popular
press when you are starting a piece to get the reader excited about the work and
emphasise that it is a topic with practical, as well as scholarly, interest.

For example, I recently co-authored a paper that sought to investigate the
effects of borrowers' emotions and personality traits on their abilities to undertake
appropriate courses of action when they unexpectedly got into difficulties in repaying
their debts. Although the paper involved setting up hypotheses, conducting an on-line
survey and running econometric models on the data, the introduction started gently
by including some summary statistics from popular websites as follows (I have
removed the footnote references here to save space):

'In recent decades, the UK has seen a rapid rise in consumer indebtedness,
which has more than quadrupled since 1990. According to personal debt
statistics from The Money Charity, total UK household debt had risen by
381% to £1669bn in 2019 from £347bn in 1990, with the average debt
per adult at £31,643. As of March 2019, average total household debt
was around £64,000, comprising of credit card balances, student loans,
personal loans and mortgage debt – an increase of 17% in just five years.'

(Rendall, Brooks and Hillenbrand, 2021).

You need to elucidate the value that your work will add in a confident, but not
arrogant, manner. What is the significance of your project? This is sometimes
called the 'so what question'. Is your research timely because of something that is
happening now? For instance, you might be studying real estate market bubbles at
a time when house prices have risen by a third in five years, and many people are
suggesting that housing might be overvalued. Are you using an empirical approach
that is new in that research area or applying established models to a different set of

data compared with existing studies? Are any of the variables you include different from those of existing studies in an interesting way?

Returning to the debt problems paper by Rendall *et al.* mentioned above, here is how we defined our contribution and arising from a lack of previous research investigating how borrowers cope with unforeseen financial problems:

> 'While there is a reasonable body of research on individual personality and psychological attributes associated with consumer indebtedness, the vast majority of extant studies focus on modelling the original decision to take on debts. Hence, to the best of our knowledge, research focusing on the factors associated with whether individuals make risky or sensible financial decisions when already in debt and experiencing financial difficulties is lacking. We argue that this latter issue is the one that is most pertinent for exploration and analysis: being in debt is not particularly problematic if one is able to manage the debt and repayment is within one's means. Rather, the problem arises when an individual finds themselves in a situation of financial difficulty, which could be due to several factors, including unanticipated unemployment or poor health affecting the ability to earn a full income. In such situations, how individuals cope with their existing debt repayments and the choices they make to manage their debts and ensure that they remain on track could mean the difference between a temporary bump in the road or a worsening spiral into indebtedness, leading ultimately to county court judgements or even, in the most extreme circumstances, the loss of their home. Therefore, it is this all too frequent but under-researched situation – unforeseen circumstances leading to a diminished ability to make debt repayments – which is the focus of the present study'
>
> (Rendall *et al., op. cit.*).

It is fine to include some references in the introduction to demonstrate early on that you are aware of where your work fits into the wider picture. But don't fill the introduction with literature review to the extent that the reasons for doing the research and the intended contribution become lost. If you need the review part to be more than a couple of pages, put it in a separate section or entire chapter that can appear right after the introduction. In general, the introductory chapter should probably only be 3-6 pages long in total.

Your investigative work is the centrepiece of your project, and so it makes sense to build the document around it so that everything coming before (i.e., the introduction and literature review) leads up to it, and everything coming after (principally the conclusions) emphasises how good it was. To support this, researchers often include a brief summary of their results in the introductory section of their papers to give a flavour of the main findings and to whet the reader's appetite. If you do this, be careful not to overdo it by including too much information here since you will also be discussing the results in more or less detail in the abstract, results chapter and conclusions. Avoid repetition where possible and always paraphrase, never copying and pasting directly from one chapter to another. For information, in the debt paper (Rendall *et al.*) discussed above, we elected not to summarise the results in the introductory section since we felt that there was already an adequate synopsis in the abstract.

It is good to finish the introduction with an outline of the remainder of the report. Sometimes this is called the 'roadmap' because it shows the reader where they will be going from here, such as: 'The remainder of this dissertation develops as follows. Chapter 2 presents a review of the literature on the role of management accountants in organisations, focusing particularly on how they provide information to senior managers to facilitate strategic decision-making. Chapter 3 then proceeds to describe the data sources, hypotheses to be tested, and the empirical methods used in the dissertation. Chapter 4 presents the results and analysis, while Chapter 5 concludes the study and offers suggestions for future research in this area.'

When writing the introduction, the roadmap can help prepare the reader for what they should expect you to cover in the rest of that chapter (or the whole project). In the introduction, you can also explain the study's span – in other words, what you will focus on and what is out of scope and so will not be covered. This will help to avoid any subsequent misunderstandings where the reader had expected you to include some aspects or to cover a topic in a particular way, and you did not. Naturally, if you have plenty of space available, each stage of the roadmap can be further broken down into a whole paragraph with a heading (e.g., 'In the data section of Chapter 3, I...'), instead of one sentence, so that more detail is presented.

The roadmap is just one aspect of the signposting that should be present throughout your dissertation. The reader should always be aware of where they are currently in the document, where they have been and where they are going. Using page numbers, headings, and a table of contents are all aspects of this, but the signposting should also be hard-coded into the writing. Use phrases such as, 'in the previous section, I did A and B; now, I will proceed to discuss C before deriving the theoretical model in section X'.

10.3.7 The literature review

Reviewing the literature and writing the review has been the subject of the whole of chapter 7 of this book so that no further details will be given here. What you have already written should be capable of being slotted directly into the dissertation draft (possibly with some minor amendments to make it fit with the rest of the material and to remove any repetition).

10.3.8 The data

If you have used secondary data in the project, it is worth beginning this chapter by stepping back and explaining why you selected this particular dataset from the source that you used. Are there features of this information that are not present in alternatives? Are the data you selected more comprehensive or more reliable than others?

The core of this section or chapter should then describe the data in detail – the source, the format, the features of the data, and any limitations relevant for later analysis. For example, are there missing observations? Is the sample period short? Does the sample include large potential structural breaks, e.g., caused by a stock market crash? Suppose that your project uses small numbers of series which are being primarily investigated. In that case, it would make sense to plot them in this section, noting any interesting features, and to supply summary statistics – such as the mean, variance, skewness, kurtosis, minimum and maximum values of each series. If the data are time-series, you should also test for non-stationarity and measures of autocorrelation, and do on. The main results will appear later in their own section following the methodology part but data summary statistics belong here.

10.3.9 Methodology

The methodology chapter or section should describe the estimation technique(s) used to compute estimates of the models' parameters. Why did you choose the approaches you did rather than others that could have been used? The models should be outlined and explained, using equations where appropriate. Again, this description should be written critically, noting any potential weaknesses in the approach and, if relevant, why more robust or up-to-date techniques were not employed.

If the methodology used does not require detailed descriptions, this chapter may usefully be combined with the data part to comprise a single chapter on 'Data and methods.' That would be ideal if the amount of material in one or both parts only runs to a few pages.

The methods and data taken together should be described in sufficient detail that somebody else could follow what you had done as a recipe. Although researchers sometimes provide brief derivations of the steps that led to a particular mathematical model that they use, in general, it is not helpful to spend time writing in detail about other methods that you did not use. Presenting extensive information about excluded models would likely cause confusion, as well as taking up valuable space. Instead, simply explain why you chose the approach that you did and describe that in detail. Similarly, it is unnecessary to run through a derivation of the final equations you used if the steps are already available in an existing study. Instead, refer the reader to that unless the algebra is required to explain how the model works or the derivation itself is new.

Whatever methods you use to collect and analyse data, your empirical work should be replicable, which means that someone else should be able to read what you have written about how you have conducted the study and understand it. That person should then be able to repeat the steps and obtain the same results as you did, so you need to explain what you did clearly and in order.

Rather than re-defining terms or variables repeatedly, refer the reader back to the part of your document where those definitions were first presented. Also, make sure that your notation is fully consistent across the whole document. It is very confusing if a particular symbol means one thing in one chapter but a totally different variable in another. If you are briefly mentioning something, you can tell the reader that you will be discussing it in greater detail subsequently in chapter Z. As often is the case, though, there is a balance: too much linking backwards or forwards will make the text confusing as you will be writing this several times.

Equations and numbering

If your document includes equations, there are two conventions regarding whether these should be numbered or not:

1. The first approach is to number every equation sequentially in the order that they appear. The equation numbers are usually placed against the right-hand margin. I prefer this approach, as it is more straightforward to implement and avoids misunderstandings.

2. A second approach is to number only equations explicitly referred to in the document's main body text. Again, the equations should be numbered sequentially in the order that they appear, but some equations will have no numbers.

All letters (Greek or Roman) should be written in *italics* when used in equations, but numbers and operators ($+$, $-$, $\times$, etc.) should not. When letters in the main body text refer to the same terms as in the equations, they too should be italicised.

10.3.10 Results

Every dissertation that includes investigative work (that is, every type excluding purely theoretical work or where the entire project constitutes a review) will include a chapter that presents the findings. The style of this part will probably be different from the introduction, literature, and conclusions since it needs to be precise and will involve some description, including the presentation of numerical data. Nonetheless, the chapter should begin with one or two introductory paragraphs that outline what it is about and what you will cover.

It would help if you then referred back to the research objectives or hypotheses you had presented in a previous chapter in the order you had shown them. You should also, in just a line or two, restate the main methods that you are using to analyse the data. A research project does not need to include any details that describe how you came to the findings you did (i.e., the personal 'journey' that you experienced), but it is good to give brief details of all of the models you also tried that you don't report.

Even if your project is predominantly a quantitative study using an extensive database, it is still of value to plot the numbers, identifying some examples to illustrate the data's nature and bring the analysis to life, making it more tangible and enjoyable to read. For instance, if you were using automated text-mining software to determine the sentiment in company statements, display one such message and highlight the words contributing to the sentiment counts. Examples of both typical and extreme cases are of interest to present as illustrations. Don't just go into autopilot and jump straight into highly complex analysis – start simply and work up from there.

Your marker will be looking for evidence that you have analysed the data systematically, in-depth and using the appropriate techniques. A common mistake is to include large numbers of tables of results but only offer a couple of lines of discussion on each. Once you have taken the time to collect the data and run the models, it is a tragic waste not to extract the maximum amount of information that you can from them.

Also, every table presented in the document should be numbered and explicitly referenced in the main text. Do not include any tables that you do not discuss since no discussion means that the table is not useful and so not needed. While tables and figures are an important aspect of almost every dissertation, you should not infer that the reader will spot information that is only contained in the tables or figures. It is still your job to identify the essential features of the tables, charts and diagrams and to point these out to the reader in your text. On the other hand, don't provide a transcript of every feature of every table and chart, which would bore the reader senseless and take up too many words.

If your approach involves the estimation of statistical models such as regressions, don't just discuss the key variables of interest to your study but also analyse the parameter estimates on the control variables – are these plausible and in line with those in existing studies? Remember to discuss the sizes, signs and statistical significances of the parameter estimates. Do they support any hypotheses that you developed in a previous chapter or refute them?

You are trying to build up a story gradually. As well as beginning with simple summary statistics and plots, next, run the models including only the variable(s) of interest on their own before finally adding control variables (covariates) and possibly include a set of results where only the controls are used and not the main variables. That way, you will have several groups of model estimates, which avoids the problem of putting in in a large amount of effort to get the results only to find that you have just one table. Merely including a single table would give the incorrect impression that there was not much work involved, making the project appear thin and weak.

A good results chapter will refer back to the literature discussed previously and explain how and why the present research findings differ from those of existing studies. This is a synthesis of what you have found from your data in the context of what was already known. Any limitations of the techniques you used for data analysis are probably best discussed in the concluding chapter rather than here. Don't just present the results, but also try to explain what they mean, put them into context, and compare them with the findings that emerged in previous studies.

Your discussion of the results should note any interesting features – whether expected or unexpected – and, in particular, inferences should relate to the original aims and objectives of the research you outlined previously. You should devote the most space in the write-up to the results that focus the most closely on your research aims. The findings should be discussed and analysed in-depth, not merely presented blandly. Comparisons should also be drawn with the results of similar existing studies if relevant – do your results confirm or contradict those of previous research? And can you reconcile any differences in your findings compared with the others – for example, because you have used a different data source or model? Each table or figure should be mentioned explicitly in the text (e.g., 'Results from the estimation of equation (11) are presented in Table 4').

Try to avoid over-claiming the strength or importance of your work or findings. For instance, it is acceptable to write, 'my results demonstrate' or 'show' or 'indicate' but don't write, 'my results prove', or 'it is indisputable that'. At best, the latter phrases appear arrogant, but at worst, these statements would be incorrect since you have not proved a result, only shown that it applies with your model and sample data.

Try to tackle any odd-looking or unexpected results head-on. Some researchers try to bury them, fearful that such findings will damage the credibility of the work and hoping that the reader won't notice. But if you have such results, and you can explain them, they could lead to particularly valuable and exciting new knowledge useful to other researchers. Present the unexpected results, state what you had been expecting and why, and then explain how and why, in your case, the findings are different. Remember, it is the anomalous results that lead to scientific revolutions, so consider them an opportunity and a source of intrigue rather than necessarily a problem.

Tips on presenting the results

It is a common stylistic flaw to include too many decimal places of accuracy in tables of results, which is unhelpful for two reasons. First, the excess accuracy is probably spurious since it is unlikely that your data would have been measured precisely enough for you to have that level of confidence in the findings. Second, it makes the numbers in the tables much harder for the reader to interpret. For instance, 0.63489271 could be reported much more succinctly as 0.635 or even 0.64. I usually find that three decimal places or three significant figures are sufficient. To save you from having to make the adjustments manually, if your statistical software provides excess precision in the output, you can use a spreadsheet to round the figures displayed before pasting the table into the document.

Furthermore, don't use 'engineering notation' in your results tables (e.g., 3.4E-2), even if the output appears in that format from your statistical software package. Instead, convert it to a decimal figure (0.034) unless it is infeasible because the number is too small or too large (e.g., 3.4E-8 or 3.4E6). Also, don't just use the default options for presenting tables or figures from a spreadsheet; instead, make an active choice based on the information you are trying to get across to the reader and how you want it to look.

Number every table and graph you incorporate in the document, and they should appear in the order to which they are referred in the text. I have seen projects where Table 2 appears before Table 1, which does not make sense, and the numbers should have been simply swapped around.

A long book with very many tables and figures is likely to recommence the numbering in each chapter – for instance, Table 3.2 would be the second table in Chapter 3, and so on. But for a typical research project, there is unlikely to be a sufficient number of tables to make doing that worthwhile, so it is more straightforward to number them sequentially as Table 1, Table 2, etc., in whatever chapter they appear. Also, ensure that every table and figure has a number and a title, and any graphs have axis labels, axis scales, and a key that explains what each line or bar is showing.

If the rules permit, and they likely will, using colour in your dissertation will make it more pleasant and entertaining to read – for example, headers can be in colour, as can figures and tables. But don't overdo it – keep the colours subtle and consistent. It is probably also best to avoid overly flamboyant table designs; instead, stick to the clean and simple formats most commonly used in academic journal articles and books. When displaying tables in the document, try to make these appear professional, clear, and of appropriate size, as they would in a published paper – try to avoid using a tiny typeface (which will be hard to read) or one that is too big (which will look silly).

Remember in your descriptions of the results, tables and figures that 'data' and 'axes' are both plurals, not singular forms, so, for instance, you would write, 'the axes are labelled...', 'the data are presented...', etc. Writing axes and data as singular are widespread grammatical errors.

Include all relevant details in your results tables. For example, if they are the estimation outputs from regression models, include standard errors or t-ratios in parentheses, and have the number of data points and the R^2 values in separate rows after the coefficients. It is also good practice, and now standard in many journals in accounting and finance, for tables to include comprehensive notes in a header or footer that explain where the information presented came from – for example, what were the data and model, and also defining any symbols or acronyms that are not obvious. Incorporating detailed notes ensures that the tables are as self-contained as possible and avoids the reader having to flip back and forth between a table and the main text (which might well be on an entirely different page) to understand what the former contains. It is also useful to number the columns in a table so that these labels can be referred to in the text to avoid confusion when discussing the results.

Virtually every empirical paper will include tables of results, but here as Table 10.2, I present one example, which is Table 4 from a pre-print version of the paper by Brooks *et al.* (2018) mentioned above, which is available in the University of Reading repository.[2] This table is a typical one from the finance literature, and has a number of characteristic features:

- It includes extensive notes explaining the variables in a header
- Each column is headed with a number so that it can be easily identified in the

---

[2]http://centaur.reading.ac.uk/73681/

body text
- Statistically significant parameters are denoted by asterisks, with $*$, $**$ and $***$ conventionally used to denote statistical significance at the 10%, 5% and 1% levels, respectively.
- It is common to place standard errors in parentheses or sometimes t-ratios, but in this case it is p-values
- The parameter estimates appear first and then other information, such as the numbers of data points or the R^2 values, appear in later rows

Try to discuss your results methodically rather than in a haphazard, seemingly random fashion. Think carefully about the ordering of not only the tables as a whole but also the columns within each table of results. For instance, it makes sense to start the discussion of the findings with the first column before moving onto the second (the next one to the right of it), and so on, in which case you may need to modify the column order accordingly. You could start with the most basic form of the model on the left-hand side before moving to incrementally more sophisticated specifications, with the full model including all the variables in the far-most right-hand column.

Also, aim to use a variety of presentational styles for the results. If you are conducting quantitative data analysis, most of the information will likely be displayed in a tabular format, but having many such tables one after another can be boring for the reader. Interspersing them with graphs (e.g., line graphs, pie charts, bar charts, etc.) will be more visually appealing. Since 'a picture says a thousand words', it might also help make the most critical points that you are trying to get across more salient, whereas they would be buried in a table and therefore unnoticed. When readers (and markers) are short of time, they might skip over a table but nonetheless glance at a picture, which would consequently make more impact.

Although, as discussed above, their inclusion is essential, don't use too much space on summary statistics and preliminaries when presenting the results, otherwise, you can quickly run up to the word limit. Prioritise the inclusion of the main findings that are the focus of the project and add additional details if you have sufficient words remaining. Give the key results first and then others that are more peripheral in a robustness checks sub-section or an appendix at the end of the document (or possibly not at all if you are very short of space). Write up the main results succinctly at first and then add further details when you know that you have spare words still available within the limit.

Many econometric and statistical software packages can output results into an attractive tabular format that can be pasted directly into a word processor, which is preferable to retyping the numbers into a table that you have created yourself. Not only will this save you from a laborious and tedious task, but it will also minimise 'transcription errors' where you make typographical mistakes. Similarly, it is always best to use a straight-through data input method when you move from one package to another (e.g., from a data provider through to a spreadsheet then the statistical software to finally getting the results into your project document).

Table 10.2: Sample table: probability of firms being acquirers

This table reports the coefficient estimates from conditional logit models for the probability of firms being acquirers. The dependent variable is equal to one for the sample acquirer and zero for the matched acquirers in the control group. The matched acquirers are firms in the sample acquirer's industry (Fama–French 10 industries), of similar size (within a 20% band of market capitalization) and of similar B/M ratio (within a 20% band of B/M). The relative size between the sample target and matched acquirers is above 5%. Detailed definitions of acquirer control variables can be found in Appendix A. Deal fixed effects are controlled for in all regressions. Robust standard errors are clustered at the deal level. p-values are reported in parentheses. Significance at the 0.01, 0.05, and 0.10 levels is indicated by $***$, $**$, and $*$, respectively.

	1	2	3	4	5	6
Ac_CrossIO	3.565***					
	(0.000)					
Ac_CrossIO_1%		8.912***				
		(0.000)				
Mvweighted_CrossIO			6.867***			
			(0.000)			
Top5Count				0.583***		
				(0.000)		
Top10Count					0.403***	
					(0.000)	
Top20Count						0.283***
						(0.000)
IO	0.683***	1.663***	1.111***	0.334***	0.305***	0.229**
	(0.000)	(0.000)	(0.000)	(0.002)	(0.007)	(0.047)
Size	1.925***	1.825***	1.995***	1.940***	1.982***	1.967***
	(0.000)	(0.000)	(0.000)	(0.000)	(0.000)	(0.000)
B/M	1.008***	0.930***	1.022***	1.023***	1.042***	1.053***
	(0.000)	(0.000)	(0.000)	(0.000)	(0.000)	(0.000)
Leverage	0.005***	0.007***	0.005***	0.005***	0.004***	0.004***
	(0.001)	(0.000)	(0.000)	(0.001)	(0.002)	(0.003)
ROA	-0.682***	-0.767***	-0.631**	-0.656**	-0.601**	-0.538**
	(0.009)	(0.005)	(0.016)	(0.015)	(0.027)	(0.046)
Cashholding	-0.119	0.013	-0.086	-0.047	-0.034	-0.046
	(0.541)	(0.945)	(0.657)	(0.808)	(0.863)	(0.814)
Sales_Growth	0.000	-0.008*	0.001	-0.004	-0.002	-0.001
	(0.931)	(0.079)	(0.785)	(0.345)	(0.548)	(0.733)
Runup	0.284***	0.299***	0.266***	0.281***	0.286***	0.295***
	(0.000)	(0.000)	(0.000)	(0.000)	(0.000)	(0.000)
Sigma	-25.615***	-26.664***	-24.916***	-25.671***	-25.351***	-25.013***
	(0.000)	(0.000)	(0.000)	(0.000)	(0.000)	(0.000)
Deal fixed effects	Yes	Yes	Yes	Yes	Yes	Yes
Observations	36,944	36,944	36,944	36,944	36,944	36,944
Actual acquirer No.	2,177	2,177	2,177	2,177	2,177	2,177
Control acquirer No.	34,767	34,767	34,767	34,767	34,767	34,767
Pseudo R-squared	0.045	0.080	0.067	0.058	0.065	0.074

In some areas within business and management, it is common to have a 'Discussion' section or chapter in addition to the Results. In that case, the latter would be reserved for the more straightforward presentation and description of the findings, with in-depth analysis, links with the existing literature and reflection on what it all means being left to the discussion part. This style is less common in accounting and finance and could lead to you having two very short pieces. Therefore, unless your Results chapter feels unwieldy (even when broken into sub-sections), a separate Discussion chapter is probably unnecessary.

10.3.11 Conclusions

The concluding part is your foremost opportunity to reflect on what you have done, why you did it and how, what aspects worked well, and areas that could be improved if the topic were to be tackled by you or someone else in the future. Being reflective and critical in this chapter is essential to demonstrate that you have developed evaluatory skills, and you can take a high-level view of your work's strengths and weaknesses. The reflection involves considering what you did, why you did that and not something else, why you chose particular methods and not others, what worked well and what worked less well and why.

Like the abstract, the concluding chapter should be able to stand alone so that it could be read by someone who had not seen the rest of the document, and it would still make sense to them. The conclusions should finish the dissertation in the same general, high-level style that the introduction began it.

The concluding chapter should comprise several elements, each of which is discussed further below:

1. First and foremost, a not-too-technical summary of the key findings of your project.
2. Next, the limitations of the work as a whole should be noted.
3. Third, some suggestions for further research in the area should be presented.
4. Finally, some projects finish off by introducing recommendations for policy or practice if these are relevant given the subject matter.

The concluding summary

This part needs to cover all aspects of the investigative process, including the motivation you identified from the existing literature and where the gap is; a restatement of your hypotheses or research aims; the methods used; and the main results. It should be written in such a way as to emphasise the contribution, so tell the reader (again) what you have done that is exciting and new and why it makes a useful contribution to knowledge and for whom. Avoid copying and pasting the wording you used in previous chapters, even though you will be covering much the same ground, albeit in less detail.

It is unnecessary to repeat details of all of the specific results discussed in the previous chapter, only the headline findings. Although the conclusions need to restate the main results, this part needs to be brief and probably not including any numerical values at all unless one or two are very notable.

It is not necessary, and probably not helpful, to discuss the issues that you faced along the road to completion – especially if these reflected a lack of knowledge or experience on your part so that it was a steep learning curve. However, it is sensible to highlight any issues that you could not resolve where they are material to the outcome and where explaining the situation will reassure the reader that you were aware of the problems and knew what you were doing.

The conclusions are not the place to introduce any entirely new ideas; instead, they should be a logical extension of what you have already found and stated in previous chapters. The concluding summary section should usually be reasonably short as a proportion of the total project length since there is no need to repeat all of the methods or results. The chapter's very final sentence is the line that will stick in the reader's mind, so try to say something memorable and perhaps even profound. For instance, in a paper that I co-authored that examined gender differences in research evaluations in business and management (Brooks, Fenton, Schopohl and Walker, 2014), we ended the conclusions with, 'Taken together these findings suggest that a shift towards the "objective assessment" of research using journal lists or other crude quantitative measures may tend to reduce diversity and in some cases may blunt women's career prospects while impeding intellectual discovery and the development of knowledge-based economies' (p. 1000).

Limitations of the study

It is good practice in a research project, although not always done, to include a sub-section in the conclusions entitled 'Limitations of the study', which does precisely what the heading suggests. Evidently, no research study is flawless, and your dissertation will not be an exception. Identifying the limitations and explaining why they apply and how they could be remedied is worthwhile since it helps to demonstrate that you are capable of being a 'reflective practitioner', able to understand and learn from problems to self-improve in the future.

The wording in this part requires careful consideration, however, since it is crucial not to undermine your research by highlighting to the reader any fatal flaws. Also, try not to give the impression that you had been lazy or thoughtless in the investigative work you have conducted. For example, the truth might be that 'I was so slow in getting my survey out that I could only leave it open for a few days and hence I got a modest number of responses.' This explanation could instead be written as 'Since I was unable to provide a monetary incentive for participants to complete the survey, it was challenging to get them to engage with it, which resulted in the sample being quite small.' The second way of wording the problem does not cast you in an unfavourable light and instead lays the blame on an unavoidable difficulty, albeit it is a slight distortion of the truth.

Therefore, try to list only relatively minor issues that would not damage the credibility of the main findings, and in particular, aspects that you could not reasonably have been expected to have dealt with in the time available. Points around the scope of the data used are an obvious choice as data availability is frequently a challenge that many researchers face and one which is not easily overcome. If you conducted a survey, was the number of participants as great as you would have liked, and was it somewhat skewed towards particular groups? If you used interviews, were there other relevant stakeholders that you would love to have had a discussion with but to whom you could not gain access, and so those you spoke to were not the real decision-makers? If you were using secondary data, was the coverage of countries or companies or the timespan as extensive as you would have liked? If you have sufficient words available, don't just make a bullet list of concerns, but explain each point and why it is relevant.

You could also discuss whether your findings could be generalised to other contexts (other companies, assets or countries, for example) or whether they are specific to the focus that you adopted. Generalisable results are in some ways more valuable, and hence if your findings are context-specific, that should be noted as a limitation in the concluding section, along with a short discussion of why that is the case.

Suggestions for further research

The 'limitations' sub-section can then lead naturally to a 'suggestions for further research' sub-section. This aspect could be used to discuss all the ideas that you might have developed relating to the project if you had another three months to work on it. A few indications of the sort of material you could incorporate here are:

- Are there additional datasets that you would have collected? Other markets, regions or countries, for example?
- If your project involved quantitative analysis, are there additional variables that could have been incorporated into the models or different ways to measure the variables?
- Were there other methods you would have used had you more time available?
- Are there emerging techniques or models that you would have tried for analysis?
- Would you have additionally used different approaches – for instance, following up quantitative analysis with detailed case studies or interviews to get a deeper insight into specific aspects of the findings or using an experiment where you are able to control the conditions?

Recommendations

A final sub-section to consider including in the Conclusions chapter is for recommendations. This aspect would step away from the results themselves towards thinking about who the end-users of your findings might be, how they might use the results, and what they should do. In other words, what are the implications of your research output for policy or practice? These could be recommendations for government policymakers, regulators, financial market practitioners, or the general public. For example:

- Your findings might identify a need for a tighter regulatory environment in a particular market
- You might have suggestions for how environmental risks could be better incorporated into accounts
- You could have identified issues with private finance initiatives
- You might have concluded that information is spreading too slowly in certain markets and approaches need to be developed to speed up dissemination
- Your research might have been able to identify which models are most effective for accurately determining value at risk so that banks could improve their processes

In each case, explain your recommendations, what the organisation or individuals should do, how the suggestions relate to your findings, and why and how they will improve outcomes for the organisation(s) or people affected by them.

While it is good practice to include some recommendations for non-academic users of the findings if these arise from your research, whether it is worthwhile to have a specific sub-section for them or the suggestions could be rolled into the rest of the concluding chapter will depend on how many words you can allocate to this aspect.

If you were engaged in research that is purely scholarly with no direct external users, this part would not be relevant. But if your original list of aims stated that you would draw recommendations for policymakers or whoever, you need to ensure that you do so.

More generally, it is essential at this stage in the process to ensure that you have addressed all of the research aims that you set yourself in the introductory chapter. If you find that you set up aims or research questions that you did not address once you came to conduct the investigative work, delete them.

10.3.12   Back matter

You have now covered the core aspects of the writing, and all that is left is the parts at the end, which are sometimes known as the back matter. This part includes the references and appendices (if used). While these will probably be read with less scrutiny than the front matter and main body of the project, they nonetheless need to be present and accurate.

10.3.13   References

A list of references should be provided in alphabetical order by the first author surname. Note that a list of references (a list of all the papers, books or webpages referred to in the study, irrespective of whether you read them or found them cited in other studies), rather than a bibliography (a list of items that you read, regardless of whether you referred to them in the study), is usually needed here. But you should check the requirements for your department, and it might be that you can include both a reference list and an extended bibliography to highlight the additional material that you read but have not cited.

All works cited should be listed in the references section using the style discussed in the literature review material of chapter 7, where an extensive treatment of referencing is given. Equally, do not list in the reference section any item that you did not cite in the project. There is no excuse for sloppy referencing. Although it is tedious to check through to make sure that none are missing and that all the information is present and in the same format for every citation, it is worth it as not doing so is to throw away easy marks.

10.3.14 Appendices

Finally, an appendix or appendices can be used to improve the study's structure as a whole when placing a specific item in the text would interrupt the flow of the document. For example, if you want to outline how a particular variable was constructed, or you had to write some computer code to estimate the models, and you think this could be interesting to readers, then it can be placed in an appendix.

The appendices should not be used as a dumping ground for irrelevant material or padding and should not be filled with printouts of raw output from computer packages. Always format any information that you include in your project to improve its presentation and make the style of appendix material the same as the rest of the document. Remove any redundant aspects (such as parts of the statistical results that repeat information given elsewhere) unless they are included as pictures that cannot be edited (e.g., screenshots).

What should go in an appendix?

Appendices can be useful for incorporating further evidence of what you have done when including it in the main body would disrupt the text's flow or would use up too many words. It makes sense to have more than one appendix where you want to include several types of material and where bundling it all into a single appendix would look odd. The following types of material can usefully be included in appendices:

- A full list of the survey or interview questions you used
- A list of variable definitions and sources
- A mathematical derivation of a core model you employed in the empirical work
- A list of all the entities used in a data sample (e.g., a list of companies or countries, if the number is too great to include in a table in the document's main body)
- Additional (non-core) tables or graphs of results such as 'robustness checks' where you estimated several different models

Any material included in appendices should still be referenced explicitly in the main document, although, unlike the evidence presented in the latter (which should be described in detail), appendix matter can be given only a one- or two-line overview (e.g., 'Tables A1 to A6 include additional results on the cross-country panel models including random effects. These are qualitatively identical to the findings presented in the main tables.')

Although appendices can add considerable value by allowing you to include additional material, they can be overdone, so try to ensure that they remain manageable in terms of both their number and their length. It would not, for instance, be appropriate to include appendices that extend to almost as many pages as the rest of the document, although I have seen this happen several times.

Further reading

There are several valuable books that you could consult if you want more detail on improving your academic writing, such as those by Bailey (2017), Coleman (2019) or Day (2018), although there are many others.

Chapter takeaways – top tips for success

⊛ Begin the 'writing up phase' as soon as possible and avoid leaving it all until the last stage

⊛ Avoid being excessively pedantic when working on the initial draft. The critical aspect is to get a first attempt written that can be improved subsequently

⊛ Write at an appropriate level and with a suitable amount of detail. You could consider your readers to be generalists in accounting and finance but not experts in the minutiae of your project topic

⊛ Before you start drafting, try to get hold of successfully completed projects and reflect on their style and structure

⊛ Ensure that each aspect of your project covers roughly an appropriate proportion of the words or space available

⊛ Adopt a scholarly, formal approach to writing but endeavour to maintain reader interest nonetheless

⊛ Use appendices where appropriate to maintain the flow in the main text, but don't make them too extensive

11. POLISHING AND SUBMISSION

Learning outcomes: this chapter covers

✓ How to improve the quality of your writing
✓ Hot to deal with feedback and criticism
✓ What to do if you are well under or over the word limit
✓ What to look out for in pre-submission checks

11.1   Why further editing is needed

You might have thought that chapter 10 ought to be the end of this book because your job is done. Unfortunately, just when you thought you had finished, you will now come to realise that there is an essential task remaining, namely editing and polishing the document. While the completion of a first draft of the whole dissertation – if that is what you have achieved by the time you reach this chapter – is a huge step forward, there is still a lot to do if you are going to maximise the mark your work obtains.

Even though the remaining aspects will be less challenging and less time-consuming, it is still nonetheless worthwhile going the extra mile to make sure that the dissertation document is as polished and refined as possible, both in terms of the writing and the structure, ordering and presentation. It is definitely worth reserving a week at the end of the allocated project time, if possible, to read the draft paper carefully at least twice. Hence the purpose of the present chapter is to provide a range of additional guidance and tips to achieve this aim.

In order for this crucial editing phase to be as productive as possible, it is valuable to find some way to distance yourself from your work because repeatedly re-reading the same material in the same format encourages the brain to become lazy, skimming over aspects of the document and making it hard to spot errors or inconsistencies. There are several approaches to achieve this distance, including deliberately varying the:

- time – wait at least a few days, or if the schedule to submission allows, a couple of weeks. In that time, the document will become less familiar and without noticing you will read it more carefully.
- medium – changing the medium could involve printing the draft if you usually read it on screen, or vice versa. The difference in the way the document looks on a screen versus on paper will make it appear less familiar
- font – changing the font size and style so that the pagination alters will also make the document seem different as the layout and positioning of the text on the page will be different
- location – even something as straightforward as working in a different place with different lighting will mix things up slightly

It is best to read the material in page order, however, even though this might be the same as you have done previously. This will enable you match the experience of the reader so that you can see if anything is out of sequence – for instance, if you had referred to some ideas or models assuming you had already presented them although they don't actually appear until a later chapter.

When you get to the editing stage, prioritise the most important aspects and don't waste time on trivial issues that will have a minimal impact on the overall quality of the work and the mark awarded, such as fiddling with presentational aspects of the references and table formatting. Make both references and tables clear and consistent, including all the relevant information. Then stop and work on more substantial aspects of the project.

Assessors are likely to consider the presentation of the document, as well as its content. It might be that this takes place formally within the mark scheme. But even if not, a poor presentation, including grammatical or spelling errors, will diminish the reader's perception of the work, and hence the mark awarded will be lower than would otherwise have been the case. Thus, students should ensure that their report's structure is orderly and logical, that equations are correctly specified, and that there are no spelling or other typographical mistakes or grammatical errors.

It is also expedient to remember that your project marker is likely to have many such dissertations to mark in a short space of time alongside many other commitments, so the better you can make the structure and presentation of the project, the easier and more pleasurable their job will be. On the other hand, bad structure and a poor standard of English are frustrating for the reader and make the task of marking the project harder than it needs to be. These problems will likely be reflected in the mark you receive. It is best to approach this as a two-stage process: fixing up the presentation and structure first before then editing the text itself, although you might have to go back to the presentation again if the editing caused you to make significant changes to the layout, such as moving substantive amounts of material around.

11.2   Polishing your project and improving its structure

The main issues to consider first are the layout of the text and its legibility. The document should be both highly readable and professional-looking.   The following sub-sections provide further tips for presenting and organising your material optimally.

11.2.1   Perfect paragraphs

Don't use an elaborate, curly font. *Gyre Chorus*, for example, might look nice on a birthday card or party invitation but not an academic research project. It is best to stick with something standard such as Times, or Helvetica. Usually, 11 or 12-point font is best, with 10-point for footnotes. Headers can either be in the same size but in bold or a couple of points larger than the main body text.

There is an optimum range of lengths for paragraphs. On the one hand, if they are too short, it makes the writing appear 'bitty' and makes it harder for the story to flow. On the other hand, paragraphs that are too long make the text dense and impenetrable, which is exhausting for the reader. Most blogs and newspaper articles tend to use shorter paragraphs (as little one or two sentences for each), but they are writing for an audience of predominantly non-specialists who want to read quickly. For academic writing, however, paragraphs tend to be longer, say four to ten lines is ideal. But again, this tends to depend somewhat on the nature of the material: the more technical the subject matter, the shorter the paragraphs tend to be.

There might be a rule concerning project document line-spacing in your department, but in general single-line spacing looks slightly more professional but is harder to read; double-line spacing is easy to read but takes up too much space on the page; 1.5-line spacing is often a good compromise. Use clear and consistent paragraph spacing – either with a line between each paragraph or a tab indent at the start of each new paragraph. Both the indented paragraph style and block paragraphs are usually acceptable but pick one of the two and don't mix them. Separating the paragraphs in one of these ways is essential since it considerably eases readability as it makes it evident when you are moving onto a slightly different thread of the argument or a new topic.

Although it is challenging to do so with subject-specific or technical words, try to maintain interest and avoid repetition by varying the words and phrases you use. Connectives such as 'however', 'but', 'additionally', and so on, are helpful to improve the flow, but even these can be overused, and the same word should not be included more than once within a paragraph or two. Avoid using vague and wordy phrases that do not really say anything, such as 'it could be stated that'. This string is ambiguous: it could be stated, but what sentiment about the matter are you expressing, and what did other researchers say?

Suppose you include the tables in the main body text rather than all gathered at the end. In that case, you will have to fiddle a bit to 'float them' around the page to avoid having large amounts of space (or 'white space' as it is known in publishing spheres), or a table splitting across two pages (which is best avoided unless a table is too large to fit onto a single page, and if that is the case, consider splitting it into two or more smaller tables).

Relatedly, adequate spacing throughout will aid the readability of the document. Don't be tempted to squash the components together to save a couple of pages (unless there is a page limit, and you are up against it). Start each chapter on a new page, leave space around tables and figures and leave an extra line of space between the end of one section and the start of the next.

11.2.2 Perfect prose: check, check and check again

Editing and polishing the document is a crucial stage in the writing process. It is an exciting aspect since you can see all of the hard work you have put in so far coming together, and the point where you can say that the project is ready to submit is getting close. While the amount of time that this stage will take should not be underestimated, it is also important not to begin too soon. In particular, if possible, it is better to complete all of the investigative work and produce a complete first draft of the entire project before commencing the editing. If you edit part of the document thoroughly and then make further changes, especially if they are substantive, there is a danger that you could fail to spot presentational or drafting issues with the newly added material. Or there might be abrupt jumps between the new and existing parts.

Even published books contain typographical errors, despite that in most cases, they have been drafted by experienced writers, copy-edited and proof-read (usually twice) by professionals; no doubt there are errors in the one you are reading too. The lesson is that small numbers of minor grammatical or spelling mistakes are almost unavoidable and are unlikely to diminish the mark you will receive. But a manuscript that is riddled with apparent errors gives the impression that the writer was careless. The reader will then worry that if the writer was sloppy with the drafting, were they similarly haphazard with the investigative work? So large numbers of typographical mistakes will not only be treated as a weak aspect of the presentation, but it might also cause the marker to be particularly fastidious in examining other parts of the work, looking even harder for errors than they otherwise would have done.

The first stage in the editing process is to make sure that you read your work a few times, ideally with several days in between as discussed in the previous section. Reciting the work aloud can help you judge whether sentences are easy or hard to read. Make sure that you read it in page order at least once from the very first page to the last. Since you likely wrote the dissertation 'out-of-order', it is easy for issues to arise with the flow of material that you otherwise might overlook. For example, you discuss a model in chapter 2 that you don't define or explain until chapter 3, but you initially did not realise because you wrote chapter 3 first. On the other hand, your marker will read the document in page sequence from beginning to end and be frustrated if they are left scratching their head for five pages until you eventually define what a particular acronym stands for.

The automated spelling and grammar checkers in word processors have made the task of polishing documents quicker and more straightforward, and the Grammarly add-in for Word is even better at spotting a range of issues. But while these packages play a vital role in improving your writing, there is also a danger of complacency since there are numerous errors that such automated software cannot identify. This means that it is still essential that you (and ideally, someone else too) go through your work carefully by hand.

An important point to consider when reading through your draft is how well the text flows both within and across sections. A pleasant experience for the reader will be like a smooth car journey where both the movement on each road and the transitions between them have no bumps or jumps. Sometimes writing can be disjointed, with the paragraphs not linking together, making it harder for the reader to follow. If that is the case, go through and add connections and linking sentences that smooth the transition from one paragraph or section to the next.

If your first language is not English, then writing an extended piece of work such as a dissertation can be particularly challenging. By reading extensively from the literature and getting tips from this book, you will have a good idea of how academics tend to write in our subject area. Don't be excessively concerned with bad grammar or punctuation, and, as stated numerous times, don't be tempted to copy someone else's work. If you can get your ideas drafted into some text, even if it is not smoothly written in perfect English initially, so long as it is understandable, it can be polished into a solid piece of prose. Your supervisor and other examiners will be well accustomed to marking work written by non-native English speakers and will be sympathetic to their cause, tending to ignore minor errors.

It is perfectly acceptable to get a proof-reader to go through your work and suggest edits to improve the spelling, grammar and other aspects of the writing style. However, you should mention their help and what they did in the acknowledgements section of your dissertation. A proof-reader will merely be improving the explanation of your ideas and not generating those ideas, and hence employing a third party to enhance the writing style will not diminish your contribution. Specialists such as these can be found relatively easily on the internet, and most will only charge a modest amount (perhaps £50–150 for a typical student project). Poor grammar, spelling and drafting are probably the easiest aspects of a bad dissertation to fix, so long as you allow sufficient time to engage the proof-reader's services and implement their suggestions.

Even if the grammar is still far from perfect when you submit the final version of the project, so long as it is readable, although avoidable, you are unlikely to lose more than a few marks. It must be at least clear what you mean in each sentence so that the reader can grasp the essence of what you are trying to get across. But the proportion of the overall mark allocated to presentation and writing style will likely be low, and of that, some marks will be awarded for the structure and formatting of the document rather than the writing itself.

Editing the project document

You will need to edit your work on several levels, and this will probably be more successful if you address each level in a separate reading rather than attempting to fix everything in one go. It might be helpful to think of editing as requiring micro-level and macro-level work.

The macro-level should be done first, and this involves reflecting on whether your dissertation covers all of the required aspects and that they are in the correct order. You will probably have to move material around – both within and across chapters – as the project draft takes shape. You also need to check for consistency of typeface, font, margin size, heading style and size, etc. Also, check that the equation, table and figure numbering is consistent and starts at 1. Are the paragraphs of an appropriate length, or do they need to be split or merged? Are any controversial statements substantiated with evidence or references?

One way to ensure that the formatting of the document is consistent throughout is to use a template. Whatever word processor you use (e.g., Microsoft Word, Apple Pages, or TeX), you can apply a template that will control all these issues without you needing to worry. All you need to do is choose the template then implement it throughout rather than choosing formats (e.g., chapter heading sizes, fonts, justification, etc.) manually.

At the micro-level, this means reading the draft very carefully, in page order, line-by-line, checking for grammatical or spelling errors, inconsistencies in spelling where both are correct (e.g., heteroscedasticity and heteroskedasticity) or hyphenation (e.g., built in or built-in; on-line or online). Are all arguments fluid and well-made? Do the paragraphs link together, or are there any abrupt movements in the writing? Are the citations correct and matching the reference list at the end?

When you start to remove material from your dissertation draft, don't just delete the words but create a new file that you can call 'spare stuff' or something similar, and paste it there. It might be that this material will come in handy later if you find that you have pruned more heavily than you needed to or you have removed the wrong parts. Regret at having deleted some content that the author later realises to be useful is surprisingly common.

The final polishing stage at the end will involve several elements. As well as the above points, there are numerous minor stylistic issues to consider:

1. Read through carefully, looking for any typos or grammatical errors, which should be removed. Look especially for incorrect words that a spell-checker

would miss (e.g., 'there' versus 'their' and 'every month' versus 'very month').

2. Ensure that the document is as readable as possible, which includes confirming that there are no excessively long sentences or containing too many clauses. It also means having paragraphs of a reasonable length – neither just two lines nor an entire page.

3. Ensure that the style is consistent throughout. Consistency is quite challenging for a novice who is unsure of what to look for, but for instance, check that:

- You have included your name and the date on the front cover (plus any other information required by the department).
- You have numbered the pages.
- Section heading styles are consistent (e.g., are the first letters of all words in headers capitalised? Do the headings have a larger font or bold or underlined typeface?) As a suggestion, use *italics* (or <u>underline</u>) for emphasis on particular words that you want to highlight or for terms in Latin (or abbreviated from Latin such as *et al.*). Use **bold** (or larger font, or **both**) for headings and titles.
- Equation numbering is consistent if present.
- The font and line spacing are the same throughout the document.
- Your use of either a justified or 'ragged' right-hand margin is consistent throughout.
- Your use of quotation marks ('single' or "double", 'smart' or 'straight') and hyphens (e.g., line-break or line break) is consistent.
- Appropriate country spellings have been used throughout (i.e., UK spellings for students studying in the UK, US spellings in the US, etc.). If you are studying in the UK, it is best to stick to UK spelling throughout, but the worst style is to mix UK and US conventions within the same dissertation. Most word processors can be configured to check for any particular country's spelling conventions, so ensure that you use the built-in function correctly.
- Tenses have been used consistently throughout. It is fine to use the past, present and future tenses in the appropriate places but be constant in their usage. For example, in the literature review, when describing the work of other scholars, you could use the present ('Brooks and Persand (2000) estimate a model with time-varying volatility and find that ...') or the past tense ('Brooks and Persand (2000) estimated a model with time-varying volatility and found that...') but do not mix the two. When writing the introductory chapter, you will need to describe what you are going to do in subsequent chapters, and this could be written as ('In chapter 2, I will review the existing literature') or in the present as ('In chapter 2, I review the existing literature'). Similarly, it is more natural to use the past tense in the concluding chapter when discussing what you have already done ('In chapter 4, I evaluated the extent to which

multinationals are able to reduce their corporation tax bills by operating in low tax jurisdictions').

- There are no 'widows or orphans' – where you have a section heading at the end of a page with no body text after it.

In many instances, the precise style is unimportant, but consistency is imperative. If in doubt about what to do regarding any aspect, just make a sensible judgement call, and it will usually be acceptable.

11.3 Dealing with feedback

Your supervisor or advisor may be willing to read through the draft and offer comments upon it before final submission. If not, maybe friends who are doing or have done similar courses can give suggestions. Any comments are useful since, after all, those that you do not like or agree with can be ignored. If your supervisor offers tips, though, they should be taken very seriously – not only because it is likely that they are highly experienced researchers who are knowledgeable about the topic, but also because the supervisor is often the first marker of projects and may not take kindly to their words of wisdom being ignored.

Actively encouraging feedback, reflecting on the comments and implementing improvements is another key skill learned as part of successful dissertation completion. Your supervisor has probably read through numerous (tens or hundreds) of projects over the years, and so their comments will be well informed and almost undoubtedly valuable.

Learning to cope with criticism is an essential skill for any aspiring scholar because critique – both giving and receiving it – is a major part of academic life. Try not to take offence at negative comments made by your supervisor or others when they are providing feedback, although this is not always easy. It can be hurtful even for senior and highly experienced staff when work they spent many weeks producing and were proud of is denigrated, particularly if the author feels that the comments are unfounded. Occasionally, there is the opportunity for academics to respond to the criticism, but most of the time, there is not. Therefore, the trick is to view any negative comments constructively and learn from them without becoming disheartened.

Don't be discouraged if your first draft is returned covered with comments and suggestions for improvement; in fact, that is a good sign that you have piqued your supervisor's interest sufficiently that they want to spend the time to help you make the work even better. If your supervisor is not engaged with what you have written, you will receive only a handful of 'high-level' comments, which are those of a very general nature that could be made by someone who had only skimmed through the draft and not read it closely.

When receiving a report or your supervisor's feedback on your work, avoid the temptation to respond immediately. The first reaction is invariably a more emotional one than how you will feel about it after a day or two. So read the comments carefully, then do something else – watch TV, go for a run, etc., and forget about it for at least 24 hours. You can then begin to concoct a response (if needed) or address the issues in your next draft. Even if you are unhappy with the comments or don't feel that they are useful, send a polite thank-you note to the person who wrote them.

Usually, you will only have the opportunity of one round of supervisory comment and written feedback on a draft, so try to submit a solid draft. The completer and more polished is the version you give in for advice, the more useful will be the suggestions you receive. Having said that, it is still better to put forward a rough draft for comments than nothing at all; hence, submit the work on time and in the best state you can, whatever that may be.

But if you are fortunate to be permitted a second turn of supervisory review, ensure that you incorporated all of the feedback from the first round of comments before asking for another set. There is nothing worse for a marker than to have taken the time to read a draft carefully and provide feedback only to find that the same issues are apparent in the next iteration, and the suggestions have been ignored. If you did not feel that your supervisor's comments were valuable in the first round, it is probably best not to ask them for feedback again.

If you have the opportunity to meet with your supervisor to discuss their comments after they have sent you their feedback, make sure you read and reflect on it first. You can then seek clarification for any points you don't understand.

Receiving and acting upon feedback provided on drafts of your work can lead to significant improvements in its quality. Suggestions from non-specialists can also be useful, particularly if you have a friend or family member with a good eye for spotting typos or inconsistencies in the presentation, as they are likely to be much cheaper than a professional proof-reader. People with dissimilar backgrounds will focus on different aspects of the dissertation, and their varying perspectives can be instrumental in helping you to refine the work before submission.

Feel free to ask as many people for feedback as possible, but you have to want their comments and if you really don't intend to make any further changes, don't feel obliged to ask people to read the work. I have been asked numerous times to comment on a colleague's grant application or promotion documentation but later realised my suggestions had been largely ignored. Often, when people say they want feedback, they don't: they are really asking for a reassuring response that what they have already written is brilliant. Comments that would require additional work, even if well-informed and well-intentioned, are not welcome. If you don't want someone to point out the weak points in what you have done so far, then it would not be a worthwhile use of that person's time to read your draft, so don't ask them.

11.4 Counting your words

Almost every dissertation, no matter whether it is for 10-credits or 30, will have an upper word limit that could be anywhere from 8,000 to 20,000, depending on the size of the project module and the amount of time devoted to it. This section discusses the issues around this figure and what to do if the draft of your project is significantly above or below the boundary.

Even if you have one eye on the word limit as you are drafting, don't merely cease writing when you reach it – you still need to devote a reasonable amount of space to the other aspects, and you need to include all of the ingredients within each chapter. Getting this balance right means that you might need subsequently to cut out some of the material that you had written. Although it can feel painful to throw away precious words that you spent time writing, it is all part of honing and refining the draft to make it as clear and sharp as it can be.

In general, the word count only involves what is written in the main body of the text – so the front matter (title page, acknowledgements, table of contents, lists of tables and figures), plus the abstract, references, tables and any diagrams, would not contribute towards the number of words. However – be careful as your school might have a policy that one or more of these aspects counts. It is good for the discussions and analysis in your project document to be detailed and including depth and richness, which will enhance the perceived quality of the writing. But it is a delicate balance. In general, try to write concisely and avoid excess verbiage, repetition or the inclusion of irrelevant or marginally relevant material, all of which will make the reader weary and irritated. Rather than enhancing the expected mark, unnecessary wordage will probably reduce it.

11.4.1 If you write too much, will you be penalised?

The word limit is one of the parameters on which you are being assessed, and so if you cannot adhere to this constraint, you have failed one of the criteria. Producing a dissertation of the right length is a skill in itself that is needed in many jobs where you need to create a report, a blog or an application with strict word constraints.

Besides, your supervisor and other markers will probably have many dissertations to mark, and if several of the documents are well in excess of the word limit, it will make their job even harder, putting them in a bad frame of mind and giving the impression that you don't care enough to heed the guidelines. There is little sense in making the final report longer than it needs to be. Even if you are not in danger of exceeding the word limit, superfluous material will generate no additional credit and may be penalised.

Despite the above advice, it is implausible that the person or people marking your project will count the number of words you write in your project, and especially if you submit it in hard copy or as a pdf, since counting would be quite challenging and time-consuming for them to do. So it is likely that the marker will use some discretion in determining whether you have exceeded the word limit, leaving you with a margin of error to play with. Some project guidelines might even formally allow for a specific, pre-defined excess over the word limit before a penalty applies (e.g., 10%), so check the rules in your school. Therefore, if you slightly exceed the word limit, you probably have little to worry about.

But if you vastly exceed the limit, or your writing is repetitive or boring, including material that is not relevant to the topic, then there is a high chance that you would be penalised. The penalty for exceeding the word limit will vary from one institution to another. It could take the form of a minimal mark reduction under the 'style and presentation' heading (such as five percentage points off the mark that you would have received) or, for extreme breaches, it could be fatal (a refusal to mark the project and a mark of zero awarded). In such a case, you would be asked to revise it and resubmit a shorter version. Even if your institution's penalty is modest, it is essential to modify your work to come close to or below the constraint.

11.4.2   What to do if you are over the word limit

If you have written too much, try to edit the draft down by removing the least important parts, moving material to an appendix or presenting it in a tabular or graphical form if these are permitted and do not count towards the number of words. Even if you are not over the word limit, it is still worth making sure that the draft does not include any redundant material. It is mentally hard to do this – throwing away words that you might have spent a long time writing is painful. I share your pain, but you need to employ the economic concept of a sunk cost: you cannot get back the time you already spent on superfluous writing, so just focus on the way to maximise your expected mark. Many people feel similarly despondent at cutting away material that they worked hard to write, but it is better to consider pruning your document as an opportunity to make the writing sharper, more concise, of greater relevance, and therefore more pleasant to read. If that means cutting words out and deleting them, then do it because your grade will be higher if your work is succinct and readable. The time spent writing the original material was not wasted since it helped you get to the version you have now.

Whenever you remove parts from the draft, ensure that what remains still makes sense and that the argument flows. Ideally, you would read again in their entireties all sections where you have made edits.

What you should do about an excess of words depends on how far over the boundary you are and how much time you have to work on the edits. For instance, if the formal limit is 10,000 words with a 5% allowance, you need to get down below 10,500. If your current count is 10,800 words, it will be straightforward to lose 300 words, but if your count is 12,800, you need to take away at least 2,300, which is more than 15% of your total. I suggest the following courses of action:

- If you only need to trim a small number of words and have sufficient time available, you could read through the draft (again) line-by-line, adjusting sentences to make them more concise and remove any redundancy. Delete any sentences or blocks of text that are not needed or repeat something you already wrote in a previous section
- If you need to take away many words, or you only have an hour or two to do it, it is unlikely that you will be able to make sufficient changes line-by-line in

the time available, so you need to be more aggressive in taking away whole paragraphs or, possibly, entire sections or sub-sections

- An obvious first place to look is the literature review since this chapter often tends to be longer than necessary in proportion to the rest of the document. Are there any parts of the review that could be removed altogether without significantly diminishing the chapter's quality? Are there models, theories or concepts that are only marginally relevant and could therefore be eliminated?

- Are there any significant repetitions across sections that could be stripped out or trimmed? For example, if you summarise the results in the introductory and concluding chapters, consider shortening these to cover just the core points

- Consider whether any material could be moved to appendices (assuming that these do not count towards the word limit, which they usually do not, but check the guidelines). For example, if you have derived a model or described your survey or your data in detail, these sorts of purely descriptive materials can fit well in appendices. Similarly, tables of variable definitions can be placed in an appendix as discussed above.

Should you ask your supervisor or the research project module convenor for an increase in the word limit if you think you will considerably exceed it?

Although there is probably little harm in asking for an increase in the limit, your request is extremely likely to be rejected since it would not be fair on other students if you were permitted to write more – potentially adding further detail and depth in the arguments – and they were not. One of the key disciplines that doing the project is supposed to imbue is the ability to work within defined parameters, one of which is the word limit.

11.4.3   What to do if you are under the word limit

Bear in mind that the word limit is usually precisely that – it is an upper constraint and not a target. If you have written a bit less than this figure, your project is probably of the right length. For example, if the limit is 10,000 words and you have written 8,000 or more, you will likely be within the range that your supervisor will expect. Provided that the project also includes all of the required elements, and each chapter is an appropriate proportion of the complete document, there is no need for undue concern about the overall length.

However, it might make your work look thin and feeble if your project is very much shorter than this figure. So, if the word limit is, say, 10,000 words, then a draft of 9,000 would be perfect; a draft of 5,000 words would probably be considered inadequate, and you could think of it as an opportunity to add depth to your arguments and analysis if you have the time remaining. In such a situation, some remedial action is needed:

- A first step is to ensure that you have included all of the required elements listed in section 10.3 of this book. If any key aspect is missing, this will provide a relatively fast way to increase the word count

- Ideally, you would go back through the whole draft to identify chapters or sections that are insufficiently detailed or where your treatment has been cursory and then expand these parts. Your writing should be detailed throughout with a depth of argument rather than skimming over the surface. For example, when you analyse the results or provide suggestions for further research, don't just offer short bullet points but thoroughly explain your reasoning
- When dissertations are brief, it is usually because the critical or evaluative parts are limited all over the document rather than a specific individual section being missing
- If your supervisor will be reading a draft, you could highlight to them that your work is currently on the short side, and they might have suggestions for which aspects should be expanded upon or further developed
- If you have placed any material in appendices, consider moving it into the main body to bulk up the latter
- As a final strategy, if you have gone through the list above and been unable to increase the word count sufficiently, or there is no time left to write a significant amount of new detail, you might consider whether it is possible to adapt the presentation of the document to give the impression of it being more substantive than it actually is. Such a step is really a last resort, but you could:
  - Use block paragraphs with line spaces between rather than tab indents
  - Ensure that each chapter starts on a fresh page
  - Slightly increase the margin sizes
  - Slightly increase the font size
  - Spread the pages out so that, for example, each table or figure is on a separate page with large section and chapter headings
  - Spread the references so that there is a line space between each one
  - Add a table of contents, list of tables and list of figures, each on their own page

In each case, take care not to make it evident that you are spreading the work out to make it look bigger than it actually is since this is slightly deceitful. So do not, for example, increase the font size to 14, which will make your deliberate repackaging job too visible.

11.5 Pre-submission Checklist

There now follows a list of points that you can tick off to ensure that you have covered all of the main features that need to be in the project. If there are any elements of the inventory below that you are unsure about whether you have incorporated or not, then check back through that chapter or section and add to it or redraft as necessary.

Front matter

- Is your title clear, relevant and succinct?

- Have you included an acknowledgements section that recognises the role of everyone who contributed to the project, including your supervisor?
- Have you included a table of contents?
- Is your abstract of the right length, comprising a summary of all aspects of the project, including the topic, main aims, methods used, key findings and conclusions?
- Is the project divided into suitable chapters and sections, with the appropriate material in each area?

Introduction

- Does your introductory chapter motivate your work and put it into context?
- Have you explained why your study is needed, and what is interesting and original about it?
- Have you briefly stated the aims?
- Have you provided an outline of the rest of the project?

Literature review

- Have you conducted a literature review summarising relevant studies from the existing body of work?
- Have you critically evaluated the work rather than just presenting it descriptively?
- Have you directed the writing of the review towards your aims and what you want to achieve in your dissertation?
- Have you used a wide range of sources, including published and unpublished academic studies as well as popular or blog pieces?
- Have you summarised what is known, and have you identified gaps in the existing literature?

Methods and Data

- How you stated your project aims and justified an appropriate methodology to achieve them?
- Have you explained the data collection approach and thoroughly described the data before embarking on a more detailed analysis?
- Are the methods and data explained with sufficient detail and clarity that another researcher could replicate the results?
- Have you explained any notation, equations or technical terms that you have included?

Results

- Do your results conform with the research aims that you established in a previous chapter?
- Have you used a varied presentation style for the results as far as possible, including both tables and charts or graphs?

- Have you discussed all of your tables of results thoroughly, explaining how they relate to your aims and objectives?
- Have you related your findings to the existing literature?
- Are your tables and figures tidy and self-explanatory with titles and notes?

Conclusions

- Have you written a concluding chapter that restates your project aims and summarises your findings?
- Have you presented some ideas for future research?
- Have you reflected on the limitations of your chosen methods and data?
- Have you outlined any implications from your findings for non-academic user groups?

References and Appendices

- Have you cited every piece of existing work upon which you have relied?
- Is there a 1:1 mapping between the work cited in the body text and listed in the references section?
- Are the references listed in alphabetical order by author surname with all details entered for every reference (including volume and page numbers for journals and place of publication for books)?
- If appendices are included, are they relevant and referred to in the main body of the document?

11.6 Project submission

Just as some students struggle to start their projects, others struggle to stop. Some people find it hard to know when to stop the investigative part of their work and get to the tidying up stage. Others agonise excessively over the writing, forever shifting the text around and redrafting. While it is always possible to make a piece of work better by working longer on it, there comes the point when further work on the project seems unnecessary – either because it is almost as good as it can be without starting again, or because time has run out and the submission deadline looms. Therefore, you will need to learn to judge when you are at this point and resist any temptation to tinker further with the draft. It will probably not be the final report you ever write, and for that reason, nor is it likely to be the best, so spend a proportionate amount of time polishing the draft and no more.

It is OK to submit your dissertation well before the deadline if it is finished. But once that is done, you will have no opportunities for any changes, so you need to be confident that you could not spend any of the remaining time doing further checks or obtaining and incorporating additional feedback. Remember: finance teaches us that options have value, and if you submit your project considerably before the deadline, you are freely surrendering an option to do more work on it.

Further reading

- Despite the title, the book by Ide (2013) is actually more a book about good grammar and writing style than proof-reading *per se*, although it could nonetheless be handy
- The book by Hampton (2019) provides many useful exercises to train you to identify common typographical errors in writing
- Similarly, Evans (2013) is a good general guide on how to proof-read, including examples and exercises

Chapter takeaways – top tips for success

⊛ Save plenty of time for final refinement and polishing at the end, which invariably takes longer than expected

⊛ Pay particular attention to the title, abstract, the start of the introduction, and the conclusions since these will remain at the forefront of the reader's mind yet are often the weakest aspects of a project

⊛ Make sure that the document is typo-, grammatical error- and spelling error-free: pay a proof-reader to do the checking if necessary

⊛ Try to include an appropriate number of tables and figures: too few makes the project look thin, while too many may become repetitive

⊛ Ensure that you remain within, or only just over, the word or page limit

⊛ Check that your project contains all of the required elements

⊛ Ask for feedback from as many people as possible. Reflect on their comments, incorporate any suggestions for improvements but don't take criticism to heart

12. STAY ON TRACK + POST-PROJECT

Learning outcomes: this chapter covers

✓ Where to find help when you are stuck
✓ How to fix problems that might occur
✓ Your options to continue research after project submission

This chapter contains two parts. Hopefully, you will never need the first aspect, which is a set of tips and guidance for what to do when things go wrong. The vast majority of students will experience a relatively smooth process from the point they start thinking about the dissertation to the submission of the final draft, but there are many ways in which things can go awry. If that happens in your case, this chapter is here to steer you out of trouble.

The second part of this chapter focuses on the opportunities that might be open to you to take the project work further if it is something that you enjoyed doing. These include publicising the findings or applying for further study.

12.1 Where to get help when you get stuck

Sometimes, you might hit a stumbling block with the project – not a complete disaster, merely a minor hitch but one which nonetheless prevents you from pushing full-steam ahead with the task at hand. Hitting a wall is most likely to occur with the investigative work, such as the statistical analysis not working correctly, bugs in your code, issues with a survey, and so on. If this happens, where should you go for help? An obvious response could be your supervisor, but you may prefer to avoid contacting them too often for fear of using up all of the available supervisory time on relatively minor matters. So what other options are available?

PhD candidates can be a precious resource for dissertation students. They tend to be 'closer to the empirical work' because they are involved with the fundamental aspects of the research process, such as data gathering and programming, that your supervisor may have left behind long ago. As I have worked through my career, I have tended to spend an increasingly large proportion of my time reading, writing, and doing administration. This has left less time available for doing data analysis. On the other hand, since PhD students are earlier in their careers, they are usually more up to date with the latest databases, literature sources, and programming languages than academic staff members. They typically hang around in the department more than the faculty, so they are easier to find and therefore frequently worth seeking out for help rather than a faculty member in the same way that you might ask a pharmacist about a minor ailment instead of making an appointment with a doctor.

While PhD students tend to be younger than the faculty, they are still more experienced and knowledgeable than undergraduate and master's students, and therefore if you want their help, you should treat them with the same professional courtesy that you would give a staff member. Your supervisor will have a formal obligation to help you with your project as part of their job. PhD students will generally not have such a responsibility, and so you need to be extra polite, e-mailing them and requesting an appointment to meet rather than just turning up (at least the first time you make contact), and anticipate that they might decline to offer support or not even reply.

Another group of people who might be able to help with certain aspects of your research are 'post-docs', variously known as post-doctoral research assistants or research fellows. However, they are relatively rare in accounting and finance compared with the natural and physical sciences, where they are employed in large numbers. Post-docs are usually full-time junior staff researchers who will have already obtained (or be very close to getting) their PhDs, and thus they will have developed relevant skills and knowledge. As for PhD students, they can be a valuable resource, but their help will again be voluntary and should not be taken for granted.

Finally, a considerable amount of relevant information and support will be available on the internet through blogsites and forums. If the problem is with data handling, statistical analysis or coding, there is likely to be a forum dealing with precisely that topic. Whichever statistical or coding package you use, there will probably be a forum for it. For example, searching for 'EViews forum' brings up the correct URL as the first hit.

For programming languages including R and Python, it is possible to get paid expert 1:1 support from organisations such as Codementor.[1] There is also a database

---

[1] https://www.codementor.io/browser-bugs-experts

of more than 20 million questions with responses regarding code debugging and other issues on theStackoverflow site that can be searched by theme, package or keyword. [2]

The following sub-section provides a list of common challenges that project students face and some suggestions on dealing with them. The points below are just ideas. While you might obtain useful advice from others, remember that your supervisor is ultimately formally charged with the responsibility for supporting your progress and will probably be marking your dissertation, so their guidance should be taken as definitive. If you are facing a more substantive issue, it is they whom you should be contacting.

12.1.1 Problems that might occur and how to fix them

I feel totally overwhelmed. The project seems like a massive piece of work, and I don't know where to start.

Conducting and writing a piece of research is always a significant undertaking, especially for those who have not done so before and consequently, many students initially approach the task completely lacking in confidence. Rather than thinking of the project as a single enormous problem, deconstruct it into a series of small ones. Follow the stages given in your department's guide on how to do a project, and try not to think too many steps ahead. So long as you follow the process in a sensible order and according to the required timescale, you will reach the endpoint by the deadline. Establish a routine, set up a work plan with timescales, and tick off each milestone as you achieve it.

As well as working on your project, you could follow up on resources to strengthen your self-confidence and build your resilience. There are plenty of free sources to support this on-line including YouTube and various websites including theSkills You Need[3] and MindTools[4] among many others.

I am just about to submit my project, and I have found an existing article or another project or thesis that has done precisely the same thing. Do I need to start again?

This is an unfortunate situation. Some students worry a lot about this possibility, but it is a surprisingly rare occurrence. Before panicking, look again. It is unlikely that the existing research is identical to your own. Perhaps the models, geographical coverage, sample period, or the interpretations of the results are different. You should acknowledge in your project any research that was in the public domain before you finished yours. It might be tempting, but it would be dangerous, to just ignore this research and pretend that you had not spotted it. To do so would be dishonest; if your supervisor/marker became aware of the existing study, it would highlight that your literature search had been deficient. Worse, it could even lead to an accusation

---

[2]https://stackoverflow.com/questions
[3]https://www.skillsyouneed.com/ps/confidence.html
[4]https://www.mindtools.com/pages/article/resilience.htm

of plagiarism if it was argued that you used ideas in the other study without giving its author(s) due credit.

But when drafting your write-up, look for and emphasise the differences between the two pieces of work, not the similarities. Try to differentiate your project from that study as much as possible. In the unlikely event that there really is little distinction between the two pieces, ask your supervisor for urgent advice. Remember that a dissertation needs only a tiny, if any, original contribution and therefore, even a minor variation between your work and the other piece would be sufficient to differentiate them.

More generally, when you think you had a brilliant project idea only to discover later that the research question, or something very similar to it, has already been investigated and written up by an established scholar, this is confirmation that your idea was indeed a good one. If you notice early in the process – for example, at the literature review stage – then it should be straightforward to modify your research aims slightly compared with those in your proposal to sufficiently distinguish your study from the one you have found. Rather than abandoning it entirely straight away, try to see if it could be re-worked or modified and improved slightly to build on the existing study, which would be much simpler and less time consuming than starting over.

I am close to completing my project, and my computer has crashed, or my laptop has been stolen, and I have lost the entire draft. What do I do?

This is probably among the worst situations a student can find themselves in. It would be easy, but not helpful at this stage, to point out that you should have kept regular, secure and separate backups of the work in such circumstances. If no such backups exist, you may have printed a draft to read through or sent an earlier draft to your supervisor or someone else to comment upon, in which case you might be able to retrieve something, even if it was not the latest version. There are several software packages and apps available that can transform pdf files to Microsoft Word documents, so if you have a hard copy, you could scan it to a pdf and try that route to get your work back.

Otherwise, especially if you can document evidence of the problems (e.g., a confirmation from IT Services that the computer is dead or a police crime number for a reported burglary), you could apply for an extension to the deadline to allow you more time to redo it. It would certainly not be fun to go over old work and write it again, but this might be the only option. You should be able to regenerate the study more rapidly the second time around.

I left working on my project right until the last minute. Now I am ill, or something else urgent has arisen, and there is no way I can complete the project in the time remaining before the deadline.

Illness is one of the most common problems that arise during the period of completing a dissertation. If the affliction is relatively minor or occurs early on during the registration period, you can probably soldier on without requiring any additional time or help. In particular, in recent years, it has become increasingly plausible to conduct almost all of the steps necessary to complete a research project on-line from home without the need to leave the house, which allows students to work through an illness where they still feel sufficiently well to do so.

If, however, the illness is sufficiently severe that it is impossible to continue to work on the project, even at home, or it occurs during a critical phase of the work (such as if it prevents you from conducting face-to-face interviews, or it happens close to the deadline when you still have much writing to do), then you must contact your supervisor to seek their guidance and probably ask for an extension. If there is no way that you could concoct a plausible project in the remaining time – especially if you have a legitimate mitigating circumstance such as a significant illness, then you should ask for additional time. You will probably need to complete a form and supply evidence that you were ill (such as a signed letter on headed paper from a doctor). However, you should still push ahead and make as much progress as possible as soon as you feel better rather than waiting to see if the extension request is approved.

I have been working steadily on the project, but I know that I am behind where I should be. Should I ask for a deadline extension, and will I get it?

Every department will have a formal process for students to ask for an extension to a piece of coursework or a project if there are mitigating circumstances that mean that the submission cannot be made on time. If you have just left everything until the last minute and cannot finish on time because there is too much to do, it is doubtful that an application for an extension would be successful.

But, on the other hand, if, despite your best endeavours, you have been unable to keep on track due to circumstances beyond your control, then it is worth putting in an application for an extension. Legitimate reasons for requesting an extension might include significant illness, technological failure, bereavement, specific learning difficulties, and caring responsibilities.

My friend's supervisor is much more senior and more famous than mine or much more supportive. Or I have been allocated a supervisor who knows much less about the topic than another member of staff. Can I switch supervisors?

Supervisors are usually allocated based on their availability and coverage of the topic (probably with a certain element of randomness in the process), but most of the time, there is no scope for students to select their own supervisor or request a change unless something has gone seriously wrong – see the next question. It would cause chaos, not to mention considerable embarrassment, if students were permitted to demand a particular supervisor on a whim.

All supervisors have their strengths and weaknesses. Although it is stereotyping somewhat, more senior academics will probably have more experience of the process and better knowledge of what constitutes a good project; but they might also be more aloof and less able to provide guidance on the detailed aspects of data collection and programming, for instance. So think positively, try to build a strong working relationship with the supervisor you have, and make use of their skills, whatever they are.

I had a massive argument with my supervisor at our previous meeting. He told me that I am behind schedule and seemed to suggest that I had not been working hard enough. I then replied that I had been ill and could have made faster progress if he had answered my e-mails quicker. Now I feel awkward, but I am stuck with my survey and need help.

Unfortunately, it is common to make remarks in a heated conversation that are ill-advised and later regretted.

Usually, the best advice initially would be to try to smooth over any difficulties, to apologise if you are at least in part to blame for the breakdown of communications and see if you can get things back on track. If this is really not possible, or you have tried this but it was to no effect, then it would be wise to make an appointment to see the 'dissertation module convenor' – this is the staff member who is responsible for organising all aspects of the dissertations and probably the same person who allocated the students to supervisors. You can explain the situation to them and follow their advice. They might be able to have a word with your supervisor to see what the issue is and how it could be resolved.

If this still fails to produce a resolution, the module convenor would be able to arrange a change of supervisor. But this would be absolutely a last resort. A change of supervisor is a drastic step only to be taken if all else fails, such as a long-term absence on their part or a serious disagreement resulting in a complete breakdown of your working relationship with them. Changing supervisors is disruptive and awkward for all parties and, therefore, only worth considering if you are near the start of the process rather than close to completing the project. In the latter case, it would be preferable just to make the best of the situation.

My supervisor is not responding to my e-mails. I am stuck, I don't know how to proceed, and getting desperate.

If it has been some considerable time (e.g., more than a week) since you wrote to your supervisor and they have not replied, even after you sent a polite reminder, then in the first instance, try some other way to contact them. The most obvious way would be to drop in to see them during their surgery or office hours. Check with other academic or administrative staff whether the supervisor has been away or off sick, which would explain their non-response.

If your supervisor has not responded because you argued during the previous meeting, or you have been contacting them daily since they were assigned to you, then you will probably have to consider that you have used up all of the available supervisory resources, and you will need to find other ways to address the difficulties you now face.

If it has been more than a week since you sent a reminder e-mail to your supervisor, your efforts to contact them through other channels have also failed, and your need for support is urgent, it is probably time to reach the dissertation module convenor – see the response to the previous question. Alternatively, you could seek help from another member of staff or a PhD student.

I can't find any relevant literature - what will I write in my literature review?

The obvious first response to this issue would be to suggest looking harder and in different places. Have you checked for published sources, working papers, theses and books using all of the resources identified in chapter 6 of this book? If that is the case, and you have still not found anything, then it might be that you have construed your topic too narrowly and excluded studies that would have been within the scope if you defined your search more widely. It is better to write a review including a range of marginally relevant material than to have nothing to write about at all.

A final possibility is that there genuinely is very little scholarly literature on the topic that you chose either because it is a very new idea that you are among the first to work on, or that it is perhaps not an amenable topic for academic-type research which is why no scholars have written about it before. This is an unlikely scenario, but if you think this might be the case, it is worth checking your supervisor's view on whether they consider it an appropriate subject for a dissertation. If the topic has received supervisory approval, then you would need to redouble your efforts to find some underpinning literature as in the first two paragraphs in response to this question. Your supervisor might also have suggestions for other places you could search for material.

There are already so many papers on my topic – how will I ever read, let alone write about, all of them?

Students also sometimes come up against the reverse of the previous problem – namely that there are simply too many relevant papers and they feel overwhelmed. Clearly, time is limited, you cannot read a hundred studies, and you will need to focus. Try to identify the most influential pieces on the topic and make sure that you read and cite those. Next, identify the handful of studies that are the very closest to what you intend to do in your project and read those. Finally, make sure you read through anything published on the topic in the last couple of years, which should incorporate the latest thinking. Following these steps should be sufficient to generate a solid literature review – remember, it does not have to be exhaustive, it just needs to set the scene for your investigative work.

I launched a survey, but I hardly got any responses

This is a pervasive problem for surveys where participants are not incentivised via payments. A first suggestion would be to try to widen the circulation list to reach a larger group of people – for example, through social media or marketing lists, newsletters, etc. Although not ideal, you could also consider encouraging friends or family to complete the survey, which is known as a convenience sample.

Finally, you could relaunch the survey but this time offering a financial incentive to those who participate. Although it would be expensive to pay every person who completes the survey, it might still pique interest by telling participants that their name would be entered into a prize draw – such as for a £50 voucher (note that of course, you would have to follow through and be prepared to pay for and award the prize to someone). A final possibility would be to use a company such as Qualtrics or Prolific who will source the participants for you, but this is likely to be very expensive, as discussed in chapter 9; Amazon Mechanical Turk (MTurk) offers a similar service but is often much cheaper and so could be within your reach financially.

I am trying to implement an empirical model using a programming language or statistical software, but it is not working, no matter what I do

It goes without saying that you should try first to debug the code yourself to identify where it is not working. There are numerous videos on YouTube showing how to do your own debugging, which is a valuable skill to learn. But if, after trying for some time, you still cannot see where the problems are, there are several places from which you could seek help. One suggestion is to upload a query and the non-working segment of your code onto a forum website as discussed in section 12.1 above, and hopefully, someone more experienced will see it and know how to solve the issue. Another possibility is finding a PhD student or post-doc proficient in that programming language (there should be plenty of them) and asking for help.

I am conducting primarily empirical research. I am applying an established model to new data, but the results are rubbish. Should I abandon the work and do something else?

Probably not. If the results are plausible but just weak, then this matters little for a dissertation. As discussed in previous chapters, the project will be marked predominantly on how well you have gone through the steps required to conduct a small piece of independent research; bad results will make the work appear less stellar than it would have been if the findings had been more robust, but it will probably hardly make any difference to the way it will be graded.

If, on the other hand, the results don't make any sense at all and are implausible – for example, the parameter estimates are way too big or too small, or they are statistically significant but with the wrong sign (e.g., a positive relationship is expected but the coefficient is negative) then you should investigate and try to identify the source of the problem. Is there an issue with the data or your implementation of the model? If possible, try to re-estimate the model using a different statistical package or code.

Or perhaps your interpretation of the results is incorrect (e.g., check the data's scaling or the way you created or transformed the variables, which is perhaps different from other studies)? Or maybe the results are plausible after all, but your expectations were wrong? Do your best to fix any problems, but if they still persist, even after you have asked others, including your supervisor, for advice, then you have no choice but to write up the findings as you see them and try your best to explain them in the drafting.

Negative results are disappointing and require some careful explanation. But they are nonetheless a vital part of the development of knowledge so that other researchers become aware of what you tried. Such findings are much more challenging for academics to publish in highly rated journals. But provided that you have followed appropriate methods and there was a strong theoretical or intuitive rationale behind the approach you used, in a dissertation setting, bad results will be viewed on an almost equal footing with good results. Your supervisor or other markers will want to see evidence that you know how to do research and write it up, and the fact that you were a bit unlucky this time will not overly worry them. They will no doubt have faced the same situation numerous times with their own research.

Therefore, don't be excessively concerned if you obtain only 'negative findings'. These can not only occur when your results seem bizarre, but more commonly also when the parameter attached to the key variable in your model is statistically insignificant, or you find no difference between treatment and control groups in an experiment, or you find that all of your hypotheses are rejected. You might obtain more favourable results by modifying the methods or data, which would be worth a try if time permits.

If your results are 'mixed' in the sense that either the parameter estimates on your main explanatory variables are insignificant, or when you examine the data in different ways, you get different conclusions, then don't be afraid to state that. It is much better to be up-front and honest about such results than to try to pretend that you have robust findings that support your hypothesis when they don't. At the level of a student dissertation, markers will be primarily looking for evidence that you know how to conduct research and interpret the results; they will be less concerned by the results themselves.

I finished the draft of my project but it is either too short or too long compared with the word limit

Usually, universities set an upper limit on the number of words that students can include in their research projects rather than a target length. This means that you cannot exceed this figure by very much (although there might be some discretion of, for example, a 5% excess which would be ignored). If your project was somewhat shorter than the word limit, that is likely to be fine, although if it was very much shorter, there could be concerns that it is missing some key elements.

If the project is far in excess of the word limit, it needs to be trimmed down as there are significant risks that you would be penalised. Some suggestions of how this could be achieved as painlessly as possible are discussed at length in section 11.4 and therefore readers are referred back to that material.

I am good at conducting data analysis and empirical work but my writing is terrible. How can I improve it?

Having great research ideas or producing high-quality empirical work is not sufficient to generate a high mark for a dissertation, since markers will be looking for a well-written draft that makes strong arguments as well. Therefore, it is essential that your writing is as polished as possible. If you are sufficiently early in the registration process, your university will probably run writing courses as part of their study skills development offerings, and you could enrol on one of those. This will provide generic advice about how to improve your writing abilities, and is likely to provide resources and exercises.

Alternatively, there are naturally a range of resources available on-line including a useful document at the University of Essex[5] and at Kibin,[6] among many others. Also, try to adopt the style used in academic articles in the field and don't be afraid to get as much feedback as possible from your supervisor, other academics and fellow students. Finally, it is perfectly reasonable to pay a professional proof-reader to help polish your final draft prior to submission. That person will be able to fix up your grammar and ensure that the spelling is spot-on. Lots of other hints and tips are available in chapter 10 and chapter 11 of this book.

I was excited to have finished a first draft of my project, but when I sent it to my supervisor, it came back covered in comments. Now I think the work is bad and it is not worth me submitting it

While it can be disheartening to receive back a piece of work that you were proud of covered in red ink with tens of comments, this does not necessarily imply that the work is of bad quality or will obtain a low mark. Some supervisors will do a very thorough job of providing feedback and even if the tone of their comments appears to be predominantly negative, that might just be their style of providing suggestions and not reflective of their view of the standard of the project. So take any feedback in good spirit and use it as an opportunity to further improve your work. If you are still worried that the comments are suggestive that your project is not up to scratch, get back to your supervisor or whoever made the suggestions and explain your concerns. It might be worthwhile to explore whether you are permitted to have a further round of feedback to see whether your revisions to the work after the first set of comments are going on the right track, or to ask for further opinions from others before you submit the final version for formal marking. Other tips on dealing with feedback are given in section 11.3.

12.2   The project is completed: now what?

Congratulations, whatever mark you receive, submitting the project is a significant milestone that represents the end of a period of hard work, and so it is time to celebrate. Once you have finally given in the project, it is quite likely that you will feel as if you never want to see it, or the underpinning material, ever again. The majority of ex-project students will feel that completing the dissertation is an experience they would never want to repeat, even if it ran smoothly and they got to the finishing line on time. Particularly if your target was just barely to scrape through with a passing mark, that might well be the end of your research journey.

---

[5]https://www1.essex.ac.uk/outreach/documents/how-to-improve-academic-writing.pdf
[6]https://www.kibin.com/essay-writing-blog/academic-writing/

Despite the amount of effort you put in and even if you are immensely proud of what you have achieved, the sad fact is that most research projects will only be read by three people: you, your supervisor, and a second marker (the moderator). That does not mean that the whole exercise was pointless, though: the main aim of the dissertation was for you to learn how to do research, and if you have acquired the skills listed in the introductory chapter to this book, it will have done its job. To repeat a well-worn cliché, it was about the journey up the mountain and not the view from the top.

On the other hand, it might be that you quite enjoyed the process and felt a slight tinge of emptiness when you realised that you would not be working on the dissertation any more after it probably took up quite a slice of your life for some time. In that case, it would be worth considering whether you could extract any additional value from the work you have already done and push it out to a wider audience.

Writing a journal article

One possibility is to consider whether your project could be redrafted into a paper suitable for publication in a journal. This route is only feasible for outstanding work (generating a mark well into the distinction or first-class category of, say, 80%+). Even then, you would need to be prepared for a lot of additional labour to have a reasonable chance of achieving a published output at the end. While the dissertation is already probably of approximately the right length (or possibly a little on the long side), it is unlikely to be in the proper format or style.

An important difference between an excellent project and a publishable paper is that the latter must include a clear, original contribution to knowledge. Bad structure, bad presentation or bad grammar can be fixed relatively easily with time, some editing and a steer in the right direction. But what cannot be remedied is if the study is simply not exciting and new enough for a journal editor to believe that it is worth working into a publishable form. It is usually a requirement that publishable papers should make a novel contribution to knowledge, which the majority of dissertations will not contain, or the contribution will be too trivial. Most projects, even if of high quality and awarded an exceptional mark, will remain unpublishable for this reason.

If you feel that your project might be publishable and you are willing to put in the effort, it is worth going back to your supervisor to seek their advice. Particularly if you have built a good rapport with them, they might be willing to work with you to transform the project into a paper. You might consider asking them to join you as a co-author, in which case you could reasonably expect that they would take on the revisions required before the paper could be submitted. They would then also provide advice on which journal would be appropriate to target, and they might also submit the article there. Equally, don't be too disappointed if your supervisor replies either that they feel the work would be hard to publish or they don't have the time to work on it with you.

A magazine or blog article

A further possibility would be to distil the project's core findings into a 500-word extended summary document that could then be drafted into a blog or magazine piece. There are numerous magazines in both accounting and finance (on-line and paper-copy) that might be willing to publish an article by a guest writer on a topic of relevance to their audience. If, after looking at some recent editions of the magazine or blogsite, you think that a considerably shortened and revised version of your project could fit the bill, have a go at writing the piece and then contact the editor. Remember, though, that the style of a popular piece will be very different from that of an article in a scholarly journal.

Further study

If you enjoyed the experience of working on the project to such an extent that you would like to do it all over again, several possibilities might be available. The first would be to consider further study – in particular for a research degree (MPhil or PhD). If that is of interest, every university department will have a set of webpages dedicated to its programme, and your supervisor would no doubt be delighted to discuss the possibilities with you. It would also be worth chatting with current PhD students about their experiences and what life might be like if you were to follow that path.

An alternative would be to consider a career that involves a research component or even one where that is the job's primary task. As well as an academic career (for which a PhD will be a requirement), there are numerous public and private sector roles for researchers, including a market researcher, quantitative analyst, government or central bank researcher. Your university's careers team would be a good resource to discuss these opportunities.

If you undertake further research, even though the topic will likely be different from the one you chose for your dissertation, the raw ingredients of the process and the final output type will be the same. The skills that you have already developed will stand you in good stead for the next research project. This experience will mean that you will probably enjoy it more: you will be more confident, make progress much more quickly, become increasingly self-reliant and able to resolve more of the issues yourself without hitting a wall. All of the tasks that took a lot of time and effort to master – where to look for ideas and material, how to write a review, how to conduct empirical work, how to approach drafting an abstract and an introduction – will all come more naturally the second time around. In essence, you can use the best aspects of how you did things for the previous project as a template for how to proceed next time.

While research never becomes effortless, the more you have already conducted, the easier it becomes to do it again. The research journey becomes a never-ending mountain-climbing tour. Once you have ascended to a mountain peak, the trip to the next one begins. Each project is different, with new experiences and new skills learned each time, and all the while, you will be contributing to the body of knowledge. The production of research generates ideas for further research in a never-ending cycle. Life as an academic researcher allows you to master your own destiny, set your own agenda of inquiry, and take it in whatever direction you choose.

Reflecting on the skills you have mastered

As well as considering whether you can make more from the work you have already done for your dissertation, it is also worthwhile to reflect on what you have learned. While the experience – both the positive and negative aspects – is still fresh in your mind, go back to the list of transferrable skills I suggested in section 1.1 that you could acquire, and construct a personalised list of these. The knowledge gained and proficiencies mastered can be worked into your CV or notes in preparation for job interviews with illustrative examples from what you did, what you learned, and how you resolved any difficulties that you faced. The dissertation work will provide you with some much more engaging material to discuss in interviews than you will obtain from the taught courses you attended, so give some thought to how you can make the most of it.

Chapter takeaways – top tips for success

⊛ Be aware of the various sources of support that are available to you if things go wrong with your project

⊛ Ask for an extension if you have a legitimate reason for falling behind

⊛ Don't panic if you identify existing work on the same topic as your thesis; instead, try to accentuate the differences

⊛ Don't be excessively concerned by odd-looking or insignificant results. Instead, think of them as an interesting puzzle to solve

⊛ Consider writing up some of your findings as a journal submission, blog piece, or magazine article

⊛ If you really enjoyed the experience of research, consider further study and discuss the possibilities with your supervisor

REFERENCES

Bailey, S. (2017) *Academic Writing: A Handbook for International Students* Routledge, Oxford, 5th edition.

Bell, A.R., Brooks, C. & Dryburgh, P.R. (2007) *The English Wool Market c.1230–1327* Cambridge University Press, Cambridge, UK.

Birks, M. & Mills, J. (2015) *Grounded Theory: A Practical Guide* Sage, London.

Booth, A., Sutton, A. & Papaioannou, D. (2016) *Systematic Approaches to a Successful Literature Review* Sage, London, 2nd edition.

Brooks, C. (2019) *Introductory Econometrics for Finance* 4th edition, Cambridge University Press, Cambridge, UK.

Brooks, C., Chen, Z. & Zeng, Y. (2018) Institutional cross-ownership and corporate strategy: the case of mergers and acquisitions *Journal of Corporate Finance* 48, 187–216.

Brooks, C., Fenton, E., Schopohl, L., & Walker, J. (2014) Gender and the evaluation of research *Research Policy* 46(6), 990–1001.

Brooks, C., Fenton, E., Schopohl, L., & Walker, J. (2019) Why does research in finance have so little impact? *Critical Perspectives on Accounting* 58, 24–52.

Carroll, J. (2012) *Effective Time Management in Easy Steps* In Easy Steps Limited, Leamington Spa.

Cassell, C. (2015) *Conducting Research Interviews for Business and Management Students*

Sage, London.

Coleman, H. (2019) *Polish Your Academic Writing* Sage, London.

Comte, A. (1880) *A General View of Positivism* Reeves & Turner, London.

Creswell, J.W. & Creswell, J.D. (2018) *Research Design: Qualitative, Quantitative, and Mixed Methods Approaches* Sage, London.

Curzer, H. & Santillanes, G. (2012) Managing conflict of interest in research: some suggestions for investigators *Accountability in Research* 19, 143–55.

Day, T. (2018) *Success in Academic Writing* Palgrave, London, 2nd edition.

Deer, B. (2011) How the case against the MMR vaccine was fixed *British Medical Journal* 342, c5347.

Denscombe, M. (2019) *Research Proposals* Open University Press, London, 2nd edition.

Dooley, D. (1995) *Social Research Methods* Prentice Hall, Englewood Cliffs, New Jersey.

Eilifsen, A., & Messier Jr., W.F. (2000) A review and integration of archival research *Journal of Accounting Literature*, 19, 1-43.

Evans, D. (2013) *Don't Trust Your Spell Check: Pro Proofreading Tactics and Tests To Eliminate Embarrassing Writing Errors* Createspace, Scotts Valley, California.

Fink, A.G. (2016) *How to Conduct Surveys: A Step-by-Step Guide*, Sage, London, 6th edition.

Fowler, F.J. (2013) *Survey Research Methods* Sage, London, 5th edition.

Friedman, M. (1953) *Essays in Positive Economics* University of Chicago Press, Chicago.

Gippel, J. (2012) A revolution in finance? *Australian Journal of Management* 38(1) 125–146.

Glaser, B.G. & Strauss, A.L. (1967) *The Discovery of Grounded Theory: Strategies for Qualitative Research* Aldine, New York.

Greener, I. (2006) Nick Leeson and the collapse of Barings Bank: Socio-technical networks and the 'rogue trader' *Organization* 13(3), 421–441.

Greetham, B. (2020) *How to Write Your Literature Review* Macmillan, London.

Hammersley, M. & Traianou, A. (2012) *Ethics in Qualitative Research: Controversies and Contexts* Sage, London.

Hampton, A.R. (2019) *Proofreading Power: Skills & Drills* Cornerstone, Little Rock, Arcansas.

Hillenbrand, C., Saraeva, A., Money, K. & Brooks, C. (2021) Saving for a rainy day… or a trip to the Bahamas? How the framing of investment communication impacts retail investors *British Journal of Management*, forthcoming.

Hinnink, M., Hutter, I. & Bailey, A. (2020) *Qualitative Research Methods* Sage, London, 2nd edition.

Holland, J., Henningsson, J., Johanson, U., Koga, C. & Sakakibara, S. (2012) Use of IC information in Japanese financial firms *Journal of Intellectual Capital* 13(4), 562–581.

Howell, K. (2012) *An Introduction to the Philosophy of Methodology* Sage, London.

Hussey, J. & Hussey, R. (1997) *Business Research: A Practical Guide for Postgraduate Students* Macmillan Business, Basingstoke, UK.

Ide, K. (2013) *Proofreading Secrets of Best-Selling Authors* Lighthouse, Raleigh, North Carolina.

Johnstone, C. (2019) *Seven Ways to Build Resilience: Strengthening Your Ability to Deal with Difficult Times* Robinson, London.

Kuhn, T.S. (1962) *The Structure of Scientific Revolutions* University of Chicago Press, Chicago.

Lancaster, T. (2019) *Avoid Plagiarism* Sage, London.

Larrinaga-Gonzalez, C. & Bebbington, J. (2001) Accounting change or institutional appropriation? A case study of the implementation of environmental accounting *Critical perspectives on accounting* 12(3), 269–292.

Loughran, T. & McDonald, B. (2011) When is a liability not a liability? Textual analysis, dictionaries, and 10-Ks *Journal of Finance* 66, 35–65.

Lovell, H. & MacKenzie, D. (2011) Accounting for carbon: the role of accounting professional organisations in governing climate change *Antipode* 43(3), 704–730.

Mattessich, R. (1989) Accounting and the input-output principle in the prehistoric and ancient world *Abacus* 25, 74–84.

Mill, J.S. (1881) *A System of Logic* Harper, New York.

Oldroyd, D. (1995) The role of accounting in public expenditure and monetary policy in the first century AD Roman empire *Accounting Historians Journal* 22, 117–129.

O'Leary, Z. (2018) *Research Proposal: Little Quick Fix* Sage, London.

Paterson, A., Leung, D., Jackson, W., MacIntosh, R. & O'Gorman, K. (2016) *Research Methods for Accounting and Finance* Goodfellow, Oxford.

Popper, K.R. (1959) *The Logic of Scientific Discovery* Hutchinson, London.

Punch, K.F. (2016) *Developing Effective Research Proposals* Sage, London.

Redfield, G. (2020) *Stop Procrastinating: Complete Step by Step Guide on How to Avoid Procrastination and Motivate Yourself Back on Track* Garrett Redfield.

Rendall, S., Brooks, C. & Hillenbrand, C. (2021) The impacts of emotions and personality on borrowers' abilities to manage their debts *International Review of Financial Analysis* 74, 101703.

Ridley, D. (2012) *The Literature Review: A Step-By-Step Guide For Students* Sage, London.

Ritchie, J., Lewis, J., Nicholls, C.M. & Ormston, R. (2013) *Qualitative Research Practice: A Guide for Social Science Students and Researchers* Sage, London, 2nd edition.

Smith, M. (2020) *Research Methods in Accounting* Sage, London, 5th edition.

Tangaarrd, L. (2016) *A Survival Kit for Doctoral Students and Their Supervisors: Traveling the Landscape of Research* Sage, London.

Tao, R. Brooks, C. & Bell, A.R. (2020) When is a MAX not the MAX? How news resolves information uncertainty *Journal of Empirical Finance* 57, 33–51.

Tucker, B. & Parker, L. (2014) In our ivory towers? The research-practice gap in management accounting *Accounting and Business Research* 44(2), 104–143.

Urquhart, C. (2012) *Grounded Theory for Qualitative Research: A Practical Guide* Sage, London.

Ventresca, M.J. & Mohr, J.W. (2017) Archival research methods, in *The Blackwell Companion to Organizations*, J.A.C. Baum (Ed.) 805–828.

Wakefield, A.J., Murch, S.H., Anthony, A., Linnell, J., Casson, D.M., Malik, M., Berelowitz, M., Dhillon, A.P., Thomson, M.A., Harvey, P., Valentine, A., Davies, S.E. & Walker-Smith, J.A. (1998) Ileal-lymphoid-nodular hyperplasia, non-specific colitis, and pervasive developmental disorder in children *The Lancet* 351(9103), 637–641.

Williams, K. & Davis, M. (2017) *Referencing and Understanding Plagiarism* Palgrave, London.

Williams, M. (2016) *Key Concepts in the Philosophy of Social Research* Sage, London.

Wilson, K. (2020) *How to Build a Healthy Brain: Reduce Stress, Anxiety and Depression and Future-proof Your Brain* Yellow Kite, London.

Yin, R.K. (2018) *Case Study Research and Applications: Design and Methods* Sage, London, 6th edition.

Index